# PAST, PRESENT, AND FUTURE

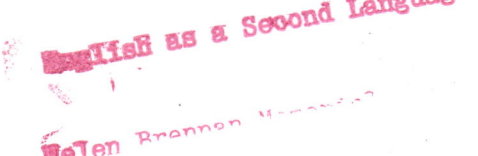

# PAST, PRESENT, AND FUTURE

## A READING-WRITING TEXT     3rd EDITION

JOAN YOUNG GREGG
New York City Technical College
of the City University of New York

JOAN RUSSELL
New York City Technical College
of the City University of New York

WADSWORTH PUBLISHING COMPANY
Belmont, California
A Division of Wadsworth, Inc.

To our parents:
Mollie Silverman
Sylvia and Harry Young

English Editor: Angela Gantner
Editorial Assistant: Julie L. Johnson
Production: Mary Douglas
Designer: Lisa Mirski
Print Buyer: Martha Branch
Copy Editor: Betty Duncan-Todd
Cover: "Transfiguration" by Alfred Russell

*Art/Photo Credits:* pp. 1, 205, 253, 314, 338 Joan Gregg; pp. 2, 5, 11, 23, 30, 31 Joan S. Russell; pp. 38, 61, 83, 113, 179, 296, 311 Serena Nanda; pp. 41, 47, 66 Hawaiian Visitors Bureau; pp. 69, 75, 150, 234 New York Public Library; pp. 80, 313 NASA; pp. 90, 275, 276 John Gregg; p. 100 Barbara Gregg; pp. 104, 121, 123, 212, 277 United Nations; p. 105 IBM; p. 134 Bernie Kraus; p. 143 Southampton University; p. 155 Gallaudet College; p. 158 Deena Burton; p. 168 The National Archives; p. 182 Rhoden Studios; p. 217 Tom Monaster for the Guide Dog Foundation for The Blind, Inc.; p. 229 Class Group, Brooklyn Friends School; p. 230 Chicago Historical Society; p. 242 Vassar College; p. 264 Nebraska Historical Society; p. 299 Tony Gahan; p. 301 Victor Jang; p. 334 International Ladies Garment Workers Union.

© 1990, 1987, 1983 by Wadsworth, Inc. All rights reserved. No part of this book may be reproduced, stored in a retrieval system, or transcribed, in any form or by any means, electronic, mechanical, photocopying, recording, or otherwise, without the prior written permission of the publisher, Wadsworth Publishing Company, Belmont, California 94002, a division of Wadsworth, Inc.

Printed in the United States of America      49

1 2 3 4 5 6 7 8 9 10—94 93 92 91 90

**Library of Congress Cataloging-in-Publication Data**

Gregg, Joan Young.
    Past, present, and future : a reading-writing text / Joan Young Gregg, Joan Russell.— 3rd ed.
      p. cm.
    ISBN 0-534-12762-2
    1. English language—Textbooks for foreign speakers.   I. Russell, Joan, II. Title.
PE1128.G66   1990
428.2—dc20

89-27420
CIP

# CONTENTS

Preface and Notes for Use of the Text  xi
Acknowledgments  xv

## UNIT I  OUR DIVERSE WORLD  1

### Chapter One
### Uncovering the Past  2

Prereading  2
  Class Discussion  2
  Free Write  3
  Vocabulary in Context  3
Reading: "Archeologists at Work"  4
  Summary Completion  6
Discussion Questions  6
Reading Comprehension  7
  Understanding the Text  7
  Answering Information Questions  8
The Reading Process: General and Specific Words; Topics  9
Vocabulary  12
  New Words  12
  Word Families: Type of Work; Person Who Does That Type of Work  13
Writing Exercises  14
  Sentence Kernels  14
  Simple Present Tense  16
  Plurals  18
  Prepositions  21
  Adverbs of Frequency  25
  Punctuation and Capitalization  27
The Composing Process  27
  Developing a Central Topic  27
  Composing a Paragraph  29
  Paragraph Topics  29
Additional Reading: "A Hero's Life"  29
Discussion Questions  32
Reading Comprehension  33
Vocabulary  35
Paragraph Topics  36

### Chapter Two
### The United States:
### Land of Many Cultures  37

Prereading  37
  Class Activity  37
  Free Write  39
  Vocabulary in Context  39
Reading: "Hawaiian Feasts and Festivals"  40
  Summary Completion  42
Discussion Questions  42

## Contents

Reading Comprehension — 43
  Understanding the Text — 43
  Answering Information Questions — 45
  The Reading Process: Identifying Main Ideas — 46
Vocabulary — 48
  New Words — 48
  Word Families: Adjectives Versus Noun Forms — 49
Writing Exercises — 51
  Simple Present Tense of *To Be*
  *There Is* or *There Isn't*, and *There Are* or *There Aren't* — 54
  *To Be* + Adjective + Noun — 56
  Capitalization and Punctuation — 59
  Pronoun Use — 60
The Composing Process — 63
  Developing a Paragraph — 63
  Composing a Paragraph — 64
  Combining Sentences to Form a Paragraph — 66
  Paragraph Topics — 67
Additional Reading: "Witching for Water" — 67
Discussion Questions — 70
Reading Comprehension — 70
  Understanding the Text — 70
  Answering Information Questions — 73
  The Reading Process: Sequencing Events in Time Order — 73
Vocabulary — 74
  Expanding Vocabulary — 74
  Using Vocabulary — 75
  Word Families: Adjective Versus Noun Forms — 76
Paragraph Topics — 78

### Chapter Three
**Steps to the Future** — 80

Prereading — 80
  Class Discussion — 80
  Free Write — 81
  Vocabulary in Context — 81
Reading: "Our Biosphere: A World of Life" — 82
  Summary Completion — 84
Discussion Questions — 84
Reading Comprehension — 85
  Understanding the Text — 85
  Answering Information Questions — 86
  The Reading Process: Identifying Specific Information — 87
Vocabulary — 89
  New Words — 89
  Word Families: Adjective Formation with *-Less* — 91
Writing Exercises — 92
  Expressing the Future with *Will* + Basic Form of Verbs — 92
  Simple Present Tense Negative Forms — 95
  Verbs + Adjectives — 96
  Singular Possessives — 98
  The Composing Process — 100
Additional Reading: "People and Computers: A Working Relationship" — 103
Discussion Questions — 106
Reading Comprehension — 106
  Understanding the Text — 106
  Answering Information Questions — 108
  The Reading Process: Identifying Specific Information — 108
Vocabulary — 110
  Expanding Vocabulary — 110
  Using Vocabulary — 111
  Word Families: Verbs Versus Nouns of Persons — 112
Paragraph Topics — 113
Unit I Review — 115

# UNIT II OUR WORLD OF LANGUAGE    121

## Chapter Four
## Voices of the Past    122

Prereading    122
   Class Discussion    122
   Free Write    122
   Vocabulary in Context    122
Reading: "Communication: Is One Picture Worth a Thousand Words?"    124
   Guided Summary    126
Discussion Questions    126
Reading Comprehension    127
   Understanding the Text    127
   Answering Information Questions    129
   The Reading Process: Linking Pronouns    129
Vocabulary    130
   New Words    130
   Word Families: Negative Adjectives with *in-*, *im-*, and *un-*    131
Writing Exercises    134
   Simple Past Tense of *To Be*    134
   Simple Past Tense of Regular Verbs    136
   Simple Past Tense of Irregular Verbs    138
   Simple Past Tense Negative Forms    140
   The Definite Article    141
   Time Expressions    142
The Composing Process    144
   Developing a Unified Paragraph with Details    144
   Sequencing Details in a Paragraph    145
   Composing a Paragraph    146
   Sentence Combining    147
   Paragraph Topics    148
Additional Reading: "The Tower of Babel"    148

Discussion Questions    149
Reading Comprehension    150
   Summarizing Through Sentence Completion    150
   Using Signals of Time Order    151
   Answering Information Questions    151
Vocabulary    151
   Expanding Vocabulary    151
   Word Families: Parts of Speech    152
Paragraph Topics    154

## Chapter Five
## Language for Living    155

Prereading    156
   Class Discussion    156
   Free Write    156
   Vocabulary in Context    156
Reading: "Signs and Signals: Communication without Voices"    157
   Oral Cloze    160
Discussion Questions    160
Reading Comprehension    161
   Understanding the Text    161
   Answering Information Questions    162
   The Reading Process: Scanning for Specific Information    163
Vocabulary    164
   New Words    164
   Word Families: Adjective and Adverb Use    165
Writing Exercises    167
   Present Continuous Tense    167
   Compound Sentence Parts with *And*    170
   Sentence Patterns with *Because*    172
   Plural Possessives    174
The Composing Process    176
   Developing a Paragraph with Logical Sequence    176

| | | | |
|---|---|---|---|
| Developing a Paragraph with Several Points | 176 | Understanding the Text | 193 |
| Brainstorming, Organizing, and Drafting a Paragraph with Several Points | 177 | Answering Information Questions | 197 |
| | | The Reading Process: Skimming for Main Ideas | 197 |
| Paragraph Construction with Three Points | 178 | Vocabulary | 199 |
| Sentence Combining to Form a Paragraph | 179 | New Words | 199 |
| | | Word Families: Verb Versus Noun Forms | 200 |
| Paragraph Topics | 180 | Writing Exercises | 201 |
| Additional Reading: "Learning to Read: Malcolm X" | 181 | Modals + Basic Form of Verbs | 201 |
| | | Verbs + Infinitives | 204 |
| Discussion Questions | 183 | Changing the Direction of a Thought: The Use of *But* | 206 |
| Reading Comprehension | 184 | | |
| Understanding the Text | 184 | Punctuation: Series of Parallel Items | 209 |
| Answering Information Questions | 185 | | |
| | | The Composing Process | 211 |
| Vocabulary | 186 | Sequencing Ideas in a Paragraph | 211 |
| Choosing the Correct Definition | 186 | | |
| Expanding Vocabulary | 186 | Composing a Paragraph | 212 |
| Paragraph Topic | 187 | Sentence Combining to Form a Paragraph | 214 |
| | | Paragraph Topics | 215 |
| **Chapter Six** | | Additional Reading: "Rabbit and Antelope: A Timeless Tale" | 215 |
| **The Cleverness of Animals** | **188** | | |
| Prereading | 188 | Discussion Questions | 218 |
| Class Discussion | 188 | Reading Comprehension | 218 |
| Free Write | 189 | Vocabulary | 219 |
| Vocabulary in Context | 189 | Expanding Vocabulary | 219 |
| Reading: "Experiments with Language Learning" | 190 | Word Families | 220 |
| | | Paragraph Topics | 221 |
| Summary Completion | 192 | Unit II Review | 223 |
| Discussion Questions | 193 | | |
| Reading Comprehension | 193 | | |

# UNIT III  OUR SOCIAL WORLD  229

| | | | |
|---|---|---|---|
| **Chapter Seven** | | Summary Completion | 235 |
| **Women of the American Past** | **230** | Discussion Questions | 235 |
| | | Reading Comprehension | 236 |
| Prereading | 230 | Understanding the Text | 236 |
| Strip Story | 230 | Answering Information Questions | 238 |
| Free Write | 231 | | |
| Vocabulary in Context | 231 | | |
| Reading: "Harriet Tubman: The Moses of Her People" | 232 | The Reading Process: Recognizing Signals of Contrast | 239 |

| | |
|---|---|
| Vocabulary | 240 |
|   New Words | 240 |
|   Word Families: Related Word Forms | 241 |
| Writing Exercises | 243 |
|   Past Continuous Tense | 243 |
|   Use of Past Continuous Tense and Simple Past Tense | 245 |
|   Complex Sentences with *When* and *While* | 246 |
|   Comparison of Adjectives | 251 |
|   Superlative Form of Adjectives | 254 |
| The Composing Process | 257 |
|   Developing a Paragraph of Contrast | 257 |
|   Composing a Paragraph of Contrast | 258 |
|   Sentence Combining to Form a Paragraph | 259 |
|   Paragraph Topics | 260 |
| Additional Reading: "Mary Wilkins Freeman: The Revolt of Mother" | 260 |
| Discussion Questions | 264 |
| Reading Comprehension | 265 |
|   Understanding the Text | 265 |
|   Answering Information Questions | 267 |
|   The Reading Process: Figures of Speech | 267 |
| Vocabulary | 268 |
|   Expanding Vocabulary | 268 |
|   Using Vocabulary | 269 |
|   Word Families: Recognizing Word Stems | 270 |
| Paragraph Topics | 271 |

## Chapter Eight
## Working Relationships: Old and New    273

| | |
|---|---|
| Prereading | 273 |
|   Class Discussion | 273 |
|   Free Write | 273 |
|   Vocabulary in Context | 273 |
| Reading: "Love and Marriage: Different Cultures—Different Ideals" | 275 |
|   Summary Completion | 278 |
| Discussion Questions | 279 |
| Reading Comprehension | 279 |
|   Understanding the Text | 279 |
|   Answering Information Questions | 279 |
|   The Reading Process: Paraphrasing | 282 |
| Vocabulary | 284 |
|   New Words | 284 |
|   Word Families: Noun Formation | 285 |
| Writing Exercises | 286 |
|   Simple Present Tense Conditionals | 286 |
|   Expressing Conditions Contrary to Fact | 288 |
|   Useful Expressions with *The* | 291 |
| The Composing Process | 293 |
|   Developing a Paragraph | 293 |
|   Developing a General Idea with Specific Details | 294 |
|   Composing a Paragraph with General and Specific Statements | 295 |
|   Sentence Combining to Form a Paragraph | 297 |
|   Paragraph Topics | 298 |
| Additional Reading: "Men's Roles, Women's Roles: A Changing View" | 298 |
|   Paragraph Completion | 301 |
| Discussion Questions | 302 |
| Reading Comprehension | 302 |
|   Understanding the Text | 302 |
|   Answering Information Questions | 304 |
|   The Reading Process: Paraphrasing | 304 |
| Vocabulary | 306 |
|   Expanding Vocabulary | 306 |
|   Using Vocabulary | 307 |

| | |
|---|---|
| Word Families: Noun Formation | 308 |
| Paragraph Topics | 309 |

## Chapter Nine
### New Directions in Family Life — 310

| | |
|---|---|
| Prereading | 310 |
|   Role Play | 310 |
|   Free Write | 310 |
|   Vocabulary in Context | 310 |
| Reading: "One Household: Two Careers" | 312 |
|   Guided Summary | 314 |
| Discussion Questions | 315 |
| Reading Comprehension | 316 |
|   Understanding the Text | 316 |
|   Answering Information Questions | 318 |
|   The Reading Process: Following Key Words | 318 |
| Vocabulary | 320 |
|   New Words | 320 |
|   Word Families: Number Prefixes | 322 |
| Writing Exercises | 323 |
|   Complex Sentences with *Before* and *After* | 323 |
|   Adverb Use | 327 |
|   Punctuation: Quotations | 332 |
| The Composing Process | 333 |
|   Developing a Paragraph | 333 |
|   Developing a Paragraph from an Outline | 335 |
|   Paragraph Topics | 337 |
| Additional Reading: "The Family: Past, Present, and Future" | 337 |
| Discussion Questions | 339 |
| Reading Comprehension | 339 |
|   Understanding the Text | 339 |
|   Summary Completion | 341 |
|   Answering Information Questions | 341 |
| Vocabulary | 342 |
|   Expanding Vocabulary | 342 |
|   Using Vocabulary | 343 |
|   Word Families: Prefix Meanings | 343 |
| Paragraph Topics | 345 |
| Unit III Review | 347 |

**Appendix A Basic Terminology for English-Language Study** — 352

**Appendix B Paragraph Correction Symbols** — 363
**Map of the World** — 364
**Map of the United States** — 366

# PREFACE AND NOTES FOR USE OF THE TEXT

This text is designed for college students at the low to intermediate level of academic reading and expository writing in English as a second language (ESL). Through extensive writing and composing exercises, students will develop competence in expressing their ideas, describing their environment, and narrating personal events using basic English structures and sentence patterns.

The readings in this text are thematically related within each of the three units. The themes of the reading selections are also the subject of the accompanying writing and composition assignments. Vocabulary is recycled throughout the units, and students are provided with an academically oriented information base for oral and written work.

This revision has a number of significant changes from the previous edition. Several new readings replace earlier ones; others have been revised to include current information; and the length and level of difficulty of the reading passages has been adjusted so that they are more developmental. The last unit now includes an adapted short story as one of its additional readings. The *process* of reading has received more attention through a revision of many of the reading comprehension exercises. More important, the *process* of composing has received greater attention, with a significant number of previous exercises either replaced by more process-oriented activities or revised to elicit brainstorming and clustering by the students in preparation for writing. In addition, a new free-write activity has been included in each chapter as a way of stimulating students to write for discovery.

## THE ORGANIZATION OF THE TEXT

As evidenced in the table of contents, the book is divided into three units. Each unit contains three chapters, whose main reading passages are loosely related to the past, the present, and the future. Additional readings, with their own condensed apparatus, follow the main section of each chapter. Each main section is arranged in the following way.

### Prereading

Varied cognitive activities engage the student with the theme of the chapter and provide motivation for the reading passage and the comprehension exercises.

### Free Write

A free-write assignment allows the student to write for discovery on some aspect of the chapter's theme or serves as a warmup to composition. Free writing encourages the student to compose freely without worrying about sentence level and correctness of specific types of organization. Free write can be used as the basis for a more formal composition later or can be used in a number of other ways detailed in the Instructors' Manual.

### Vocabulary in Context

This preliminary vocabulary exercise directs attention to the words that comprise the new word list and are the basis of the vocabulary exercises. Here the student is encouraged to find meanings by using context clues.

### Reading Passage

The focus of the reading passages is some subject or issue that relates to the overall theme of the unit. The level of the reading passages is, in general, more difficult than the writing exercises because our experience and the professional literature suggests that most viable college ESL students are able to read at a higher level of proficiency than they are able to write. Each reading passage is followed by a comprehension exercise of a cumulative type, such as summarizing.

### Discussion Questions

Following each reading passage are questions for discussion that tap both the student's own experience and the information presented in the passage. These questions are usually more conceptually challenging than the level of the material presented in the writing exercises because many ESL college students are mature adults with a wide variety of life experiences and an ability to express complex ideas, albeit in imperfect English. The principles of fluency and communication rather than that of correctness underlie the discussion questions. Although instructors may wish to use the material from the oral discussions as a basis for essay writing, it is not necessary nor always appropriate to do so. The discussion questions are valuable in and of themselves as a base for student interaction and as a simulation of mainstream academic settings.

## Reading Comprehension

In this section, students practice both literal and inferential reading skills. They learn to recognize paragraph topics, central ideas, significant details, and supporting examples, as well as understand the more basic paragraph patterns such as development by time order, spatial arrangement, and enumeration of reasons. Several chapters include more general academic study skills such as outlining or summarizing. Students are encouraged to apply the skills learned in the reading comprehension exercises to their composing processes as well.

## Vocabulary

A new word list directs attention to selected words in the reading passage and provides a number of exercises for their receptive and productive use. It is helpful for the instructor to pronounce these words aloud with the students and encourage them to use them in their own writing. Both dictionary work and contextual and semantic strategies are incorporated in the various vocabulary exercises. Each vocabulary section offers a special word family activity for broader vocabulary enrichment.

## Writing Exercises

The structures comprising this section reflect current consensus about those items that form the foundation of ESL writing or the first half of an ESL "grammar" course. Emphasis is on basic tenses; sentence boundaries, components, and word order; and signal expressions and clause markers necessary for coherence at this introductory level. Although most exercises in this section operate at the sentence level, they compel the student to apply linguistic principles, make choices, and master sentence-level correctness as a prelude to writing longer connected discourse. Review of such items as articles, pronouns, and prepositions is included throughout, but the material is not intended to be comprehensive because most college ESL students have studied these items before.

## Composing Process

There is increased emphasis in this edition on brainstorming and clustering as prewriting activities, and students are encouraged to see writing as a multidrafting process, with editing for correctness the last of several steps. As any instructor who incorporates process approaches in his or her teaching recognizes, however, it is almost a paradox to speak of encapsulating process writing within the covers of a text. Because ESL students at this level often come from educational systems where composing is not part of the English curriculum, we have tried to provide some guidance and structure in the activities that comprise this section. Instructors will be the best judges of the degree to which their students will benefit from the topic frameworks provided by the text.

Brainstorming, the process of generating subtopics and details for an essay by jotting down the ideas that come to mind in regard to a given topic, may be done by students individually or by the class as a whole, with all the items listed in the chalkboard.

Clustering, the step following brainstorming, groups items together in some logical organization (depending on the assignment) to serve as an informal outline or basis for the essay. Because clustering is probably a new activity for many ESL students, and one that taps cognitive skills that may not be developed to the same degree, this activity is best done, at least for the first few essays, as a class, with the instructor using the chalkboard to display the students' responses.

## Unit Review

Each unit of three chapters has its own review, which includes vocabulary work, reading exercises, and composing assignments. The unit review is a cumulative activity that may be done either at home or in class.

## Appendices

Appendix A contains a basic terminology for English-language study and a list of principal parts of irregular verbs.

Appendix B contains the paragraph corrections symbols sheet. Instructors may wish to mark the symbols from the paragraph corrections symbol sheet in the margin or body of the student's essay, or they may simply circle or underline the points at which the error occurs and direct the student to the paragraph corrections symbols sheet to determine the nature of the error and the means of correcting it. Students should spend at least a short period immediately following the return of their papers making the corrections as a prelude to rewriting. This process can be done in pairs so that students can help each other before turning to the instructor as a last resort for corrections. This pair-correction process adds an oral/aural dimension to composition correction and reinforces the idea that writing is communication with another.

# ACKNOWLEDGMENTS

It gives us great pleasure to acknowledge the contributions of our colleagues at New York City Technical College who have provided us with valuable insights in language skills instruction. We would also like to acknowledge our colleagues in TESOL who have been so generous in sharing their ideas at conferences and in publications. A special thanks to Beth Pacheco for her support throughout the project and to Elayne Rinn for her help in preparing the manuscript.

We are especially grateful to Margaret Maron for her important contribution to the reading, "Witching for Water."

Reviewers to whom we are thankful for their constructive suggestions are Mary S. de Benedetti, Miami–Dade Community College; Suzanne Izzo, Georgetown University; and Laura Rossi-Le, Bunker Hill Community College. Reviewers of the present edition are Donald Campbell, University of the Pacific; Theresa Dalle, Memphis State University; Eston Evans, Tennessee Technical Institute; Cynthia Fong, Bunker Hill Community College; James Layton, Illinois Eastern Community College; Myra Redman, Miami–Dade Community College; and Mary Thurber, City College of San Francisco.

For their photographs we would especially like to thank Serena Nanda, Ravinder Nanda, and John Gregg.

To John, Alfred, and Paisley who have experienced the pleasures of learning a second language, we also dedicate this text.

# UNIT I

# OUR DIVERSE WORLD

The beauty of our diverse world

# CHAPTER ONE

# UNCOVERING THE PAST

**PREREADING**

**Class Discussion.** These pictures show things from earlier times. How are they similar to things that we have today? How are they different? What are some ways we can find out about the past?

Silver coin, Persian, third century A.D.

Triumphal arch, Roman, 1st century B.C.

Seated god, Mexico, *circa* A.D. 300

Clay pitcher, Turkey, 18th century B.C.

# Chapter One   Uncovering the Past

> *Free Write.* Some objects in a home may have special meaning to a family. Perhaps they belonged to an older generation, or they may be souvenirs of a past travel experience. Write about one such object in your home. Describe it as fully as you can. Is it an ordinary, useful object or an extraordinary one? How old is it? How did your family acquire it? What meaning does it have for you?

**Vocabulary in Context.**   The words in this exercise will appear in the reading passage.

Circle the word or words that mean the same as the italicized word in each set of sentences. The first one is done for you.

1. A visit to a museum is a pleasant *activity* on a Sunday afternoon. Going with friends is really a nice (thing to do.)

2. Some museums have exhibits of modern art, the art of today, but many people prefer to see *ancient* art and objects. So they usually go to museums that display the art objects of the distant past.

3. There is a *splendid* exhibit of Egyptian art at the Metropolitan Museum in New York. Visitors can see the beautiful statues, paintings, and other objects made by the ancient Egyptians.

4. People like to see the *extraordinary* animal exhibits at the Museum of Natural History. They are especially interested in seeing the remarkable display of dinosaurs and woolly mammoths, animals that are extinct, that no longer exist.

5. The museums of New York are often *crowded*. During the week they are packed full with schoolchildren and on weekends with tourists and families.

6. Museum visitors like to read the labels on the exhibits and to *examine* the objects carefully. But it is often difficult to look closely at them when the exhibit is crowded.

7. The labels on the exhibits give *accurate* information about the objects on display. They often can't give exact dates for the objects, but they always tell you where the objects were found.

8. Sometimes there are maps of the *area* in which the objects were found. It is always interesting to look at the region of land to see exactly where the objects came from.

9. The objects of the past can *reveal* the life of the people of the past. Objects such as animal bones can tell us something about the kind of life that existed thousands of years before human beings.

10. Museums are wonderful places because they *preserve* the works of human beings and the remains of life before humans appeared on earth. Museums are places that save the past for all of us to enjoy.

## READING

### Archeologists at Work

[1] How do we learn about the past? History books can tell us about past events, but in many places the past lies in the earth. It lies beneath the streets in such cities as Rome and Paris or under fields of grain in China and Greece. The past lies buried deep in the jungles of Mexico and Guatemala. The past is hidden in crowded places and in lonely countrysides. When ancient people died, they left behind a record of their lives. Archeologists work to uncover this record. Archeologists from around the world dig in the earth to reveal new information about the history of nations.

[2] Archeologists spend long days of hard work preserving the record of life in the past. First, they must clear an area, measure it, and draw an accurate plan of the ground. Then they dig slowly, layer by layer. They usually use such hand tools as small picks, spades, and brushes. The archeologist uses a brush to clean the soil away from an object as it comes out of the ground. Archeologists always take photographs of each layer of earth. They make notes of each discovery and mark the place on the plan. The objects are carefully removed from the soil and brought to the laboratory. There the archeologists examine them in detail and write their reports. In this way, the past lives again in the archeologist's notebooks and in the objects themselves.

[3] Archeologists find different kinds of objects that helped ordinary people to pass their lives. They unearth the pots, jars, and dishes from which family members ate and drank; the tools they used for sewing; the weapons with which they hunted animals or killed one another. Occasionally, children's toys and games lie among the household ruins. Archeologists always search carefully for religious objects. They sometimes find small statues in the shape of animals or humans. These figures may represent the gods that the people worshipped. Other discoveries include simple jewelry made of stone beads or bone. Even in their graves, ancient people wore necklaces, earrings, and hair ornaments to decorate their bodies. All these objects reveal information about the daily activities and social customs of countless ordinary people.

[4] The rich and powerful people of the past also left a record. When they died, they were often buried with splendid items of gold, silver, and rare stones.

# Chapter One  Uncovering the Past

Archeological work includes piecing together broken objects found in the ground. Does this look like interesting work to you? Why or why not?

Grave robbers sometimes find such treasures before archeologists do. But Dr. Walter Alva was fortunate. He recently discovered a tomb of the Moche people of Peru. It contained the bones of a ruler, three other men, and two women, possibly the ruler's wives. The objects included face masks, beads shaped like peanuts, and knives, all made of gold. In the 1920s, Sir Leonard Woolley had the good fortune to find the grave of Shub-ad, the queen of Ur in ancient Iraq. Such items as jewelry, furniture, vases, statues, musical instruments, and weapons, all made of the most expensive materials, filled the grave. There were also wagons, carts, and a special carriage for the queen. Shub-ad, like the Moche ruler, was buried with members of her household. From the work of archeologists like Alva and Woolley, we learn a great deal about powerful rulers and the extraordinary artistic and technical skills of their people.

[5]   Sometimes archeologists discover written records of the past. Ancient people usually wrote on stone, clay, or bone objects. Many types of texts exist from ancient times: government regulations and codes of law; reports of armies in battle; poems about heroes, gods, and goddesses. There are school exercises in mathematics and language as well as business and personal letters. One letter from the Middle East reveals the advice of a father to his disobedient son:

> Night and day I am disappointed in you. Night and day you waste your time in pleasures. All your relatives are unhappy about your behavior. Come now, be a man. Don't stand about in the public square or wander in the streets. My

son, do you want to achieve success? Go to school. It will be a benefit to you. Get the advice of the older generations. Ask them for help. Be a good friend. Show your humanity to others.

This text is about 4000 years old. Was this disappointed father very different from some modern parents?

[6] The earth holds information of other times, of life and death, war and peace, work and play, and the ordinary and extraordinary. Archeologists uncover the past and preserve it. They help us to understand that the past is still present and that it belongs to all of us.

**Summary Completion.** Fill in the blank spaces with the correct word from the reading passage.

The past lies in the (1) _____. Archeologists dig in the earth to reveal new (2) _____ about life in ancient times. They work very (3) _____ to preserve the objects that come out of the ground. Some of the objects come from places where ordinary (4) _____ lived, so we learn about family activities and social (5) _____. From the tombs of rich and powerful people, archeologists may find extraordinary (6) _____ that show the technical skills of ancient people. Archeologists sometimes discover (7) _____ on clay, stone, or bone. Everything that archeologists uncover helps us to (8) _____ the past. Perhaps the people of the past weren't very (9) _____ from us.

## DISCUSSION QUESTIONS

1. Museums around the world display objects and works of art from ancient times. Name a museum where you can see such items. Tell what objects are especially interesting in that museum. What culture do the objects represent? What facts about the past do the objects reveal? Should objects be returned to museums in their country of origin?

2. Some people want to buy ancient objects or works of art found by archeologists. But these discoveries belong to the country in which they were found. Should people be allowed to buy these things and keep them in their homes to enjoy privately? Or should they be in museums in the country in which they were found, for everyone to enjoy?

3. Sometimes archeologists want to dig in areas where people live. They think it is important to look for ancient objects beneath village houses or in certain areas of a city. Do you think that governments should make people move from their homes so that archeologists can dig? If a government allows this to happen, what should it offer the people in return? Would you want to move from your home if this happened to you?

4. Many modern cities have old buildings with historic importance. These buildings are often very beautiful and well constructed. But some landowners want to tear them down to build high-rise office buildings or expensive apartments. Should these old buildings be torn down? What could be done to save these buildings and make them more useful?

## READING COMPREHENSION

1. **Understanding the Text.** Choose the correct answer.
    a. According to Paragraph [1], which statement is true?
        (1) We learn about the past only in history books.
        (2) Archeology is a way of learning about the past.
        (3) Ancient people were interested in learning about the past.
    b. In Paragraph [2], the fifth sentence, the word *it* refers to
        (1) a brush.
        (2) the soil.
        (3) an object.
    c. In Paragraph [2], the sentence before the last, the word *There* means
        (1) on the plan.
        (2) in a notebook.
        (3) in a laboratory.
    d. Archeologists dig in a special way
        (1) to destroy the record of the past.
        (2) to save the record of past life as much as possible.
        (3) because they want to keep ancient objects for themselves.
    e. Ordinary people of the past left behind objects showing that
        (1) there was no religion in ancient times.
        (2) they had only the basic needs of food, clothing, and houses.
        (3) they had more than just the basic things in life.

**f.** According to Paragraph [3], the graves of ordinary people
  **(1)** sometimes contain jewelry.
  **(2)** only contain bones.
  **(3)** never contain kitchen items.

**g.** The information in Paragraph [4]
  **(1)** gives further information about ordinary people of the past.
  **(2)** gives us a view of ancient society different from Paragraph [3].
  **(3)** describes how archeologists found some ancient tombs.

**h.** From the objects found in Peru and Iraq, we can say that
  **(1)** some ancient people probably believed in an afterlife.
  **(2)** rich people probably lived a simple life.
  **(3)** ancient people had little technical or artistic skill.

**i.** Ancient texts give us
  **(1)** information only about public affairs.
  **(2)** information about public as well as private affairs.
  **(3)** no information about education.

**j.** In Paragraph [6], the words in the pairs *war and peace, life and death, work and play, the ordinary and extraordinary*
  **(1)** are the same in meaning.
  **(2)** refer only to the past.
  **(3)** are the opposite in meaning.

2. **Answering Information Questions.** Answer the following questions in complete sentences. Then write your own summary of the reading passage using some of your completed answers.

  **a.** Why do archeologists dig in the earth?
  **b.** What special tools do archeologists use?
  **c.** Why does an archeologist use a brush?
  **d.** Where do archeologists examine the objects?
  **e.** What items occasionally lie among the household ruins?
  **f.** What do we learn from the extraordinary objects found in Peru and Iraq?
  **g.** What materials did ancient people usually write on?
  **h.** What kind of letters and exercises exist from ancient times?
  **i.** How old is the father's letter to his son?

**Chapter One  Uncovering the Past**

3. **The Reading Process: General and Specific Words; Topics.** A general word is a word used for a large group or class of things. A specific word is used to give us a special detail or example of a more general word.

---
General word: people          General word: student
Specific word: queens         Specific words: archeology student
---

a. For each set of words, mark *G* next to the more *general* word(s) and *S* next to the more *specific* word(s). The first one is done for you.

(1) tool _G_          (6) men _____
    brush _S_             kings _____
(2) city _____        (7) business letters _____
    Rome _____            writing _____
(3) notebook _____        school lessons _____
    book _____        (8) occupation _____
(4) ball _____            farming _____
    doll _____            teaching _____
    toy _____         (9) silver _____
(5) chair _____           metal _____
    furniture _____       gold _____

b. In the blank space write a general word that names the group of specific words. The first one is done for you.

(1) picks    spades    shovels  _tools_
(2) Mexico    China    Guatemala    Italy _____
(3) farmers    schoolboys    soldiers    queens _____
(4) chairs    desks    beds    bookcases _____
(5) ring    bracelet    necklace    beads _____
(6) jars    pots    dishes _____
(7) dress    hat    shirt _____
(8) notes    letters    compositions _____
(9) statues    paintings    drawings _____

(10) piano    guitar    violin    harp _____

(11) guns    spears    bombs _____

(12) wheat    oats    barley _____

(13) dictionary    atlas    encyclopedia _____

(14) biology    chemistry    physics _____

(15) wagons    trains    sleds _____

c. The topic of a paragraph or a passage is the general idea or general subject. We use general words to talk about topics. Read the following paragraph. Look for the sentence that tells the topic, or the general subject of the paragraph. In the list that follows the paragraph, circle the item that tells the topic, or general subject.

The ancient hunters of Europe left behind splendid paintings on cave walls. There are paintings of animals such as wild horses, reindeer, and bison. Figures of humans holding weapons sometimes appear near the animals. There are painted finger marks and handprints in some caves. In other caves there are rows of painted dots and lines, or strange signs. Cave paintings are thousands of years old, but their colors are still quite strong.

(1) human figures painted in caves
(2) paintings of animals on cave walls
(3) strange signs made by ancient hunters
(4) ancient cave paintings
(5) the colors of cave paintings
(6) finger and hand prints of the cave painters

The first sentence of this paragraph states the topic: *paintings on cave walls*. The correct choice from the list is item 4. Item 4 is the most general idea of the paragraph. The other items are specifics, or details that support the topic.

Circle the correct answer for the following items about the reading passage.

(1) The topic of Paragraph [2] is

    a. tools of the archeologist.
    b. what archeologists do in a laboratory.
    c. how archeologists work.

A fragment from Queen Shub-ad's tomb shows activities of the Queen's life on earth.

(2) The topic of Paragraph [3] is
   a. children's toys and games from ancient times.
   b. ordinary family objects discovered by archeologists.
   c. discoveries of ancient tools and kitchen items.

(3) The topic of Paragraph [4] is
   a. discoveries in the ancient tombs of powerful people.
   b. the gold and silver objects found in a queen's tomb.
   c. wagons, carts, and carriages discovered by Sir Leonard Woolley.

(4) The topic of Paragraph [5] is
   a. government records from the past.
   b. school exercises from the ancient Middle East.
   c. written records of past life.

(5) The topic of the whole reading passage is
   a. learning how archeologists dig for ancient objects.
   b. discovering the past through archeology.
   c. preserving extraordinary objects from ancient tombs.

## VOCABULARY

1. **New Words.** Pronounce the words following your instructor.

| Verbs | Nouns | Adjectives | Adverbs |
|---|---|---|---|
| preserve | area | crowded | |
| reveal | activity | ancient | |
| examine | | splendid | |
| | | extraordinary | |
| | | accurate | |

*Using Vocabulary.* Write a complete sentence in answer to the question. Use the italicized word in your answer. The first one is done for you as a possible answer.

a. Does your friend ever *reveal* secrets to you?

*My friend never reveals secrets to me.*

b. Do you ever *reveal* your secrets to a friend?

c. Where do people go to see *ancient* objects?

d. Why is a giraffe an *extraordinary* animal?

e. What do you like to do on a *splendid* summer day?

f. Is your neighborhood usually *crowded* with shoppers on Saturday afternoon?

g. What is your favorite sports *activity* or weekend *activity*?

h. Should a country try to *preserve* its ancient temples or tear them down?

i. Where can you find *accurate* information about a person's address?

j. Where do archeologists *examine* the objects they find?

k. Are there inexpensive restaurants in your *area* of the city?
_____

2. **Word Families.** Study the following lists:

| **Type of Work** | **Person Who Does That Type of Work** |
|---|---|
| archeology | archeologist |
| art | artist |
| science | scientist |
| writing | writer |
| teaching | teacher |
| photography | photographer |
| history | historian |
| mathematics | mathematician |

*Sentence Completion.* Choose the correct word in parentheses to fill in the blank space in each sentence.

a. (archeology, archeologist) An _____ digs in the earth to find hidden objects. We learn about the people of the past through _____ .

b. (art, artist) Pablo Picasso was a famous Spanish _____ . His _____ is in museum collections all over the world.

c. (farming, farmer) In the past, _____ was the usual type of work. An ancient _____ probably made his own tools.

d. (history, historian) Sir Moses Finley is a professor of ancient _____ _____ . Many books about ancient society have been written by this famous _____ .

e. (photography, photographer) A good _____ always takes interesting pictures. In _____ it is important to know how to compose a picture.

f. (writing, writer) Composing a mental picture is the job of a _____ _____ . Think about composing a clear, interesting picture in your own _____ .

g. (science, scientist) Geology is the branch of _____ that

deals with the rocks that compose the earth. Dr. Mary Landers is a well-known _____ in the field of geology.

h. (teacher, teaching) Does your _____ enjoy _____ this class?

i. (psychology, psychologist) A _____ studies the human mind. Teachers of young children often take courses in child _____.

j. (astronomy, astronomer) One of the most difficult subjects is _____, the study of the planets and stars. An _____ spends long hours looking through a telescope.

k. (mathematics, mathematician) You have to know _____ well to be an astronomer. Understanding the laws of nature in space isn't difficult for a _____.

Now fill in the blank spaces in the following sentences with information about yourself.

I want to be a (an) _____. I am taking courses in _____.

## WRITING EXERCISES

### Sentence Kernels

1. **Verbs.** The verb is the heart of the English sentence. There cannot be an English sentence without a complete main verb. The main verb is the word that tells us the state of being, the feeling, or the action of a person, place, or thing.

> An archeologist *digs* in the ground.

*Recognizing Verbs.* Underline the verbs in the following sentences:
a. The earth holds many secrets about the past.
b. An archeologist writes everything in a notebook.

c. Archeologists discover objects of gold and silver.
d. They never keep these objects for themselves.
e. We learn about the past from these ancient objects.

2. **Subjects.** The subject of a sentence answers the question, *Who* or *what* is doing the verb action?

> *An archeologist* **digs** in the ground. (Who digs?)

*Recognizing Subjects.* Go back to sentences *a, b, c, d,* and *e*. Circle the subject of each underlined verb.

3. **Identifying Verbs and Subjects.**

   a. Read the following paragraph carefully. Find the complete main verb in each sentence. Put each verb in the Verb column of the chart that follows. Then find the subject of each verb. Put the subject in the Subject column. The first one is done for you.

   (1) Professor Ortiz teaches archeology in Mexico City. (2) He has permission to dig in certain areas of the city. (3) His students help him in the field. (4) They follow his instructions carefully. (5) They receive course credit for their work. (6) The professor writes a report about their discoveries at the end of the dig.

| Subject | Verb |
|---|---|
| 1 *Professor Ortiz* | *teaches* |
| 2 | |
| 3 | |
| 4 | |
| 5 | |
| 6 | |

Now respond to the following questions orally, in short answers. The first set of answers is given to you.

Sentence (1): What does Professor Ortiz teach? *Archeology.* Where? *In Mexico City.*

Sentence (2) What does he have permission to do? Where?

Sentence (3) Where do his students help him?

Sentence (4) What do they follow? How?

Sentence (5) What do they receive? For what?

Sentence (6) What does the professor write? About what? When?

Now place the chart of Subjects and Verbs on the board. With your books closed, reconstruct as closely as possible the paragraph about Professor Ortiz and his students.

b. Write a short paragraph about someone you know who has an interesting job. Check each sentence for a subject and a verb. Make it clear to your reader who your subject is and what his or her actions are.

## Simple Present Tense

The Simple Present tense is used to tell a fact or describe something that is generally true. It is used to tell about things that people usually do (not what they are doing right now). All the verbs in your Verb column are in the Simple Present tense.

> **Archeologists *dig* in the ground. (This is something they usually do.)**

Study the following Simple Present tense forms.

|  | Singular | Plural |
|---|---|---|
| First Person | I dig | An archeologist and I dig<br>We dig |
| Second Person | You dig | You dig |
| Third Person | An archeologist digs<br>He/She/It digs | Archeologists dig<br>They dig |

Notice that only the Third Person Singular form has the extra *s* at the end.

1. **Sentence Completion.**

    In the blank space, write the correct verb form from the pair in parentheses. First you must find the subject. Is the subject singular or plural? Choose the verb that agrees in number with its subject.

Dr. Diana Warren is a famous archeologist. She (work, works) (1) _____ in Italy. Many archeologists (dig, digs) (2) _____ with her. They (bring, brings) (3) _____ the past to life. But Dr. Warren also (discover, discovers) (4) _____ the past of New York City. She sometimes (dig, digs) (5) _____ on Staten Island or in lower Manhattan. She (look, looks) (6) _____ for objects from the Dutch or English periods. Her discoveries (give, gives) (7) _____ us an interesting picture of daily life in those times. Many secrets of New York (lie, lies) (8) _____ beneath the city streets. As Dr. Warren (say, says) (9) _____, "Everyday we (walk, walks) (10) _____ on top of our history."

2. **Scrambled Sentences.** The words in each item form a complete English sentence, but they are out of order. Rewrite the words in the correct order so they form a correct sentence. Punctuate the sentence. Remember to look for the verb first. Then find its subject.

| ground . archeologists maps the draw of |
|---|
| *Archeologists draw maps of the ground.* |

a. everything    an archeologist    .    writes    in a notebook
b. us    .    tell    archeologists    a lot    the past    about
c. find    sometimes    and    archeologists    .    bones    weapons
d. of the past    .    discover    also    written records    they
e. carefully    these    .    the archeologists    records    preserve    ancient

3. **Controlled Writing.** Rewrite the following paragraph. Change the subject *Paula and Brian* to the singular subject *Paula*. Change the pronoun *they* to *she*. Change all the verbs to the Third Person Singular. Your first sentence will be the following: *My friend Paula is an archeologist.*

My friends Paula and Brian are archeologists. They know a lot about the past. Every summer they dig in Turkey. Usually they find pieces of pots and dishes, but sometimes they discover gold and silver objects. Paula and Brian always write me postcards and send me splendid photographs of Turkey. They want me to visit them there one summer. They want to show me their extraordinary discoveries.

## Plurals

An *archeologist* is one person. *Archeologist* is singular. *Archeologists* refers to more than one person. *Archeologists* is plural.

1. **Regular Plurals.** Most regular plural nouns are formed by adding *s* to the singular form.

| Singular | Plural |
|---|---|
| a place | places |
| a toy | toys |

Regular plurals of nouns ending in *y* preceded by a consonant are formed by changing the *y* to *i* and adding *es*.

| Singular | Plural |
|---|---|
| a discovery | discoveries |

Regular plurals of nouns ending in *sh*, *s*, or *x* are formed by adding *es* to the singular form.

| Singular | Plural |
|---|---|
| a class | classes |
| a wish | wishes |
| a tax | taxes |

Regular plurals of nouns ending in *f* or *fe* are formed by changing the *f* or *fe* to *v* and adding *es*.

| Singular | Plural |
|---|---|
| a knife | knives |

Note that the plural of the nouns *belief, chief,* and *roof* are formed by adding *s* only.

*List Completion.* Fill in the blank spaces with the correct singular or plural form.

| Singular | Plural |
|---|---|
| a secret | _____ |
| a goddess | _____ |
| _____ | areas |
| a body | _____ |
| a piece | _____ |
| _____ | objects |
| a boy | _____ |
| a country | _____ |
| _____ | boxes |
| _____ | games |
| a dish | _____ |
| a story | _____ |
| a brush | _____ |
| _____ | lives |

When a singular noun is not specific, we use the indefinite article *a* or *an* in front of it. When we write plural nouns, we do not use *a* or *an*.

2. **Irregular Plurals.** Irregular plurals do not follow one pattern. Study the following list of irregular plurals.

| Singular | Plural |
|---|---|
| a man | men |
| a woman | women |
| a child | children |
| a mouse | mice |
| a tooth | teeth |
| a foot | feet |

*Sentence Completion.* Choose the correct word in parentheses to fill in the blank space in each sentence.

a. (place, places) Archeologists go to many _____ to dig in the earth.

b. (Child, Children) _____ like to dig in the sand at the beach.

c. (object, objects) An archeologist is always happy to find a gold _____ in the earth.

d. (man, men) Most _____ a thousand years ago were farmers.

e. (bone, bones) Archeologists sometimes find animal _____ when they dig in the earth.

f. (plan, plans) Archeologists make careful _____ of the places where they dig.

g. (woman, women) A _____ of the past usually made her own clothing.

h. (story, stories) Do you like to read _____ about men and women of the past?

i. (piece, pieces) Chinese people of the past often wrote on _____ _____ of bone.

3. **Sentence Rewriting.** Follow the directions.

   a. Change the italicized words in each sentence to plurals. Write your new sentence on the line. The first one is done for you.

   (1) I keep *a brush* and *a broom* in my kitchen closet.

   *I keep brushes and brooms in my kitchen closet.*

(2) I would like to visit *a country* where I can see *an* ancient *temple*.

_____

(3) I write *a letter* to *a friend* when I have time.

_____

(4) Sometimes I make *a* long-distance phone *call* to *a relative*.

_____

(5) *An archeologist* must write *a report* about the discoveries in the field.

_____

(6) My cousin always wears *an* expensive *dress* to *a party*.

_____

b. Change the italicized words in each sentence to singular. Write your new sentence on the line. The first one is done for you.

(1) I want to put up *shelves* and buy *bookcases* for my bedroom.

*I want to put up a shelf and buy a bookcase for my bedroom.*

(2) My friend is taking *courses* in geology. He has excellent *teachers*.

_____

(3) I usually buy *toys* as birthday *gifts* for young *children*.

_____

(4) I always have *pens, pencils,* and *erasers* in my bookbag.

_____

(5) *Archeologists* must make accurate *plans* of the ground.

_____

(6) *Students* should buy pocket *dictionaries* for English *classes*.

_____

## Prepositions

Prepositions are short but important words in English. They show the relationship among things, people, and places. The words *in, on, to, from, at, between,* and *next to* are just a few of the many prepositions. Some prepositions indicate direction, some indicate a place, and some indicate a time.

> Archeologists take the objects *from* the field *to* the laboratory. (direction)
> I keep my books *on* the desk. I sit *at* the desk to study. (place)
> I get up *at* 7:00 A.M. I usually work until late *at* night. (time)

1. **Prepositional Phrases of Direction.** A prepositional phrase is a group of words that begins with a preposition and includes a noun or pronoun indicating a person, place, or thing. The prepositions *to* and *from* will begin a phrase that includes a noun.

   > She comes *from* New York. She goes *to* Turkey in the summer.

   *Answering Questions with Prepositional Phrases.* Write the answers to the following questions in complete sentences. Use a phrase with *to* or *from* in each sentence. Underline the prepositional phrases of direction in your sentences.

   a. What country do you come from?
   b. Where do you often go on a warm day?
   c. Do you walk to school, or do you take a bus or train?
   d. Is the plane ride from New York to London one hour or six hours?
   e. Do you go home from school alone or with friends?

2. **Prepositional Phrases of Place.** A prepositional phrase of place will include a preposition and a noun. The phrase will tell *where* someone or something is located.

   > She sits *next to her friend*. She keeps her books *under the chair*.

   a. *Recognizing Prepositional Phrases of Place.* Study the following list of some common prepositions of place. Then read the paragraph about an ancient Roman house. Underline the prepositional phrases of place. The first one is done for you.

   | | | |
   |---|---|---|
   | at, at the back of | around | on, on the side of |
   | under | beside | behind |
   | next to | inside | among |
   | by | in, in the center of | |

The entrance of a Roman house was a simple doorway <u>next to the shops</u> on the street. Inside the doorway there was a courtyard. The roof of the courtyard had an opening in the center, and under the opening there was a basin on the ground to collect the rainwater. Around the courtyard were a few small bedrooms. At the back of the courtyard was another room that the Romans used for eating or studying. A large open garden was located behind that room. Here the Roman family sat by the fishpond or among the fruit trees and enjoyed their free time. Sometimes they ate in a dining room on the side of the garden. The plan of an ancient Roman house was simple, and it gave the family a lot of privacy.

This modern Turkish potter is working with the same materials potters used in ancient times.

    **b.** *Sentence Combining.* In some areas of the world today, as in ancient times, the potter is an important member of a village community. The following sentences describe the potter in the photograph. The second and third sentences in a set contain a prepositional phrase of place. Combine each set into one complete sentence. Leave out unnecessary words. The first combination is done for you.

    **(1)** The potter works everyday. He is in his shop. The shop is next to his house.

*The potter works every day in his shop next to his house.*

(2) He keeps the clay. The clay is in a tub. The tub is in a corner of the shop.

(3) There is a potter's wheel. It is near the window. The window is on the other side of the shop.

(4) To make a pitcher, the potter throws a lump of clay. The clay is on the wheel.

(5) The clay spins around by means of a pedal. The pedal is under the wheel.

(6) The potter moves his hands. His hands are over the clay to form a beautiful shape.

(7) He uses his fingers. His fingers are around the neck of the pitcher to create an interesting design.

(8) Sometimes he paints a design. The design is around the body of the pitcher. Or sometimes it is just on the neck.

(9) He dries his pitchers. They are outside the workshop. They are in the sun.

Now think of a place where you work, study, or pursue a hobby. Describe some features of the place and your activities there. Use prepositional phrases as appropriate.

c. *Answering Questions.* Write a complete sentence using a prepositional phrase of place.

(1) Where is the best place for a telephone in the home?

(2) When they are not in the closet, where do you sometimes find your shoes?

(3) Where is the light switch in your kitchen?

(4) Where does a house cat like to sleep to keep warm?

(5) In which room do you usually study?

(6) Where do you like to sit in a movie theater?

(7) In what city does your best friend live?

(8) Where is the best place for a reading lamp?

3. **Prepositional Phrases of Time.** Study the list of prepositional phrases that answer the question *when*?

| | | |
|---|---|---|
| in the morning/afternoon/ evening | on July 4 | at 6 A.M./P.M./ o'clock |
| in the summer/winter | on holidays | at lunch time |
| in May/August | on the weekend | at night/noon/ midnight |

| in the past | on Friday/Sunday | at the end/beginning of the day/semester |

*Sentence Completion.* Fill in the blank spaces with *at, in,* or *on* to complete the prepositional phrase of time.

a. We always talk about the day's events _____ dinnertime.
b. _____ weekends I usually go to bed _____ midnight.
c. _____ the beginning of the semester I'll buy my new textbooks.
d. I'll take a trip to Boston _____ Easter or _____ the summer.
e. My parents pay all their bills _____ the beginning of every month.
f. My friend from Colorado will visit me _____ July.
g. _____ Saturdays I usually go shopping _____ the afternoon.
h. Americans celebrate Independence Day _____ July 4.
i. I attend school _____ night because I work _____ the morning and afternoon.
j. I get home _____ 11:00 P.M. I'm very tired _____ the end of the day.

## Adverbs of Frequency

Adverbs of frequency tells us how often we do things or how often something happens. The words *always, usually, frequently, often, sometimes, occasionally, rarely,* and *never* are adverbs of frequency. Study the following chart.

| always | usually | frequently often | occasionally sometimes | rarely | never |
|---|---|---|---|---|---|
| 100% of the time | | less than half of the time | | | none of the time |

Review Paragraphs [3], [4], and [5] of the reading passage for the use of these adverbs. With your class, discuss the position of these adverbs in the sentences.

1. **Dictation.** Write each sentence as your instructor dictates it.

    a. My friend often goes to Mexico in the summer.
    b. She always visits the museums there.
    c. She rarely writes me letters from Mexico.
    d. She usually sends me splendid picture postcards.

e. I never throw the postcards away.
f. Sometimes I look at them in my spare time.

2. **Sentence Composing.** Write a complete sentence following the directions for each item. The first one is done for you.

   a. Tell where you sometimes study your English lessons.
      *I sometimes study my English lessons in the school library.*
   b. Tell when you usually eat dinner.
   c. Tell where children often play after school.
   d. Describe what an artist always needs.
   e. Tell what article of clothing you rarely wear in the summer.
   f. Tell what you frequently do in your spare time.
   g. State what time you usually go to bed on weekdays.
   h. Tell who you occasionally visit on weekends.
   i. Tell what you never do on a test.
   j. Tell where your teacher usually stands.
   k. Explain what you always do before a test.

3. **Sentence Combining.** Combine each group of sentences into one sentence. Add the adverb of frequency in parenthesis to your sentence in the appropriate position. Leave out all unnecessary words. The first combination is done for you.

   a. In early autumn I take a walk. I walk through the fields. The fields are in back of my house. (often)
      *In early autumn, I often take a walk through the fields in back of my house.*
   b. I look around. I look for ancient American objects. I look in the soil. (always)

   c. Objects appear in great numbers. They appear on top of the soil. They appear among small stones. (sometimes)

   d. Objects lie on the ground. They lie under larger rocks. (occasionally)

e. I collect the objects carefully. I collect them from the ground. I take them back to my house. (always)

f. I examine the objects. I examine them with a magnifying glass. (usually)

g. I keep these objects. They are in a special cabinet. They are in my living room. (always)

h. My friends come to see my collection. It is an interesting collection of ancient American artifacts. (frequently)

## Punctuation and Capitalization

In English every new sentence begins with a capital letter. Every complete sentence ends with a period. The names of countries, states, and cities begin with capital letters. Punctuate and capitalize the following paragraph.

> my friend robert is an archeologist every summer he digs in mexico or colombia he digs for objects from the past he usually finds pots and dishes sometimes he finds gold and silver next summer robert and i are going to mexico together i want to see his interesting discoveries

Only one English pronoun is always capitalized. It is capitalized at the beginning of a sentence and within the sentence. Do you know which pronoun this is? Can you find it in the paragraph? Did you capitalize it?

## THE COMPOSING PROCESS

1. **Developing a Central Topic.** The topic of a paragraph is the general idea or general subject. Once you have a topic for writing, you can develop a paragraph by brainstorming for specifics to support the topic.

Read the following paragraph. Then with your classmates discuss the questions.

Archeologists usually have a busy day. They eat breakfast at 6:00 A.M. Then they go to work in the field. They dig until 11:00 A.M. They have an early lunch and take a rest in the afternoon. After that, they return to the field and work until sundown. In the evening, after dinner, they write their reports or work in the laboratory. Sometimes they have free time to relax or read a book. They usually go to bed late.

What is the topic of this paragraph?
In which sentence does the topic appear?
How is the topic developed?
Is there a logical order to the sentences? What kind of order?
Do all the specific sentences support the topic?

**a.** Use the following topic to develop a paragraph similar to the one about archeologists: My Busiest Day. Before you write, make a list of specific activities on the lines provided. Then arrange your items in time order, from earliest to latest.

_____    _____    _____    _____

_____    _____    _____    _____

_____    _____    _____    _____

Begin your paragraph by telling your reader about your topic. Write your first version using your list of activities. Exchange papers with a classmate. Does your partner understand your schedule? Can he or she suggest ways to make your writing clearer? Rewrite your paragraph making any necessary corrections. Check for correct use of the Present tense, pronouns, prepositional phrases, and adverbs of frequency.

**b.** Weekend schedules or a day off from work or school are usually pleasurable times. Think of a family member (brother, sister, parent) or a friend and his or her Saturday, Sunday, or day off. In the following outline, list that person's activities in short note form. Then develop the items into a paragraph about the person. Begin with a topic sentence. Review your version, make corrections, and rewrite.

in the morning    _____

_____

_____

in the afternoon _____
_____
_____

at night _____
_____
_____

2. **Composing a Paragraph.** In Paragraph [2] of the reading passage, you are told about the steps archeologists follow when they work in the field. Compose a paragraph based on the topic: Preparing for a Party or Having Guests for Dinner. Some items are listed for you. Add others after you discuss the topic with your classmates. Begin your paragraph with a sentence that introduces the reader to your topic. Develop the paragraph in time order.

   prepare special foods _____ _____
   get dressed _____ _____
   clean the house _____ _____

3. **Paragraph Topics**

   a. Write a paragraph telling what you do on a typical summer day when you are free. Tell where you like to go and with whom you usually go. Include the different activities in which you take part on such a day. Begin with an appropriate topic sentence.

   b. Compose a paragraph that describes the steps you take to do a certain activity. Here are some suggestions for topics: washing a car, dressing a baby, taking a photograph, making a sandwich. You and a classmate may want to brainstorm and collaborate on the paragraph. Begin with a sentence that introduces your topic.

## ADDITIONAL READING

### A Hero's Life

Ancient people wrote stories on clay tablets. The Sumerians, a group of people who lived in the Middle East 3000 years ago, wrote the story of their hero Gilgamesh in this way. Gilgamesh wanted to uncover mysteries and gain knowledge. He wanted to understand the meaning of life and death. The legend of Gilgamesh is 3000 years old, but it reveals something about the joys and sorrows of life at any time and in any place.

Ancient people wrote stories on clay tablets such as this fragment from Sumer. Many tablets were needed to record the story of Gilgamesh.

When his tale begins,* Gilgamesh is the young king of Uruk, a city in the land of Sumer. He rules his people with a strong hand, but he is restless and ambitious. He wants to do great deeds and become famous throughout the world. His people want to be left in peace, so they pray to the sky god Anu for help. "O Great Anu," they cry, "create a companion for Gilgamesh, someone who is equal to him in strength and courage. Then they can go away together on adventures, and we will be left in peace."

In response, the god creates Enkidu to be Gilgamesh's best friend. At last, Gilgamesh has someone he loves and trusts, a comrade who will join him in great deeds.

Together Gilgamesh and Enkidu set out to find fame and wealth. They travel to the faraway land of the Cedar Forest. They want to cut down the trees and bring the wood back to build temples to all the gods of the land. This is a dangerous task. The giant Humbaba guards the forest against all enemies. Humbaba has great powers. He hears everything, he breathes fire, and he never sleeps. As the two companions come near the home of this giant, they begin to feel afraid and weak. They wait a little to overcome their fear. Then they attack. Humbaba fights for his life but knows that the two together are stronger than he is. "Let me go free, and the trees will be yours," the giant begs.

Gilgamesh and Enkidu must decide if their enemy should live or die. It is a difficult choice, but they decide to kill him. When Humbaba is dead, they cut down the trees and return to Uruk with the wood. Then Gilgamesh builds his temples to all the gods.

*Stories about the past are often told in the Simple Present tense to make them more real to the reader or listener.

The Sumerians were very respectful of their gods and goddesses and built many temples to honor them. Here is a statue of a worshipper found in a temple in Sumer.

Now Gilgamesh is a hero in his city and famous throughout the land. Immediately, the goddess Ishtar falls in love with him. "Take me as your bride," she says, and offers him all kinds of splendid gifts.

Gilgamesh refuses her. "You are cruel to those you love. You never remain faithful to those who love you," he responds.

Ishtar becomes very angry and calls on Anu for help. "Father Anu, send down to earth the Bull of Heaven to punish Gilgamesh for this insult," she demands.

Anu agrees, and the bull falls on the land of Sumer. It kills hundreds of people. Then it attacks Enkidu. To save his friend, Gilgamesh stabs the bull in the neck. With the death of the bull, the people are free from fear.

Everyone in the land is joyful, but sadness soon follows. The gods decide that Enkidu must die as punishment for the death of the bull. He falls sick. Day after day he suffers, and Gilgamesh cries for him. Finally Enkidu's life ends and Gilgamesh loses a dear friend, a brother. He waits for the body to return to life, but he soon understands the meaning of death. "I too will die someday and lie in the earth forever."

Gilgamesh cannot rest or be at peace. He is afraid of death. He wants to discover the secret of everlasting life. He leaves Uruk to find the Far-Away, the only man who has everlasting life. It is a long and difficult way to the home of this wise man, down an unknown road. Along the way he meets a mysterious woman and tells her of his wish. "Accept death," she tells him. "Eat and dance, marry and have children, for these things make men happy."

Gilgamesh cannot accept her advice. In pain and sorrow, he continues on the dark road. At last, after many hardships, he arrives at the Far-Away's home. "Oh Far-Away, I wish to question you about the living and the dead. How can I find everlasting life as you did?" he asks.

"Everything changes," explains the Far-Away. "No one lives forever. I am free of death as a special gift from the gods. No one else can have that gift."

Then the Far-Away tells the story of the mysterious ways of the gods. At the end he says, "You, Gilgamesh, must return to Uruk and live the way all men live." He gives his guest new clothes for the journey home. Gilgamesh leaves with understanding in his heart.

Old and tired, he arrives home. He is worn out from his difficult travels and his suffering. But he is proud of his city of Uruk, the beautiful towers and temples, the high walls of brick, and the rich fields of grain for his people. Gilgamesh is wise now, not sad. He accepts death and life. His people shout, "O Lord Gilgamesh, greatly we praise you." They say that they will write his story, a hero's life, for others to read in the future.

## DISCUSSION QUESTIONS

1. A hero is an extraordinary person. Every culture has its heroes, usually leaders who have helped their people. Discuss the deeds of a leader that you think of as a hero.

    Some people think of movie stars, singers, and sports figures as heroes. What qualities do those people have that make them seem like heroes? Do you think of any entertainer or sports person as a hero? Why?

2. We all suffer at the death of a friend or relative. How do we show our sorrow at such a loss? Describe the various ways we comfort each other at such times.

3. We know that we cannot stay young forever. However, there are ways to keep our bodies and minds active for a long time. What are some of the ways people can stay youthful in mind and in body?

    Do you think that people spend too much time and money on trying to stay young in body? What kinds of things do advertisements in newspapers and magazines and on TV try to sell to keep us young? Do you believe these ads? Give reasons for your opinion.

4. Everything changes; nothing lasts forever. Think of the different kinds of love:

between parents and children, brothers and sisters, husbands and wives, and close friends. How much do these relationships change throughout life?

## READING COMPREHENSION

1. **Understanding the Text.** Choose the correct answer or follow the directions.

    a. When the tale begins, Gilgamesh

    **(1)** is not happy just being the ruler of Uruk.
    **(2)** prays to the gods for a companion.
    **(3)** wants to be left in peace.

    b. Gilgamesh and Enkidu leave their city

    **(1)** to guard the Cedar Forest.
    **(2)** to find fame and wealth.
    **(3)** to find everlasting life.

    c. Write the sentence from the tale that best describes the powers of Humbaba:

    _____

    d. In this tale, we learn that a great hero

    **(1)** never needs the help of a friend.
    **(2)** can sometimes feel afraid and weak.
    **(3)** is always brave and strong.

    e. Gilgamesh and Enkidu seem to feel sorry for their enemy Humbaba when they face him. Which expression from the story shows this?

    **(1)** Humbaba has great powers.
    **(2)** It is a difficult choice.
    **(3)** This is a dangerous task.

    f. Gilgamesh doesn't want to marry Ishtar because

    **(1)** he is afraid of her father Anu.
    **(2)** he isn't in love with her.
    **(3)** he doesn't trust her love for him.

    g. After Enkidu's death, it states: *Everyone in the land is joyful, but sadness soon follows.* Write the part of this sentence that is important for the next part of the story.

    _____

**h.** Gilgamesh travels far and wide

    **(1)** to ask the advice of a mysterious woman.

    **(2)** so he can forget the death of his best friend.

    **(3)** because he wants to be saved from death.

**i.** At the home of the Far-Away, Gilgamesh

    **(1)** asks the gods for the special gift of everlasting life.

    **(2)** finds out how everyone can live forever.

    **(3)** learns that his wish for everlasting life is hopeless.

**j.** At the end of the story, Gilgamesh and his people seem to have

    **(1)** the same relationship as at the beginning of the story.

    **(2)** a better relationship than at the beginning of the story.

    **(3)** a worse relationship than at the beginning of the story.

**k.** In the following list, mark *G* for the *general* item and *S* for the *specific* items.

beautiful gardens and temples _____

rich fields of grain for the people _____

the proud features of Uruk _____

high walls of brick _____

**l.** In the following list, circle the items that show that Gilgamesh is a very real human being in this story.

    **(1)** He kills a giant. **(2)** A goddess falls in love with him. **(3)** He has a good friend. **(4)** He accepts death and life. **(5)** He kills the Bull of Heaven. **(6)** He suffers over the death of a friend. **(7)** He cuts down a whole forest. **(8)** He is proud of his city. **(9)** He sometimes feels weak and afraid. **(10)** He is worn out from his travels.

**m.** Choose the sentence that best expresses the meaning of this tale.

    **(1)** The love of one's city is the most important kind of love.

    **(2)** It is better to have good friends than to be married.

    **(3)** The struggle for wisdom and self-knowledge will bring us peace.

**2. Answering Information Questions.** Answer the following questions in complete sentences. Use a separate sheet of paper.

    **a.** Who is Gilgamesh?

    **b.** Who do the gods create to be Gilgamesh's best friend?

    **c.** To where do Gilgamesh and his friend travel?

d. Why is their task dangerous?
e. What must the two men decide about their enemy?
f. What does the Bull of Heaven do in the land of Sumer?
g. What happens to Enkidu?
h. Why does Gilgamesh leave Uruk the second time?
i. What does the mysterious woman advise Gilgamesh?
j. What is Gilgamesh proud of at the end of the story?
k. Is Gilgamesh sad or wise now?

## VOCABULARY

1. **Expanding Vocabulary.** Choose the word(s) that have the same meaning as the italicized word in the sentence. Use your dictionary only if necessary.

    a. Gilgamesh is *restless;* ruling his people isn't enough for him.
    
    **(1)** patient   **(2)** inactive   **(3)** not quiet

    b. Gilgamesh wants to be famous throughout the world; he is *ambitious*.
    
    **(1)** wants to succeed   **(2)** feels lazy   **(3)** is trustful

    c. Gilgamesh and Enkidu are good *companions*. Together the *comrades* set out on an adventure.
    
    **(1)** heroes   **(2)** warriors   **(3)** friends

    d. They *travel* to the faraway land of the Cedar Forest.
    
    **(1)** hurry   **(2)** go on a journey   **(3)** move their home

    e. A giant guards the forest, so cutting down the trees is a dangerous *task*.
    
    **(1)** discovery   **(2)** object   **(3)** job

    f. Ishtar wants to marry Gilgamesh, but he *refuses* to be her husband.
    
    **(1)** doesn't agree   **(2)** expects   **(3)** would like

    g. Ishtar is *insulted* by Gilgamesh's reply and becomes angry.
    
    **(1)** offended   **(2)** destroyed   **(3)** frightened

    h. Enkidu falls sick; day after day he *suffers*.
    
    **(1)** feels angry   **(2)** is in pain   **(3)** gets better

    i. Gilgamesh cannot *accept* the advice of the mysterious woman; he refuses to be an ordinary man.
    
    **(1)** understand   **(2)** reveal   **(3)** take or agree with

2. **Using Vocabulary.** Answer the questions in a complete sentence. Use the italicized word in your answer.

   a. Where do you want to *travel* someday?
   _____

   b. What is a difficult household *task* for you?
   _____

   c. Which friend of yours would be a good traveling *companion*?
   _____

   d. What do you do when someone *insults* you?
   _____

   e. What can a parent do to soothe a *restless* baby?
   _____

   f. When you *accept* an invitation to a party, what gift do you usually bring?
   _____

## PARAGRAPH TOPICS

1. Write a paragraph about the things you do before you travel to a new place. Before you begin, brainstorm for some specifics with a partner and add them to the items provided. Select those items most important to you to write about and organize them in logical order of time. Begin your paragraph with a sentence that introduces the subject of planning a trip.

   pack bags            _____

   buy tickets          _____

   read about the place _____

2. It is important to have good companions. Write a paragraph about a companion you have. Describe the qualities of that person. How does that person help, advise, or guide you? In what activities do you both participate? Do you ever disagree with each other? Begin your paragraph with a sentence that introduces the person to the reader.

# CHAPTER TWO

# THE UNITED STATES: LAND OF MANY CULTURES

## PREREADING

**Class Activity.** The people of the United States come from many different cultural backgrounds. Look at the following photographs of Americans. These people represent different ethnic groups in America. Choose a partner in your class. Interview the person to find out the information on the list. Fill in the list with that information.

Name of student _____

Native country _____

Native language _____

National holiday _____
(in native country)

Basic foods of native country _____

Favorite food _____

Favorite American holiday _____

Favorite city _____

Is the person from the same background as yours or a different background from yours? _____

Is any of the information the same as yours? Yes _____  No _____

If yes, then list the information that is the same.

_____  _____  _____

_____  _____  _____

**38** Unit I  Our Diverse World

The United States is a land of many cultures. Its people come from many different homelands.

## Chapter Two  The United States: Land of Many Cultures

> ***Free Write.***  Immigrants face many problems when they first come to the United States. Write about your first experiences, or those of your relatives, with language, housing, food, social customs, or other difficulties.

**Vocabulary in Context.**  The words in this exercise will appear in the reading passage. Choose the word(s) that mean the same as the italicized word in each sentence.

1. People like to *celebrate* important events in their lives such as birthdays, weddings, and graduations.

    a. examine          b. honor          c. ignore

2. An *occasion* like a wedding usually has a *ceremony* in a place of worship with many people attending.

    a. event            b. area           c. occupation
    a. chance           b. crowd of people  c. formal observance

3. On special occasions, people like to do things in a traditional way, as their *ancestors* did before them.

    a. past family members   b. children   c. activities

4. When *immigrants* first come to the United States, they usually feel more at home when they practice their *native* customs.

    a. foreign products   b. people from other homelands   c. citizens of the United States
    a. original           b. accurate                       c. new

5. By practicing their traditions, people can pass them on to their children, grandchildren, and other *descendants*.

    a. fathers and mothers   b. people born after them   c. neighbors

6. All over the United States, people enjoy eating *delicious* meals prepared according to national customs.

    a. ancient          b. heavy          c. flavorful

7. Everyone enjoys going to street fairs and festivals to see people of different nationalities *perform* folk dances in native dress or to watch other activities.

   **a.** do        **b.** reveal        **c.** preserve

8. Sometimes the dances and the music *represent* something important in the history of the people who perform.

   **a.** tell lies about        **b.** stand for        **c.** obey

## READING

### Hawaiian Feasts and Festivals

[1] The United States is a land of many cultures. Its people have come from different homelands and have brought their own customs from all parts of the world. Although they live and work in a modern, changing society, they want to preserve their traditions and pass them on to their children. So, in their daily lives many Americans continue to speak their native languages as well as English. They cook traditional foods. They practice their own religions and have their own way of thinking about life and death. In addition, they set aside time to celebrate the important occasions of their native culture with special ceremonies.

[2] Every part of the United States has special celebrations, depending on the particular national groups that live in the area. In Hawaii, America's island state in the Pacific Ocean, there are many people of Asian ancestry. Many of these Asians are of Japanese, Chinese, or Polynesian descent. Immigrants from China and Japan arrived in Hawaii in great numbers during the past century. The early Polynesians came to Hawaii from South Pacific islands more than a thousand years before any other people. The Asians left rich traditions for their descendants to follow. Today, Hawaiians honor the memory of their ancestors with special feasts and festivals.

[3] For people of Japanese ancestry in Hawaii, the O-bon Festival is a special occasion. The ceremonies honor dead relatives and friends and are an important part of the Buddhist religion as practiced in Japan. They take place in July and August on Oahu, the main island of Hawaii. People gather in the courtyards of Buddhist temples, dressed in traditional robes called *kimonos*. To the music of drums and flutes, men and women perform their native folk dances in honor of the dead. In the evening there are further ceremonies at the seashore. People place paper lanterns on tiny wooden boats, which represent the souls of the dead. They set hundreds of these boats in the water and watch as they float out over the dark ocean. The lights guide the souls to a peaceful sleep on the waters until the next year when they will be honored again.

[4] Chinese-Hawaiians hold the Moon Festival to honor the memory of their ancestors and their native land. The Moon Festival occurs in August on the night

Chapter Two   The United States: Land of Many Cultures            41

Twelve-foot leis are draped on the statue of Kamehameha I in Honolulu during ceremonies honoring the Hawaiian king. Visitors can see these rites June 11, Kamehameha Day, followed by a big Hawaiian parade.

of the full moon. Unlike the Japanese festival, the Chinese celebration is a simple family occasion. Family members gather in a garden or large open-air space in the light of the moon. They drink tea and feast on delicious moon-shaped cakes filled with meat or sweets, depending on family custom. If the family is from northern China, the cakes have meat in them; if the family came from southern China, the cakes have sweet fillings. The cakes, an important food on this occasion, represent an event in Chinese history. A long time ago, the people of China used round cakes in a special way: they sent secret messages to each other in them. The messages gave instructions for the people of the north and south to join together to fight against the evil emperor who ruled them at that time. The trick worked and the people were able to overthrow their ruler. By recalling this event in the Moon Festival, the Chinese people help to keep their native traditions alive and their family ties strong.

[5]   Like the Japanese and Chinese people, the Polynesians in Hawaii have strong, deep-rooted traditions. They have the same love of the sea as their ancestors and are skillful sailors, swimmers, and fishermen. Some of the men still catch fish with spears as their great-grandfathers did. Sometimes they have a fishing party called a *hukilau*. All the neighbors help catch fish in big nets and then cook the fish on the beach. Sometimes they have a *luau*, an outdoor feast under the trees. Traditional foods of the Pacific Islands are popular at a *luau*. The main dish is usually a whole roast pork cooked in an underground oven, or *imu*. The people sit on the ground to eat in the style of their ancestors. At the end of a *luau*, dancers

perform the *hula*, the sacred dance of the ancient Polynesians. The graceful movements of the dance tell stories of their long trip over the dangerous waters of the Pacific to find the peaceful islands of Hawaii. In the early autumn, the Polynesians hold the great Aloha Festival. The word *aloha* means "welcome," and they invite all Hawaiians to see the special events in honor of their ancestors. One of the most exciting activities is boat racing in outrigger canoes, the same kind of boats that the early Hawaiians used to sail the Pacific Ocean.

[6]   Hawaii is only a small part of the United States. Its feasts and festivals are just a few of the many celebrations that take place in America throughout the year. Our lives are richer when we take part in these special occasions. We are fortunate to be in a land of many cultures.

**Summary Completion.**   Fill in the blank spaces with the correct word from the reading passage.

The United States is a land of many (1) _____. People like to preserve their traditions and pass them on to their (2) _____ _____. Many of Hawaii's (3) _____ are of Asian ancestry. The people who came from Japan, China, and the South Pacific left rich (4) _____ for their descendants to follow. The Japanese perform ceremonies in memory of dead (5) _____ _____ and friends. The Chinese celebrate the Moon Festival to honor the (6) _____ of their ancestors. The Polynesians also have (7) _____, deep-rooted traditions, and follow in many ways the customs of the past. Hawaiian feasts and festivals are only a few of the celebrations that take place in (8) _____. On these special occasions our lives are (9) _____ when we take part in them.

## DISCUSSION QUESTIONS

1. Some people think that the United States should be a "melting pot" where all people have the same American culture. They think immigrants should give up their old ways of thinking and enter the mainstream of American life. What do you think of this idea? What are the benefits of preserving the old traditions? Are there times when it is better to do things in a modern American way? Discuss both sides of this issue.

2. What problems would a person face if he or she wanted to go against family tradition and become completely Americanized? Might a person become ashamed of his or her native customs and cause a break in the family relationship? How would you advise a person who was struggling against the past?

3. Who has more difficulty with the American life-style, an older immigrant or a younger one? Does it help to live in a neighborhood with other people of the same nationality? What services are available to help new immigrants in your neighborhood?

## READING COMPREHENSION

1. **Understanding Text.** Choose the correct answer or complete the given items.

    a. Paragraph [1] discusses

    **(1)** specifically the people of Hawaii.
    **(2)** the people of the United States in general.
    **(3)** the different kinds of foods that Americans generally cook.

    b. In Paragraph [1], the second sentence, the pronoun *Its* refers to _____ _____ and the pronoun *their* refers to _____ .

    c. What three groups of people in Hawaii are introduced in Paragraph [2]?

    **(1)** _____
    **(2)** _____
    **(3)** _____

    d. The _____ were the first people to arrive in Hawaii.

    e. Next to each Paragraph number write the name of the group that is discussed.

    **(1)** Paragraph [3] _____
    **(2)** Paragraph [4] _____
    **(3)** Paragraph [5] _____

    f. The O-bon Festival is held

    **(1)** to honor the memory of those who have died.
    **(2)** in a garden in the light of the moon.
    **(3)** to recall the brave deeds of ancestors.

**g.** The pronoun *They* in Paragraph [3], the third sentence, refers to the words

   **(1)** the Buddhist religion.
   **(2)** dead friends and relatives.
   **(3)** the ceremonies.

**h.** In the next-to-last sentence of Paragraph [3], the first pronoun *They* refers to _____. The other pronoun *they* in the same sentence refers to _____.

**i.** In the last sentence of Paragraph [3], the pronoun *they* refers to

   **(1)** the lights.
   **(2)** the souls.
   **(3)** the waters.

**j.** From the description of the ceremonies in the O-bon Festival, what kind of occasion is implied by the author?

   **(1)** It is a serious occasion, but the people are not sad.
   **(2)** It is a very joyful occasion, with lots of noise and laughter.
   **(3)** It is uninteresting and dull for the people who participate.

**k.** Write the sentence from Paragraph [4] that shows a contrast between the Moon Festival and the O-bon Festival.

   _____

**l.** To show the difference between the Japanese O-bon Festival and the Chinese Moon Festival, write *J* next to the items that describe the O-bon Festival. Write *C* next to the items that describe the Moon Festival. Write *J and C* if the item represents both festivals.

   **(1)** religious ceremony performed _____
   **(2)** drink and eat _____
   **(3)** recall ancestors _____
   **(4)** use something to represent something else _____
   **(5)** stay outdoors _____
   **(6)** music and dancing _____
   **(7)** wear native costumes _____
   **(8)** celebrate a historical event _____

**m.** In Paragraph [4], the eighth sentence, the last word *them* refers to

   **(1)** messages.

(2) the people of China.

(3) round cakes.

n. The ancient Chinese won their war against the emperor by

(1) filling round cakes with meat and sweets.

(2) using round cakes to send each other messages.

(3) making cakes in the shape of the full moon.

o. According to the information in Paragraph [5], the Polynesians in Hawaii

(1) continue to practice some ancient traditions.

(2) never do things as their ancestors did.

(3) catch fish only with spears.

p. Write the meanings of the following Polynesian words:

(1) *luau* _____

(2) *hukilau* _____

(3) *aloha* _____

(4) *imu* _____

(5) *hula* _____

q. The movements of the *hula* describe

(1) the trip that the ancient Polynesians took to reach Hawaii.

(2) stories about present-day Polynesians.

(3) events in modern Hawaiian history.

2. **Answering Information Questions.** Write a complete sentence in answer to the following questions.

a. When and where do the O-bon ceremonies take place?

b. What religion are these ceremonies part of?

c. What dances do men and women perform in the O-bon Festival?

d. What happens in the evening?

e. Where do people place paper lanterns?

f. What do the boats represent?

g. When does the Moon Festival occur?

h. Where do family members gather for this festival?

i. What do they drink and eat?

j. What do the moon-shaped cakes represent?

k. What happens at a Polynesian *hukilau*?

**l.** What kinds of food are popular at a *luau*?

**m.** What happens at the end of a *luau*?

**n.** What festival do the Polynesians hold in early autumn?

3. **The Reading Process: Identifying Main Ideas.** A main idea states the topic or subject of a passage. It also tells something important about the topic. A main idea is a *general* statement. It helps the reader to understand the writer's *basic* idea. It does not give specific details. Look for the main idea sentence in the following paragraph.

   The Honolulu Academy of Arts is the cultural center of Hawaii. There you can see Chinese paintings by Ma Fen and other masters. There are works by skillful Japanese artists. The Academy also has fine examples of Buddhist religious art. In addition, it has the best collection of Korean pottery outside of Asia.

   Underline the first sentence. It tells you the main idea of this paragraph. It tells the topic: *the Honolulu Academy of Arts*. It also tells something important about the topic: The Honolulu Academy of Arts is *the cultural center* of Hawaii. The first sentence is the most general statement in this paragraph.

   Read the next paragraph and underline the sentence that contains the main idea.

   Kim Fong is Chinese, Polynesian, and Portuguese. Daniel Sato is part Japanese, part Korean, and part French. Josie Hall's grandparents came to Hawaii from Spain, and her father is from San Francisco. John Doi's father is a Filipino immigrant, and his mother is part Irish and part Norwegian. In Hawaii there are many people of mixed ancestry such as these.

   The last sentence is the main idea sentence. It tells the topic: *people of mixed ancestry*. It also tells something important about the topic: *There are many people in Hawaii of mixed ancestry.*

   **a.** Read the following paragraphs. Then write in the topic of the paragraph and the main idea of the paragraph on the lines provided.

   (1) Flowers are a favorite expression of love and friendship in Hawaii. When visitors arrive in Hawaii, they usually receive a wreath of flowers called a *lei*. A *lei* is worn around the neck or as a crown on the head. There are flowers in shops and in hotel rooms to make people feel welcome. There is even a special holiday called Lei Day on May 1. If you are there on that day, you will be greeted everywhere with smiles and flowers.

Chapter Two   The United States: Land of Many Cultures   47

The graceful movements of the hula dance tell stories of Hawaii's past. The *lei* and *ti* leaf skirt are part of the traditional Hawaiian ceremonial dress. Describe a traditional dance in your culture.

Topic: _____

Main Idea: _____

(2)   Special foods of the Pacific Islands are popular at a *luau*. For the main dish, there is roast pork, served with sweet potatoes, *poi*, and other vegetables. Fish is also served, especially salmon and swordfish. Tropical fruits such as bananas, pineapples, papayas, and mangoes end the delicious meal.

Topic: _____

Main Idea: _____

**b.** Read Paragraphs [3], [4], and [5] of the reading passage earlier in this chapter. For each of these paragraphs write the topic, and copy the sentence that expresses the main idea of the paragraph.

(1) Paragraph [3]:

　　Topic: _____

　　Main Idea: _____

(2) Paragraph [4]

　　Topic: _____

　　Main Idea: _____

(3) Paragraph [5]

　　Topic: _____

　　Main Idea: _____

c. Write the main idea of Paragraph [3] on a separate sheet of paper. Then summarize the paragraph in your own words.

## VOCABULARY

1. **New Words.** Pronounce the words following your instructor.

| Verbs | Nouns | Adjectives | Adverbs |
|---|---|---|---|
| celebrate | ancestor | native | |
| perform | descendant | delicious | |
| represent | ceremony | | |
| | immigrant | | |
| | occasion | | |

a. *Expanding Vocabulary.* Fill in each blank space with a word from the New Word list.

(1) In the United States we _____ Independence Day on July 4. It is always a happy _____ .

(2) An _____ to the United States can learn to speak English by attending classes. Many foreign students are bilingual; they speak English and their _____ language.

(3) An _____ on my father's side was a soldier in the American Revolution. My mother is a _____ of a Dutch family that settled in New York in the seventeenth century.

(4) It is traditional for an American bride to wear a white dress for her wedding _____. A white dress _____ purity.

(5) At many festivals the people _____ their native dances. _____ food is usually sold at these festivals.

**b.** *Using Vocabulary.* Write a complete sentence in answer to the following questions. Use the italicized word in your statement.

(1) In your opinion, what kinds of fruit are *delicious*?
_____

(2) Where do you like to go to *celebrate* your birthday?
_____

(3) Is Thanksgiving Day a special *occasion* in your family?
_____

(4) What holiday is important in your *native* country?
_____

(5) Who usually *performs* a wedding *ceremony* in your place of worship?
_____

(6) Do most *immigrants* have an easy time or a difficult time when they first come to their new homeland?
_____

(7) What does the $ sign *represent*?
_____

(8) How can you find out more about your *ancestors*?
_____

(9) Is your uncle a *descendant* of yours?
_____

**2. Word Families: Adjectives Versus Noun Forms.** A noun is the name of a person, place, or thing. An adjective describes a noun. An adjective usually goes before the noun.

> She is from *Hawaii*.
>           (noun)
>
> Most *Hawaiian men* are *excellent swimmers*.
>    (adjective)  (noun)   (adjective)  (noun)
>
> (What kind of men? Hawaiian. What kind of swimmers? Excellent.)

In English some adjectives and nouns are related to each other in meaning, but they have different forms. Study the following lists.

| Noun | Adjective |
| --- | --- |
| America | American |
| Korea | Korean |
| (the) east | eastern |
| (the) west | western |
| richness | rich |
| tradition | traditional |
| culture | cultural |

*Sentence Completion.* Choose the correct word in parentheses to fill in the blank space in each sentence.

a. (west, western) California is a _____ state.

b. (culture, cultural) Mexican cowboys went to Hawaii and introduced the knowledge of horses from their own _____ .

c. (America, American) There are fifty stars on the _____ flag, one for each state.

d. (tradition, traditional) The _____ gift to visitors in Hawaii is a long necklace of flowers, called a *lei*.

e. (ancestor, ancestral) Many Americans save money to take a trip to their _____ homeland.

f. (kindness, kind) Visitors to Hawaii find _____ and friendly people to welcome them.

g. (Hawaii, Hawaiian) *Aloha* is the _____ word for welcome or good-bye.

**h.** (Korea, Korean) There aren't many people from _____ in Hawaii, but their number is growing every year.

**i.** (richness, rich) Immigrants from Scandinavia, Portugal, Spain, Ireland, and Holland have added to the _____ of life in Hawaii.

## WRITING EXERCISES

### Simple Present Tense of *To Be*

The Simple Present tense of *to be* connects the subject with the rest of the sentence to show the existence of a person, place, or thing. It also describes or gives information about a person, place, or thing.

> **Hawaii *is* in the Pacific Ocean. (shows existence)**
> **Gold and silver *are* metals. (describes or gives information)**

Study the Simple Present tense forms of the verb *to be*.

|  | **Singular** | **Plural** |
|---|---|---|
| First Person | I am (I'm) | The teacher and I are<br>We are (we're) |
| Second Person | You are (You're) | You are (You're) |
| Third Person | The teacher is<br>He is (He's)<br>She is (She's)<br>It is (It's) | Teachers are<br>They are (They're) |

The negative forms are *am not (I'm not), are not (aren't),* and *is not (isn't).*

**1. Sentence Kernels with *To Be*.** Read the following paragraph and number each sentence.

    Hawaii is the fiftieth state of the United States. But it isn't part of the mainland. The state of Hawaii is a chain of islands in the Pacific Ocean. The islands are the tops of great underwater mountains. The mountain tops are quite high in some parts of the islands. Mauna Kea, the highest mountain, is almost 14,000 feet. Some areas aren't very mountainous. The farms are in the lowlands.

## Unit I  Our Diverse World

In the following chart fill in the verb of each sentence in the Verb column. Then fill in the subject in the Subject column. Mark *S* if the kernel is *singular*. Mark *P* if the kernel is *plural*. The first one is done for you.

|  | Subject | Verb | S or P |
|---|---|---|---|
| Sentence 1 | *Hawaii* | *is* | *S* |
| 2 | | | |
| 3 | | | |
| 4 | | | |
| 5 | | | |
| 6 | | | |
| 7 | | | |
| 8 | | | |

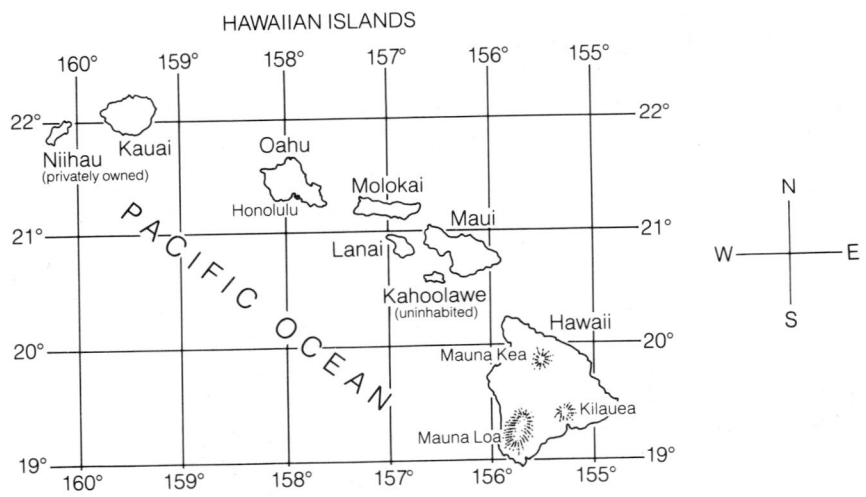

2. **Sentence Completion.** Fill in the correct form of the verb *to be* in the following sentences. The first blank in each pair is positive. The second blank in each pair is negative. The first one is done for you.

a. Many people in Hawaii ____*are*____ of Japanese ancestry, but they ____*aren't*____ Japanese citizens.

**Chapter Two  The United States: Land of Many Cultures**  53

b. English _____ a difficult language for some people. A new language _____ easy to learn at a certain age.

c. I _____ in my first year of college. I _____ ready to graduate.

d. *Poi* _____ a basic food of the Polynesian people. This vegetable _____ a basic food for most Americans.

e. Wheat, corn, and rice _____ basic foods for most people of the world. Coffee, tea, and sugar _____ necessities of life.

f. The Pacific Ocean _____ the largest body of water on earth. The Atlantic Ocean _____ as deep or wide as the Pacific.

g. Mauna Loa and Kilauea _____ mountains in Hawaii. These two mountains _____ as high as Mauna Kea.

h. These three mountains in Hawaii _____ volcanoes. Volcanoes _____ ordinary mountains because they sometimes erupt, or blow up.

i. Honolulu _____ a seaport and the capital of Hawaii. But this city _____ on the island of Hawaii.

j. What _____ the capital of New York State? It _____ New York City.

k. What _____ the famous holidays in your native country? These holidays are exciting, _____ they?

3. **Answering Questions.**  Write a complete sentence in answer to the following questions. Look at the map of Hawaii for your answers.

   a. What ocean are the Hawaiian Islands in?

   _____

   b. Which is the largest island of the chain?

   _____

## Unit I  Our Diverse World

c. Is Lanai the smallest island?

d. Are Mauna Kea, Kilauea, and Mauna Loa on the island of Maui?

e. Which island are these three volcanoes on?

f. Which island is directly east of Niihau?

g. Is Kauai privately owned?

h. Which island is the farthest west?

i. Which island is farther south, Oahu or Maui?

j. Which island is between Molokai and Kauai?

k. Is Lanai about 1° south of Niihau, or 10° south?

l. On which island is the city of Honolulu?

m. Is Honolulu on the coast or inland?

n. Which two islands are closest to Hawaii?

o. Is Kauai about 6° west of Maui, or about 3° west?

## *There Is* or *There Isn't* and *There Are* or *There Aren't*

When the subject of the verb *to be* is not a specific person or thing, we usually use the expression *there is* or *there are* + a noun. The negative forms are *there isn't* and *there aren't*.

## Chapter Two  The United States: Land of Many Cultures

|       | Verb   | Subject       | Rest of Sentence              |
|-------|--------|---------------|-------------------------------|
| There | is     | a festival    | on Oahu in August.            |
| There | isn't  | much rainfall | in the summer.                |
| There | are    | many beaches  | all along the coast.          |
| There | aren't | any roads     | on some parts of the islands. |

The subject is not *there*. The subject comes after the verb. When the subject is plural, the verb must be plural.

**1. Sentence Completion.**

   a. In the following paragraph fill in the blank spaces with *there is* or *there are*. Use the negative where the directions say so. The passage is about Niihau, one of the Hawaiian Islands.

   (1) _____ only 300 people on Niihau. (negative)

   (2) _____ any airplane service to the island. (negative)

   (3) _____ any visitors, except those who are invited by the people living there. (4) _____ lots of sheep, horses, and wild pigs, but (negative) (5) _____ any dogs. The people can't farm because (negative) (6) _____ much fresh water. (7) _____ a public school for the children, but young people must leave Niihau if they want to continue their education. Many of them return because (8) _____ peace on the island. (negative) (9) _____ any police officers or private telephones. The people on Niihau want to preserve their ancient way of life.

   b. Use *is/are* or *there is/there are* to fill in the blank spaces in the following paragraph. Use the negative where indicated.

   Holidays (1) _____ usually happy occasions. Thanksgiving Day (2) _____ an especially happy occasion in the United States. In some cities (3) _____ special events like ball games or parades. In New York City (4) _____ an extraordinary parade with balloons of Mickey Mouse, Superman, Santa

Claus, and other popular characters. This parade (5) _____ always crowded with children and their parents. In most homes (6) _____ usually a traditional feast of turkey, cranberry sauce, and pumpkin pie. Many people eat too much. But this holiday (7) _____ a time for fun and relaxation. It (negative) (8) _____ a time to think about diets.

2. **Sentence Composing.** On a separate sheet of paper, write the answers to the following questions in complete sentences. Use *there is, there isn't* or *there are, there aren't* in your answers. The first one is done for you.

   a. How many states are there in the United States?
      *There are fifty states in the United States.*
   b. Is there a map of Hawaii in this book?
   c. How many verbs are there in this sentence?
   d. Are there any Portuguese students in your class?
   e. Is there any water on the moon?
   f. Are there any Chinese restaurants near your school?
   g. How many ounces are there in a pound?
   h. How many volcanoes are there on the island of Hawaii?
   i. Are there any people on the island of Kahoolawe?

## *To Be* + Adjective + Noun

Study the sentences in the chart.

| Subject | Verb | Article | Adjective | Noun |
|---|---|---|---|---|
| An archeologist | is | an | active | person. |
| Japan | isn't | a | large | country. |
| Polynesians | are | | skillful | fishermen. |
| Dogs and cats | aren't | | extraordinary | animals. |

Adjectives don't change for plural nouns. Adjectives never add an *s* for plural nouns. Do we use the article *a* or *an* for plurals?

1. **Sentence Building.** Draw a line from the subject on the left to the correct adjective–noun phrase on the right.

**Chapter Two   The United States: Land of Many Cultures**   57

|    | Subject | Adjective–Noun |
|----|---------|----------------|
| a. | Japanese | delicious fruit |
| b. | a lion | small state |
| c. | gold | serious student |
| d. | an apple | difficult subject |
| e. | *aloha* | Asian language |
| f. | Hawaii | expensive metal |
| g. | I | American city |
| h. | Mauna Loa | wild animal |
| i. | Los Angeles | Polynesian word |
| j. | chemistry | active volcano |

Now write a complete sentence with the Simple Present tense of the verb *to be*, using your matched items. Your first sentence will be the following: *Japanese is an Asian language*.

2. **Sentence Building with Plurals.**   Now rewrite each sentence from Exercise 1 using the following plural subjects.

   a. Japanese and Chinese
   b. lions and tigers
   c. gold and silver
   d. apples and oranges
   e. *aloha* and *hukilau*
   f. Hawaii and Delaware
   g. my brother and I
   h. Mauna Loa and Kilauea
   i. Los Angeles and New York
   j. chemistry and astronomy

   Your first sentence will be the following: *Japanese and Chinese are Asian languages*. Remember that the article *a* or *an* is not used with plurals.

3. **Sentence Completion.**   Write an appropriate subject and the correct form of the verb *to be* for the given adjective-noun combinations. Use the positive or negative form of the verb as appropriate for your meaning.

   _____ **dangerous sport.**
   _____ **native speakers of English.**

   a. _____ exciting city.
   b. _____ Asian countries.
   c. _____ cold area of the world.

d. _____ my best friend.
e. _____ deep bodies of water.
f. _____ interesting subject.
g. _____ useful tools.
h. _____ my native language.
i. _____ extraordinary animal.
j. _____ convenient forms of transportation.

4. **Sentence Combining.** The first sentence in each group states the subject. The second sentence states the adjective. The third sentence states the place *where* or the time *when*. Place the adjective in the correct order, and add the prepositional phrase to make one complete sentence. Leave out any unnecessary words.

> (1) Canton is a city. (2) The city is important. (3) The city is on the Asian mainland.
> *Canton is an important city on the Asian mainland.*
>
> (1) There is a restaurant. (2) The restaurant is Chinese. (3) The restaurant is in my neighborhood.
> *There is a Chinese restaurant in my neighborhood.*

a. (1) Niihau is an island. (2) The island is privately owned. (3) The island is in the Hawaiian chain. _____

b. (1) There are animals. (2) The animals are wild. (3) The animals are on some of the Hawaiian Islands. _____

c. (1) There are beaches. (2) The beaches are splendid. (3) The beaches are along the coast. _____

d. (1) The Dominican Republic is an island. (2) The island is beautiful. (3) The island is in the Caribbean Sea. _____

e. (1) There are hotels. (2) The hotels are expensive. (3) The hotels are near the sea. _____

f. (1) There are seashells. (2) The seashells are interesting. (3) The seashells are on the beach. _____

g. (1) There are lots of activities. (2) The activities are cultural. (3) The activities are during the summer. _____

h. (1) There are workers. (2) The workers are skillful. (3) The workers are in my native country. _____

i. (1) A dictionary is a book. (2) The book is basic. (3) The book is for language students. _____

j. (1) There is a dictionary. (2) The dictionary is English. (3) The dictionary is on the shelf in my bedroom. _____

k. (1) There are many dictionaries. (2) The dictionaries are different. (3) The dictionaries are in my college library. _____

## Capitalization and Punctuation

The names of all specific places, or proper nouns, are capitalized. The adjectives made from proper nouns are also capitalized. A question mark (?), not a period, is placed after a sentence that asks a question.

1. Correctly punctuate and capitalize the following paragraph.

many people in the united states are bilingual they can speak english and the language of their ancestors some people in the city of new orleans, louisiana, speak french and english some people in the states of minnesota and wisconsin still speak swedish, german, and other european languages many people of mexican ancestry live in the southwest and near the rocky mountains they know spanish very well are there many americans of asian ancestry what are some asian languages which languages do the people of hawaii speak do you know any polynesian words

2. Review the following paragraph for correct punctuation and capitalization. Make corrections as necessary.

   Most people in the United states and Canada speak English. We sometimes call these two places Anglo-America. Most people in Mexico, the caribbean Islands, and south america speak Spanish, French, and portuguese. We often call these places Latin america there are many latin americans in New York and Los Angeles. Are you from a latin american country. do some of your classmates speak spanish or french. What countries are they from?

## Pronoun Use

An understanding of pronoun use will help you follow a writer's ideas and help you write clearly for your reader. You can use pronouns to replace subjects, objects, or possessives in a sentence. Pronouns must agree in number, person, form, and gender with the nouns they replace. Study the following pronoun chart and examples.

|  | Subject | Object (of verb or preposition) | Possessive | Possessive Adjective (+ noun) | Reflexive |
|---|---|---|---|---|---|
| **Singular** | I<br>you<br>he<br>she<br>it | me<br>you<br>him<br>her<br>it | mine<br>yours<br>his<br>hers<br>— | my (tradition)<br>your (tradition)<br>his (tradition)<br>her (tradition)<br>its (tradition) | myself<br>yourself<br>himself<br>herself<br>itself |
| **Plural** | we<br>you<br>they | us<br>you<br>them | ours<br>yours<br>theirs | our (traditions)<br>your (traditions)<br>their (traditions) | ourselves<br>yourselves<br>themselves |

**Chapter Two    The United States: Land of Many Cultures**    **61**

> ***We* always have a big celebration for *our* son's birthday.**
>   (plural first person subject)     (plural first person possessive adjective)
>
> **The Fourth of July is a festive holiday in the United States. People celebrate *it* with parades and fireworks.**
>   (singular third person object)

1. **Sentence Completion.**  Read the following paragraph about parades and festivals in New York. Then fill in the blank spaces with the correct form of the pronoun in parentheses.

    People in New York love parades and festivals. (Them, They, Their) (1) _____ have (it, us, them) (2) _____ for varied occasions. Each ethnic group has (its, their, your) (3) _____ own day of celebration. For example, there are parades for Puerto Rican Day and Turkish Day. There are Haitian, Greek, and Italian festivals. For these

People in New York love parades and festivals. Thousands of West Indians take part in the West Indian Day parade each year.

events, people dress in (they, his, their) (4) _____ native costumes, play folk music, and perform traditional dances. The performers and the spectators enjoy (yourselves, themselves, ourselves) (5) _____ a great deal. If (your, yours, you) (6) _____ are in New York in January or February, (you, I, it) (7) _____ can attend the Chinese New Year festival. (Its, She, It) (8) _____ is one of the most exciting celebrations in the city. This celebration will make (yours, ours, your) (9) _____ trip to New York worthwhile.

2. **Pronoun Reference.** Circle each pronoun, and draw an arrow to the noun that it is replacing. The first one is done for you.

Halloween is a favorite celebration for children. (They) like to dress up in costumes and go to their neighbors asking for treats like candy or cookies. Last year at a school in New York, the students decided to do something different. They wanted to collect money for children in other countries. The third and fourth graders decided that they would pick a country, study it, and dress like its children. So, on Halloween one student named Kenneth wore a straw hat with the words *Puerto Rico* on it. "My father is from there," he explained. Another student, Jonathan, wore a robe with a Chinese dragon on it. "I want to help Chinese children. They need money there," Jonathan said. The seventh and eighth graders didn't wear any costumes. They decided that the more adult they looked, the more money they would collect. The principal of the school, Mrs. Velez, said she was very proud of the children for thinking of others instead of themselves on Halloween.

3. **Sentence Completion.** Fill in the blanks with the correct pronoun.
   a. St. Patrick's Day is a great day for Irish people in New York. _____ is celebrated on March 17 with a big parade down Fifth Avenue. Thousands of people line the streets to watch _____ . Many of _____ wear something green to signify _____ love of Ireland.

**b.** Atlantic Avenue in Brooklyn is famous for _____ stores featuring Middle Eastern food products. My wife and _____ live in the neighborhood, so _____ often go there together to buy such items as dried fruits, nuts, and olives. The owners are very friendly. _____ always welcome _____ with smiles.

**c.** Aliki, a young American woman of Greek descent, is getting married next month. _____ will have a traditional wedding in a Greek church. _____ relatives from Greece will come over here for the ceremony. _____ are all happy that Aliki is following the old customs.

**d.** John is unhappy because _____ doesn't have a traditional grandmother. _____ grandmother doesn't bake cakes or baby-sit for _____ . _____ is out playing tennis and dancing in the evening. John wants to put an ad in the local paper. _____ will say: "Wanted: one old-fashioned grandmother."

## THE COMPOSING PROCESS

1. **Developing a Paragraph.** A paragraph is a group of sentences about one topic, or subject. A good paragraph contains a main idea sentence that states the topic and often gives the writer's opinion or point of view about the topic. A main idea sentence can appear anywhere in the paragraph, but usually it is at the beginning. Students learning to write paragraphs should place the main idea statement first in the paragraph.

   *Arranging Sentences to Form a Paragraph.* In the following exercise, each set of sentences has a single topic. Each set of sentences contains a main idea statement and sentences of detailed information about the topic. Rearrange each set so that the main idea statement comes first and the details follow it. Write all the sentences in correct paragraph form on a separate sheet of paper.

   **a.** In some Hawaiian workshops, people make *leis* of silk or paper.
   There are excellent workers who create articles of bone and stone.

Some of the workers carve beautiful bowls and plates of wood.
Many Hawaiians are skilled workers in arts and crafts.
Some Hawaiians are skillful at weaving grass mats, baskets, and hats.

b. You can have a fine meal of Polynesian roast pork.
Japanese restaurants serve a delicious dish of raw fish called *sashimi*.
A visitor can try *kim chee*, a Korean vegetable specialty.
There are restaurants in Hawaii that serve traditional French and Spanish food.
There are so many kinds of food for a visitor to enjoy in Hawaii.
The Chinese make excellent dumplings filled with meats or sweets.

c. In this set you must arrange the sentences in logical order. Use words like *then, after,* or *other* to guide you in arranging the correct order. There are prepositional phrases of time and other phrases to help you find the correct sentence order.

In the afternoon you can go down to the beach and watch the boat races.
After dinner there are performances of hula dancing.
There are exciting things to see and do at the Aloha Festival in Hawaii.
Hawaiians wear traditional clothing of skins and feathers for these ceremonies.
In the evening you can eat outdoors at a luau.
Then there are other water sports to watch, such as surfing and diving.
There are ceremonies in the morning to celebrate events in Hawaiian history.
There are other forms of entertainment at night, such as concerts and stage plays.
After the water sports you can attend the boxing and wrestling matches.

2. **Composing a Paragraph.**

   a. Write a paragraph describing a holiday, festival, or special occasion that is celebrated in your native culture. Include details about the significance of each aspect of the celebration. Begin by filling in the topic and the main idea sentence on the lines provided. Then use the sentences in the list to guide you in writing your paragraph. Write your paragraph on a separate piece of paper and use correct paragraph form.

   Topic: _____

   Main Idea: _____

Your main idea statement should tell the name of the holiday, your opinion about the holiday (important, enjoyable), and the name of the country in which it is celebrated. Your main idea statement will be the first sentence of your paragraph.

(1) State the reason for the celebration. Tell when it was first celebrated. (Is it ancient or more recent?)

(2) Tell when it takes place. Explain why it is celebrated at this time.

(3) Describe what special costumes the people wear. Explain the significance of any unusual clothing.

(4) Tell what the people carry or use (flags, statues, paper animals) in the celebration. What is the meaning of these items?

(5) Describe any performances (dancing, music, shows, or other entertainment) that take place. Explain how these performances relate to the occasion.

(6) Tell what special food or drink is prepared. What is the reason for these special preparations?

(7) Describe other activities during the day or night in which people participate. (Perhaps there are sports events, games, or firework displays.) What meaning do these events have for the occasion?

(8) Explain how the people feel during the celebration. Are they proud, serious, sad, joyful, enthusiastic. Tell why the people feel as they do at this time.

(9) Tell how you in particular feel about this celebration.

b. In the United States, immigrants from all over the world still practice their native customs. What are some of the customs or traditions that you or your family members maintain? Brainstorm items and add them to the following list. You may want to work collaboratively with another person of the same background.

### Traditions I Maintain

*language*  *religion*  _____

*food*  _____  _____

Choose two or three items from your list that are important to you and your family. Write a paragraph in which you describe each custom, who participates, and when and where the custom is maintained. Begin your paragraph with a main idea sentence that states the topic and expresses your opinion or feeling about it. Review your paragraph with a partner for correct grammar and clarity of presentation.

3. **Combining Sentences to Form a Paragraph.** Combine each set of sentences into longer, more interesting statements to form a paragraph about a festival in New Orleans. Leave out all unnecessary words. Place adjectives before nouns to combine sentences. Use the word *and* to combine sentences where appropriate. Write your complete paragraph on a separate sheet of paper.

   a. (1) New Orleans is a city.
      (2) It is in Louisiana.
   b. (1) There is a festival there.
      (2) It is exciting.
      (3) It is in the winter.
      (4) It is called Mardi Gras.
   c. (1) During Mardi Gras there are parades.
      (2) They are throughout the city.
   d. (1) There are marching bands.
      (2) There are floats with people in costumes.
      (3) The costumes are extraordinary.
   e. (1) The people on floats toss out trinkets.
      (2) They toss out candy.
      (3) This is for the children watching the parades.
   f. (1) People dance in the streets.
      (2) They dance all day and night.
   g. (1) They wear masks.
      (2) The masks are interesting.

Early Hawaiians used outrigger canoes like this one to sail the Pacific Ocean.

(3) The masks cover their faces. (Use *to cover*)
- h. (1) Everyone enjoys eating the food.
  - (2) The food is delicious.
  - (3) The food is French-Creole.
  - (4) They eat outdoors or in restaurants.
- i. (1) There are other carnivals such as this.
  - (2) They are in different parts of the country.
- j. (1) But New Orleans has the largest celebration.
  - (2) It has the most colorful celebration.
  - (3) The celebration is in the United States.
- k. (1) It is a place to visit.
  - (2) It is wonderful at Mardi Gras time.

4. **Paragraph Topics.**

   a. Make up a holiday. Your paragraph will be clear if you ask yourself the following questions:

   Who would you honor? What would you celebrate?
   What day of the year would it take place?
   How would people celebrate it? (activities, costumes, food, music)
   What special part would you play in this celebration?

   b. People usually dress according to the customs of their country. In the United States, it is customary to dress according to the activity of the moment. Write about the different kinds of clothing you wear for various occasions: for example, school, work, evening out, at home, sports activities.

## ADDITIONAL READING

### Witching for Water

[1] People who live in cities rarely think about their water supply. When they are thirsty or need water to cook or bathe, they simply turn on the tap. Their water usually comes from a reservoir outside the city. A reservoir fills up with rainwater and melted snow from mountains and the water flows through pipes to the city. In rural areas, however, there aren't any reservoirs to supply farmhouses with water. People who live in the countryside obtain their water from an underground spring, and so they must dig a well. When a well goes dry, they must dig another in a different place. It is an important and difficult task to find the right place for a good supply of well water.

[2]   How do people make a choice about where to dig a well? There is no scientific method of detecting underground water, but there is a traditional "magic" way. It is called water witching, or dowsing. Some farmers in the United States practice this ancient folk custom. They use a divining rod, a switch from a tree, as their tool. Of course, they must have a special ability too; not everyone can be a dowser. Dowsers think that they have a reliable method of searching for hidden springs of water. Margaret Maron, a writer of mystery stories, agrees with them.

[3]   Mrs. Maron was born and raised on a farm in North Carolina, but moved to New York when she got married. Then in 1968 her mother gave her three acres of land at the edge of the family farm to build a vacation house, which later became her permanent home. Mrs. Maron and her husband went back to North Carolina to make all the arrangements. Here is Mrs. Maron's account of "witching for water":

[4]   This particular lot had been the site of my grandparents' house, a pinewood farmhouse that was built in the 1880s and burned to the ground in 1954. During those seventy-five years, at least three wells had been dug on the grounds. They provided fresh water for humans and animals and then went dry. My mother reminded us of this and I jokingly said, "Perhaps we should bring in a dowser to witch us a well." Mother laughed and said, "If you want, we can ask Mr. Randall Woodall. He's a dowser."

I knew that Mr. Randall was a tobacco farmer, the same age as my grandfather, but I didn't know that he had the mysterious powers of a dowser. My husband and I were thrilled with the idea of folk magic, so mother asked him and he agreed to come.

Mr. Randall arrived on our property a few days later. He was a tall man with white hair and a weather-worn face. He was dressed in a neat blue shirt, faded overalls, and high-top shoes. He was a little shy as we showed him around the property, but as soon as he started to work, he seemed quite sure of himself.

He began by cutting a switch from a hickory tree. He picked a young green shoot. "A green shoot is full of water, and like calls to like," he explained. The switch was slightly thicker than his thumb and about four feet long. He held one end of the stick in each hand, elbows at his side, forearms parallel to the ground, and palms down. He held the hickory stick so tightly that his knuckles turned white and the stick bent out in front of him like a half-loop.

We told Mr. Randall where we wanted to build our house, so he began to walk back and forth over that general area. Occasionally the tip of the stick began to shake slightly, but Mr. Randall paid no attention. "They don't mean much of nothing. Jest little streamlets. We're looking for something stronger," he explained.

After he had walked for about twenty minutes, the hickory loop suddenly made a strong downward movement. Mr. Randall slowed his steps and swept over the area with the stick more thoroughly. As he moved away from the "strong spot," the loop would swing back up until it was parallel with the ground. But, as he returned to that area, we watched in fascination as the end of the loop bent downward again with great force. It seemed as if something in the earth were pulling it.

"Dig here," he told us. "Hit's 'bout as strong a sprang as I've ever felt."

So we hired a man to come out and dig the well in that spot. He went down sixty feet and found thirty feet of water. That was over twenty years ago. About two years ago there was a terrible dry spell, and all our neighbors' wells were going dry. My husband and I went out and took the cap off our well and measured the depth of the water. It had only gone down eighteen inches!

Mr. Randall promised us "hit won't never run dry," and I for one believe him.

[5]   People in many parts of the world have a folk-magic tradition. Folk magic helps people make a choice when they do not have all the information they need to solve a problem. A dowser helped Mrs. Maron make a difficult choice. In her case, the "magic" worked well.

[6]   What do scientists think of dowsing? They say there is no connection between the use of a divining rod and the discovery of water. They believe that the downward motion occurs because the dowser, without knowing it, stops squeezing

Some farmers in the United States practice the ancient folk custom of dowsing for water. A farmer in Maine is holding a divining rod that is pointing down to a strong spot in the ground.

the rod and relaxes his muscles. It is just accidental, a matter of chance, that water is later discovered in places where the movement occurred. What do you think? Would you take a chance on a dowser?

## DISCUSSION QUESTIONS

1. People face difficult problems in their daily lives. Discuss the ways people have of solving the following problems: personal relationships, family relationships, school and study problems, housing, illness. When do people need professional help in solving their problems? When do friends or family members provide the best help? Should people keep their problems to themselves or express them to others?

2. Tossing a coin is a way to make a choice about something. Think of other "folk customs" that people use to make choices, for example, in playing games and sports. Did you ever make a serious choice about something by tossing a coin or other "magic" way?

3. People usually go to a doctor when they feel sick. However, some people prefer to treat minor illnesses with folk medicine, special home cures. They drink herb tea, or have other ways to treat themselves. Discuss some of the home remedies that you or others you know use for illness. Do you believe that folk medicine cures an illness? When should people not rely on folk medicine to cure an illness? Who believes more in folk medicine, older people or younger people?

## READING COMPREHENSION

1. **Understanding the Text.** Choose the correct answer or follow the directions.

   a. Which statement is true according to Paragraph [1]?
      
      (1) It is just as easy for rural people to obtain water as it is for city people.
      
      (2) Reservoirs supply farmhouses with a steady stream of fresh water.
      
      (3) In rural areas, people use well water for their daily needs.
   
   b. According to the information in Paragraph [2],
      
      (1) scientists have their own method of detecting hidden springs.
      
      (2) some farmers practice a form of folk magic to detect hidden springs.
      
      (3) dowsers use a scientific method of detecting hidden springs.

**c.** What was the situation on Mrs. Maron's property?

    **(1)** There was a good well, but it was in the wrong place for the house.
    **(2)** There was a house, but no well.
    **(3)** There was no well for the house that she was going to build.

**d.** When Mrs. Maron first spoke to her mother about a dowser,

    **(1)** she said it in a joking way.
    **(2)** she was really serious about calling one in.
    **(3)** her mother did not approve of the idea.

**e.** Mark *T* for the statement that is *true*, *F* for the statement that is *false*, and *P.T.* for the statement that is *probably true* about Mrs. Maron.

    **(1)** She had never heard about dowsing before 1968. _____
    **(2)** She knew about dowsing before 1968 because she was raised in an area where it was practiced. _____
    **(3)** She never knew before 1968 that Mr. Randall was a dowser. _____

**f.** Mrs. Maron decided to have Mr. Randall come to her property because

    **(1)** her mother told her to do it.
    **(2)** she and her husband were excited about seeing some folk magic.
    **(3)** she knew Mr. Randall and wanted to see him again after so many years.

**g.** Write the sentence from Mrs. Maron's account that describes how Mr. Randall looked.

_____

**h.** Write the sentence that describes Mr. Randall's clothes.

_____

**i.** Mark *T* for *true*, *F* for *false*, or *N.I.* for *no information* about Mr. Randall in this story.

    **(1)** He was a full-time dowser. _____
    **(2)** He was a young man. _____
    **(3)** He sometimes spoke English ungrammatically. _____
    **(4)** He had found water many times in the past. _____
    **(5)** He came dressed in work clothes. _____
    **(6)** He was a well-digger. _____

(7) He earned his living as a tobacco farmer. _____

(8) He didn't take payment for his dowsing service. _____

j. From the description of Mr. Randall holding the stick in his hands, draw a simple side view figure showing the position of the arms and hands and how the stick looked. Use the space provided.

k. Mr. Randall chose a green shoot from a hickory tree because it was full of water and *"like calls to like."* This expression means that

(1) the water in the shoot will attract water in the ground.

(2) Mr. Randall likes water.

(3) the young shoot looks like the hickory tree from which it came.

l. Mrs. Maron wrote her account using some of Mr. Randall's exact words and pronunciation. In the following items the italicized words are either used incorrectly or are spelled incorrectly. Write the correct form of the word on the line.

(1) They don't mean much of *nothing*. _____

(2) *Jest* little streamlets. _____

(3) *Hit's 'bout* as strong a *sprang* as I've ever felt. _____

_____   _____

(4) *Hit* won't *never* run dry. _____   _____

Chapter Two   The United States: Land of Many Cultures   73

Divining rods are used to detect metals, oil, and other minerals in the ground. This drawing of 1556 shows divining rods in use for finding metals.

   m.  Mrs. Maron believes in the mysterious powers of dowsers because

   **(1)** she is a writer of mystery stories.
   **(2)** her well has been full of water for over twenty years.
   **(3)** Mr. Randall was a mysterious man.

2. **Answering Information Questions.**   Write a complete statement in answer to the following questions.
   a. Where do city people get their water from?
   b. Where do country people obtain their water from?
   c. What happens when a well goes dry?
   d. Is there a scientific method of detecting underground water?
   e. What is the "magic" way of detecting water called?
   f. Where do some farmers practice this ancient folk custom?
   g. How does folk magic help people?
   h. What do scientists say about dowsing?

74  Unit I  Our Diverse World

3. **The Reading Process: Sequencing Events in Time Order.** Time order is important in relating an event. Recalling a series of activities in sequence helps the reader to reconstruct the event correctly.

   a. The following items are about Mrs. Maron's property in North Carolina. Number the sentences in correct order according to the time the event takes place. Number 1 will be the first thing that happened. Number 5 will be the last.

   (1) The farmhouse burned down. _____

   (2) Mrs. Maron lives there now. _____

   (3) Mrs. Maron's grandparents lived in that house. _____

   (4) Mrs. Maron built a house on the property. _____

   (5) A pinewood farmhouse had been built on the property. _____

   b. When the following sentences are put in correct time order, they will make a paragraph about the steps Mr. Randall took to dowse for water. Arrange the sentences correctly and write them in a paragraph on the lines provided.

   (1) In some places the stick would shake slightly.

   (2) He told Mrs. Maron to dig there.

   (3) First he cut a switch from a hickory tree.

   (4) Then he began to walk back and forth over the property.

   (5) But he paid no attention to those spots.

   (6) He held the stick with both hands so that it formed a loop.

   (7) Then he found a strong spot.

   (8) He walked around some more.

   _____
   _____
   _____
   _____
   _____
   _____
   _____

# VOCABULARY

1. **Expanding Vocabulary.** Choose the word(s) that mean(s) the same as the italicized word in each sentence. Use a dictionary only if necessary.

    a. People who live in cities *obtain* their water from reservoirs located outside the city.

    **(1)** drink    **(2)** keep    **(3)** get

    b. People who live in *rural* areas usually obtain their water from a well.

    **(1)** crowded    **(2)** tropical    **(3)** agricultural

    c. Farmers depend on underground springs to *supply* them with water for drinking, bathing, and cooking.

    **(1)** provide    **(2)** measure    **(3)** show

    d. It is impossible to *detect* an underground spring without digging in the earth, or perhaps asking a dowser to help you.

    **(1)** destroy    **(2)** discover    **(3)** hide

    e. Dowsers think that their way of searching for water is *reliable*.

    **(1)** dependable    **(2)** silly    **(3)** delicious

    f. Mrs. Maron was *thrilled* with the idea of seeing a dowser at work.

    **(1)** annoyed    **(2)** bored    **(3)** excited

    g. Mr. Randall kept his forearms *parallel* to the ground as he held the dowsing stick.

    **(1)** away from    **(2)** in the opposite direction from    **(3)** extending in the same direction as

    h. When he found a strong spot, he went over the area more *thoroughly* to make sure it was the right place to dig.

    **(1)** quickly    **(2)** frequently    **(3)** completely

    i. There is no scientific *method* of detecting underground springs, so dowsing may be as good as any other *method* of finding water.

    **(1)** technique    **(2)** problem    **(3)** discovery

2. **Using Vocabulary.** Answer each question in a complete statement. Use the italicized word in your answer.

    a. Are the lines in the letter V *parallel*?

    _____

b. What do the guards at an airport use to *detect* a weapon in a suitcase?

c. Are you *thrilled* when someone gives you an expensive gift?

d. Which people have more fresh air to breathe, people in cities or people who live in *rural* areas?

e. Is it easy or difficult to *obtain* information about registration in your school?

f. Do elementary schools *supply* the children with books for their studies?

g. When do you clean your house *thoroughly*, during the week or on weekends?

h. In your experience, are older people or younger people more *reliable* as baby-sitters?

i. Which is a quicker *method* of learning new words, using a dictionary or getting the meaning from the context?

3. **Word Families: Adjective Versus Noun Forms.** Study the following list of nouns and adjectives.

| Noun | Adjective |
|---|---|
| difference | different |
| evidence | evident |
| importance | important |
| intelligence | intelligent |
| patience | patient |
| (in)dependence | (in)dependent |
| convenience | convenient |
| depth | deep |
| height | high |
| width | wide |
| length | long |
| warmth | warm |

# Chapter Two    The United States: Land of Many Cultures

*Proofreading.*   Each sentence uses the italicized word in either a correct way (as a noun or adjective) or incorrectly. If the sentence is *correct*, mark *C* in the blank. If an italicized word is used incorrectly, write the correct form of the word on the line.

**a.**  (1) Before you buy a sofa, you should measure its *length*.
_____

(2) You don't want it to be too *length* for the space you have.
_____

**b.**  (1) It isn't *convenience* to be without a car in a rural area.
_____

(2) I prefer to live in a city because of the *convenience* of public transportation. _____

**c.**  (1) There are many *depth* bodies of water on the earth's surface.
_____

(2) The Pacific Ocean has a *deep* of seven miles in some parts.
_____

**d.**  (1) *Intelligent* is something we like in our pet dogs and cats.
_____

(2) Farmers don't usually keep pigs as pets, but they admire pigs for their *intelligent*. _____

**e.**  (1) It is *important* to know the traditions of your own national group.
_____

(2) If we learn about each other's traditions, we can understand their *important* and respect each other more. _____

**f.**  (1) Parents need a lot of *patience* in taking care of their children.
_____

(2) If parents are not *patience*, there may be trouble in the family.
_____

**g.**  (1) What is the *high* of the Empire State Building? _____

(2) It isn't as *high* as the Twin Towers of the World Trade Center.
_____

**h.**  (1) We all understand the *different* between the word "to" and "too."
_____

(2) Do you know that "there" is *different* from "their"?
_____

i. (1) We need wool clothing to keep *warmth* in cold weather.
_____

(2) In *warmth* weather, we usually wear clothing made of cotton.
_____

j. (1) The fruits, flowers, and other vegetation of a particular area are *dependent* on the climate of that area. _____

(2) Because there is very little rainfall in Egypt, vegetation there is *dependence* on water from the Nile River. _____

*Sentence Construction.* Write a complete sentence in which you use the given item. The first one is done for you as one possibility.

a. convenient way to travel
   *The bus is a convenient way to travel over short distances.*

b. the difference between the words "no" and "know."
   _____

c. different kinds of animals
   _____

d. the deep end of the swimming pool
   _____

e. evidence against the thief
   _____

f. to become independent
   _____

## PARAGRAPH TOPICS

1. Many people prefer to live in a city because of the many conveniences it offers. Write a paragraph in which you describe the various conveniences that your city offers its people. The following list may help guide you in writing your paragraph:

   public transportation            different kinds of schools

job opportunities            entertainment

cultural activities            parks, beaches, or other recreational areas

Begin your paragraph with a main idea statement that introduces your topic and your viewpoint.

2. Living in the countryside can be rewarding. Write a paragraph in which you describe life in the countryside. If you have lived in a rural area, write about your experience. The following items may help guide you in writing your paragraph:

fresh air            lots of trees and flowers

peace and quiet            places to swim or go fishing

grow vegetables            learn about nature

Begin your paragraph with an appropriate main idea statement.

# CHAPTER THREE

# STEPS TO THE FUTURE

## PREREADING

**Class Discussion.** Study the following entry from the *Webster's New World Dictionary*, pocket-size edition:

> *pre.dict* (pri-dikt′), v.t. & v.i. [LL. *prae*, -before + *dicere*, tell], to make known beforehand; foretell; prophesy—predict′ a-ble, adj.—prediction, n.

What does the dictionary tell you about the entry word? What do the abbreviations mean?

Apollo II astronaut Edwin E. Aldrin, Jr., leaves his footsteps on the surface of the moon. What predictions can you make about living on the moon in the future?

Chapter Three Steps to the Future   81

> *Free Write.* What are your predictions of the future? What will the world be like when the next generation of children is grown?

**Vocabulary in Context.** The words in this exercise will appear in the reading passage. Choose the word that means the same as the italicized word in each sentence.

1. Scientists can *observe* the stars through a telescope.
   a. watch closely   b. hear clearly   c. instruct

2. They also send spacecraft to *explore* the planets.
   a. explain about   b. record   c. go over closely

3. Nine planets *revolve* around the sun.
   a. return   b. remain   c. turn

4. The air around the Earth *protects* it against the sun's dangerous rays.
   a. attacks   b. guards   c. provides

5. The Earth has air and water *necessary* for life.
   a. needed   b. traditional   c. unimportant

6. Without the Earth's special *environment*, there would be no life.
   a. planet   b. surroundings   c. rays

7. There are many *varieties* of plants and animals on Earth.
   a. kinds   b. areas   c. millions

8. If we don't take care of our planet, we may *destroy* some of the life on it.
   a. save   b. disturb   c. ruin

9. There must be a *balance* of all kinds of life forms to have a good life on Earth.
   a. harmony   b. culture   c. responsibility

10. If you enjoy the beach, it would be *irresponsible* of you to leave your trash in the sand.
    a. very kind   b. expected   c. totally careless

## READING

### Our Biosphere: A World of Life

[1]   In the past, many people liked to think that life existed on other planets in our solar system. It was an exciting thought. Perhaps we had friendly neighbors out there. Perhaps we had enemies. Today we know that we have no neighbors in our solar system. All the planets have been visited by Earth's robot explorers. According to the scientific information, no planet but Earth has the air, water, and vegetation necessary for life.

[2]   Earth has the best position among the nine planets that revolve around the sun. Neither too near or too far from the sun, it receives the necessary amount of heat and light. High up in the air, the ozone layer protects us from the sun's dangerous rays. As Earth revolves, the seasons change. Winds blow rain clouds over the land, and our fields are green with vegetation. Without this special environment, there would be no life on Earth. If we change this environment, we may destroy some of life's treasures.

[3]   Earth was formed over 4 billion years ago. At first it was a dead object of rock, like the moon now, without air or water. It took millions of years to develop into a biosphere, a world of life. Now Earth is the home of over 13 million different plant and animal species. All the varieties of living things depend on the sun, on air and water, and on each other. The sun will shine for millions of years. Will we be able to keep Earth a special place in the solar system?

[4]   The future doesn't look bright. There are environmental problems everywhere with harmful effects on our health and on all of nature. These problems may be at home with our drinking water, at the beach where garbage floats in the ocean, in our polluted rivers and streams where fish can no longer live, and on our farmlands and woodlands where acid rain falls. Scientists warn us that our problems will get worse. In some parts of the world, whole forests are being cut down. As a result, wildlife species become homeless and may even die out. Moreover, scientists predict that, without our forests, Earth's climate will change. They say that the continued use of fuels such as coal and oil will add to the climate problem. These fuels and other chemicals pollute the air and slowly destroy the ozone layer that protects us from the sun's dangerous rays. This will result in higher temperatures, droughts, and severe storms all across the globe.

[5]   Can we live on our land without spoiling the environment? In the desert of Arizona, scientists are performing an experiment. They are building a huge structure of glass and steel. Called Biosphere II, it will be a completely enclosed world which can support plant, animal, and human life without the help of our main biosphere, Earth. The structure, covering two and one-half acres of land, will contain a variety of environments: a tropical rain forest, a desert, a grassland region, and a farming area. In addition, there will be a thirty-five foot deep ocean and a fresh water and saltwater swamp. In each environment, several thousand

Health problems are caused by smoke from cars, factories, and homes. Describe the quality of the air, water, and other features of your environment.

species of plants and animals will live just as they do in the outside world. Eight researchers will live along with them. According to the plan, they will not come out for two years.

[6] The purpose of Biosphere II is to observe and understand Earth's delicate balance of nature. How will it work? Thousands of plants will give off oxygen for humans and animals; the carbon dioxide exhaled by them will keep the plants alive. Solid wastes must be reused as fertilizer for food crops and water plants. Water plants will feed fish in the man-made ocean. The research scientists will eat bananas and papayas that grow in the rain forest and vegetables grown in the farmland area. All fruits and vegetables will be free of chemical pesticides. Ladybugs will be used to protect vegetation from harmful insects. There will be chickens and goats to provide eggs, meat, and milk, but the researchers will get their protein mostly from fish.

[7] The people taking part in this project will have a variety of skills. There will be a plant specialist, an animal specialist, mechanics, and technicians who will constantly test the environment for safety. They will be shut off from everything except sunlight. They will, however, have very comfortable rooms to live in and a large library. They can communicate with the outside world by telephone and computer. Except in an emergency, they will not leave the structure until the experiment is done.

[8] Creating a perfect balance of nature is a difficult task. Nothing can be wasted because each part of nature depends on another part. As one researcher says, "It will take three thousand blooming flowers every day to feed a pair of hummingbirds . . . and there are a lot of unknowns. But the more we learn about our world, the more we will care about its future."

[9]  Biosphere II will show us how Earth was before humans created environmental problems. But we can't turn our biosphere back to that time. Nor can we go on with irresponsible human activities that will lead to further destruction. No one wants Earth to become like the planet Venus—a world of carbon dioxide, acid rain, and 900° temperatures!

[10]  Stories about the future—in books and in movies—show people living in biospheres on other planets, on the moon, or in space. But Earth is our real home, our only home. "How strange and wonderful is our home, our earth, with its swirling atmosphere, its flowing and frozen rivers, its climbing creatures, the things with wings that hang on rocks and soar through fog, the furry grass, the scaly seas . . . how utterly rich and wild. . . ." With these words, the writer Edward Abbey expressed his love of nature. All of us, governments, private companies, and we as individuals must act responsibly in our home. We must work to make it safer for a brighter future.

**Summary Completion.**  Fill in the blank spaces with the correct word from the reading passage.

Earth is the only (1) _____ with the necessities of life. Our environment supports a great variety of plant and animal (2) _____. But we are in danger of losing our treasures because of environmental (3) _____. Chemicals are polluting our water and (4) _____. Scientists predict that our (5) _____ will change because we are destroying the ozone layer. The Biosphere II project will create a perfect balance of (6) _____. The researchers hope to (7) _____ more about our world and how to take better care of it. Humans cannot continue their irresponsible (8) _____ that lead to further destruction. Earth is our only (9) _____, and we must plan well for a better future.

## DISCUSSION QUESTIONS

1. What kinds of pollution do you notice in your neighborhood? Discuss such things as noise, garbage, gasoline fumes, smoke from chimneys. What can ordinary citizens do about each of these problems? Which problems are the responsibility of the city government? Do you know of any laws against pollution?

2. Gasoline fumes cause terrible pollution in our cities. Should cars be banned from city streets? Would better public transportation help keep cars off the streets? What kind of transportation system would you like to see in your city?

3. Discuss the movies you have seen that portray alien creatures from outer space. Are these creatures like us in any way? Are they shown as more intelligent than we are? Do they have similar feelings? What is their environment like? Do you believe, as some scientists do, that some form of intelligent life exists on remote planets outside our solar system?

## READING COMPREHENSION

1. **Understanding the Text.** Choose the correct answer or follow the directions.

    a. According to Paragraph [1], all the planets in our solar system
       - (1) have been visited by human astronauts.
       - (2) have not yet been explored.
       - (3) have been explored by unmanned spacecraft.
    
    b. The topic of Paragraph [2] is
       - (1) the sun's dangerous rays.
       - (2) Earth's special environment.
       - (3) our changing seasons.
    
    c. In Paragraph [3], we learn that
       - (1) life always existed on Earth.
       - (2) Earth is now like the moon.
       - (3) Earth is a biosphere.
    
    d. In Paragraph [4], the author
       - (1) gives us a description of our environmental problems.
       - (2) offers some suggestions for improving our environment.
       - (3) describes our environment in positive terms.
    
    e. The purpose of Biosphere II is
       - (1) to see how long researchers can live in an enclosed place.
       - (2) to understand Earth's delicate balance of nature.
       - (3) to observe the exchange of carbon dioxide and oxygen between plants and animals.

**f.** Biosphere II will be free of chemical pesticides. This is because

  **(1)** chemical pesticides are harmful to the environment.

  **(2)** chemical pesticides cost too much money to use.

  **(3)** there won't be any harmful insects on the plants.

**g.** The researchers in Biosphere II

  **(1)** will live without sunlight.

  **(2)** will remain in there even in an emergency.

  **(3)** will enjoy balanced meals.

**h.** In Paragraph [9], we are told that

  **(1)** we can change our environment to the way it was.

  **(2)** we must change our activities to save our environment.

  **(3)** we have an unchanging environment.

**i.** In Paragraph [9] there is the phrase *irresponsible human activities*. Check (√) the items that would be considered irresponsible actions.

  **(1)** Dumping chemicals in rivers and lakes _____

  **(2)** Keeping endangered species of animals in zoos _____

  **(3)** Burning garbage _____

  **(4)** Drilling for oil in national wildlife areas _____

  **(5)** Hunting elephants, lions, and tigers _____

  **(6)** Establishing fast, cheap public-transportation systems _____

  **(7)** Recycling newspapers _____

  **(8)** Cutting down whole forests _____

  **(9)** Throwing garbage on the streets _____

  **(10)** Using the sun's energy to heat homes _____

**j.** In Paragraph [10], the writer Edward Abbey expresses

  **(1)** his appreciation of all of nature.

  **(2)** his concerns for the future.

  **(3)** his love of modern society.

2. **Answering Information Questions.** Answer each of the following questions in a complete sentence.

  **a.** What protects us from the sun's dangerous rays?

  **b.** What happens to wildlife species when forests are cut down?

c. What will happen to the climate without our forests?
d. Where are they building Biosphere II?
e. What kinds of food will the researchers eat?
f. What kind of rooms will they live in?
g. What kind of world is the planet Venus?

3. **The Reading Process: Identifying Specific Information.** Specific information sentences give the details or facts in a paragraph. These sentences support the main idea of a paragraph. Details and facts explain the main idea sentence by answering the questions *why, when, where, how, what, who,* and *which* about the main idea. Specific information sentences can also give examples of something or give a time order of when things happen.

   a. In the following paragraph, the main idea sentence is italicized. Read the specific information sentences carefully and answer the questions at the end of the paragraph orally with your class.

   *In the future, robot machines will take the place of human beings in difficult and dangerous jobs.* Robot machines will have arms to do all the unsafe work in factories. They will look for minerals deep underwater where no humans can go. Some robots will have special eyes to find people in burning buildings where firefighters can't go. Robots with special fingers will work in hospitals helping doctors with delicate operations. Perhaps robots will work in space, on the moon, or on other planets.

   (1) Do the specific information sentences give examples of something, or do they give a time order?
   (2) Name all the things that answer the question *where* and underline them in the paragraph.
   (3) What kind of work will robots do in factories?
   (4) What will robots look for deep underwater?
   (5) How will robots help doctors?
   (6) Do all the specific information sentences support the main idea?

   b. In the following exercises, you will be asked for specific information about the reading passage. Follow the directions for each item. Write your answers in brief form on the lines.

   (1) Look through the reading passage to find answers to the following *how* questions.

88  Unit I  Our Diverse World

    (a) How many planets are there in the solar system? _____

    (b) How old is Earth? _____

    (c) How many different plant and animal species exist? _____

    (d) How many acres of land will Biosphere II cover? _____

    (e) How many researchers will live in this structure? _____

    (f) How long will they stay there? _____

    (g) How will they communicate with the outside world? _____

    (h) How many flowers does it take to feed two hummingbirds? _____

(2) According to Paragraph [4],

    (a) there are environmental problems everywhere. List the places where these problems occur according to the paragraph.

    _____ _____ _____

    _____ _____ _____

    (b) *What* are the two harmful effects of cutting down our forests?

    _____ and _____

    (c) What will be the result of the destruction of the ozone layer?

    _____ _____ _____

    (d) Which fuels are given as examples of air pollutants?

    _____ and _____

(3) Biosphere II will contain a variety of environments. What kinds are included?

    _____ _____ _____

    _____ _____ _____

(4) What foods will the different environments provide for the researchers?

    _____ _____ _____

    _____ _____ _____

(5) What will be used instead of chemicals to control harmful insects in Biosphere II? _____

(6) What kind of specialists will inhabit Biosphere II? _____ , _____ , _____ , and _____

**(7)** Who wrote the words in quotation marks in Paragraph [10]?

_____

## VOCABULARY

1. **New Words.** Pronounce the words following your instructor.

   | Verbs | Nouns | Adjectives | Adverbs |
   |---|---|---|---|
   | explore | balance | necessary | |
   | observe | environment | irresponsible | |
   | revolve | variety | | |
   | protect | | | |
   | destroy | | | |

   a. *Expanding Vocabulary.* Choose a word from the list that correctly completes the sentence.

   (1) A loving home _____ is important for children.

   (2) On the Fourth of July, I always go up on the roof to _____ the fireworks.

   (3) If you tell lies, you may _____ your relationship with those who trust you.

   (4) It isn't _____ to copy these sentences on a separate sheet of paper.

   (5) There are parts of this city I haven't been to, but I'll _____ them sometime in the future.

   (6) My friend's garden is blooming with such a wonderful _____ of flowers.

   (7) When you prepare a meal, you should consider a good _____ between proteins and carbohydrates.

   (8) To leave a young child alone in the house is an _____ action.

   (9) In many areas of the world, there are strict laws to _____ endangered species of animals.

Unit I  Our Diverse World

Many species of animals like this caiman are dying out because people shoot them for their skins.

    (10) As Earth and the moon travel around the sun, they also _____ on their own axes.

**b.** *Using Vocabulary.* Write a complete sentence in answer to the following questions. Use the italicized word in your statement.

    (1) Can people *observe* the stars best in a city or in the countryside?

    (2) What kind of *environment* must a palm tree have, a warm one or a cool one?

    (3) Is special clothing *necessary* for work in outer space?

    (4) Are there many or few *varieties* of fruit available in the summer?

    (5) Can air pollution *destroy* ancient buildings and statues?

    (6) Does the sun *revolve* around the Earth?

    (7) Would you like to *explore* the moon someday?

(8) What kind of clothing do you wear in the winter to *protect* you from the cold?

_____

(9) Is there a *balance* of work and play in your life?

_____

2. **Word Families: Adjective Formation with -*Less*.** Some English adjectives can be formed by adding the suffix *-less* to a noun. The suffix *-less* means *without*.

> **The moon is a world without *life*. (*Life* is a noun.)**
> **The moon is a *lifeless* world. (*Lifeless* is an adjective.)**

Study the following list of nouns and adjectives.

| **Nouns** | **Adjectives** |
|---|---|
| life | lifeless |
| air | airless |
| hope | hopeless |
| care | careless |
| tree | treeless |
| home | homeless |
| pain | painless |
| sleep | sleepless |

*Sentence Completion.* Choose the correct word in parentheses to fill in the blank space in each sentence.

a. (home, homeless) We can see _____ cats in some neighborhoods at night.

b. (sun, sunless) During the winter in North America there are many _____ days.

c. (pain, painless) Do you usually have _____ during your visit to the dentist?

d. (meat, meatless) If farmers don't keep a lot of animals, people will eat many _____ dinners.

e. (hope, hopeless) We must all have _____ that the future will be brighter.

f. (star, starless) In the past, sailors couldn't sail their ships across the ocean without a _____ to help them.

g. (sleep, sleepless) Astronomers spend _____ nights watching the stars through telescopes.

h. (water, waterless) Scientists used to think there were rivers on Mars, but now they know that the planet is _____ .

i. (tree, treeless) A traveler will see a _____ environment at the North and South Poles.

j. (care, careless) We must treat the Earth with _____ or we will destroy it.

k. (life, lifeless) Where there is _____ , there is hope.

## WRITING EXERCISES

### Expressing the Future with *Will* + Basic Form of Verbs

*Will* + the basic form of a verb is one way of expressing action that will be completed in the future. This form usually expresses a person's opinions, beliefs, plans, or hopes about the future. It also expresses the idea of determination, promise, or inevitability.

> I'm sure he will return. (belief)
> The snow will melt when it gets warmer. (inevitability)
> I will never forget you. (promise)

Study the following verb forms.

|  | Singular | Plural |
|---|---|---|
| First Person | I will travel (I'll travel) | My friend and I will travel<br>We will travel (We'll travel) |

| | | |
|---|---|---|
| Second Person | You will travel (You'll travel) | You will travel (You'll travel) |
| Third Person | A scientist will travel<br>He/She/It will travel<br>He'll/She'll/It'll travel | Scientists will travel<br>They will travel (They'll travel) |

Notice that the auxiliary verb *will* never changes its form. Notice also that the main verb that follows *will* is always in its basic form. The negative form of *will* is *will not (won't)*.

1. **Recognizing Verb Forms.** Read the following paragraph. It is a student's plan for the next few days. Underline each complete verb form expressing the future. Then with your class discuss the questions that follow the paragraph.

    (1) We often have quizzes in our English class. (2) The next quiz will be in a few days. (3) Later today I'll go to the library and put my notes in order. (4) Tomorrow afternoon I'll work at my friend's house. (5) She knows English better than I do. (6) She will help me with verb tenses. (7) When the test comes, I will be well prepared.

    Which two sentences use only the Simple Present tense? Why?
    What future time expressions occur in sentences (2), (3), and (4)?
    Sentence (7) uses the Simple Present tense in the *when* clause and *will* + basic verb in the main clause. Write a sentence of your own using this pattern.

2. **Paragraph Reconstruction.** In the following chart, fill in the subject of each sentence in Exercise 1 in the subject column. Fill in the complete verb form in the Verb column. Place the items in the chart on the board. Read the paragraph in Exercise 1 several times. Then close your book and reconstruct the paragraph as closely as possible.

| | **Subject** | **Verb** |
|---|---|---|
| (1) | | |
| (2) | | |
| (3) | | |
| (4) | | |
| (5) | | |
| (6) | | |
| (7) | | |

3. **Controlled Writing.** The following paragraph about Rome, Italy, is written in the Simple Present tense; the information in it is factual. Pretend that the paragraph is a prediction about the future of New York City. Change the name *Rome* to *New York*. Change the verbs to express the future in each sentence. Your first sentence will be the following: *New York will have a new law.*

   Rome has a new law. The government doesn't allow cars in special areas of the city. The people of Rome and visitors from other cities explore these areas freely. The streets are crowded with people. There isn't any noise of car engines. The people stroll around and stop to look at interesting buildings or shop windows. They sit outside and have coffee or ice cream without breathing bad air. The children of Rome play ball in the middle of the street. They ride their bicycles without danger. There is a very pleasant environment in these areas of Rome.

4. **Sentence Composing**

   a. Answer the following questions in complete sentences on a separate sheet of paper.
      (1) Where will you go when summer comes?
      (2) What will you buy your best friend for his or her next birthday?
      (3) What will you do when you graduate from this school?
      (4) Where will you go next Saturday night?
      (5) Who will you visit the next time you have a vacation?
      (6) What will you do when you leave school today?
      (7) What will you have for breakfast tomorrow morning?
      (8) What will you buy when you have enough money?
      (9) At what time will you be in school tomorrow?
      (10) When will this semester be over?

   b. Write a complete sentence stating what you will do if you are faced with the given situation. The first one is done for you.
      (1) Your teacher announces a test for tomorrow.
         *I'll review all my notes.*
      (2) You need to look up some information about a subject.
      (3) You don't know the meaning of a word in a reading passage.
      (4) Your little brother has a problem with his math homework.

(5) Your friend is in the hospital.
(6) Your younger sister has trouble in school.
(7) Your best friend tells you a secret. (Use the negative.)
(8) You don't understand the teacher's explanation.
(9) Your pet cat or dog is sick.
(10) You are invited to a party, but you don't want to go alone.

## Simple Present Tense Negative Forms

The negative form of the Simple Present tense is the auxiliary verb *don't* + *base verb* for all persons, singular and plural, except the Third Person Singular. The Third Person Singular forms the negative by *doesn't* + *base verb*.

> **I (You, We, They)** *don't travel* **by bus very often.**
> **The planet Venus** *doesn't have* **a suitable environment for life.**

1. **Answering Questions.** Write the answers to the following questions in complete sentences. Use the Simple Present tense negative form of the verb only when appropriate. The first two are done for you.

   a. Does a car run without gas?
   *A car doesn't run without gas.*

   b. Does this book have many writing exercises?
   *This book has many writing exercises.*

   c. Does your school library charge students for borrowing books?
   d. Do art museums allow people to touch the paintings?
   e. Do most of your friends go to bed late?
   f. Does the moon have air and water necessary for life?
   g. Does a salesperson earn as much as the company's boss?
   h. Do banks let customers borrow money without paying interest?
   i. Does traffic noise bother you very much?
   j. Does the word *too* mean the same as the word *also*?
   k. Do you consult a doctor when you have a mild headache?
   l. Does smoking harm a person's health?

2. **Sentence Composing.** Compose a complete sentence in response to the following items. The first one is done for you as a possible response.

   a. Tell which three vegetables you don't like.
      *I don't like carrots, peas, or spinach.*
   b. Tell which two fruits you don't like.
   c. Tell one thing you don't like about your school.
   d. Name two sports you don't know how to play.
   e. Tell which item your mother, father, or other family member doesn't have, but would like to have.
   f. Write which two household items you don't own, but would like to have.
   g. Name an item you don't need because you have one.
   h. Tell what your little brother, sister, cousin, or other child doesn't like to do.
   i. Tell what expensive article of clothing you don't have, but will buy some day.
   j. Name what kind of weather you don't like.
   k. Tell one thing your teacher doesn't want the students to do in class.
   l. Tell one thing a young family member doesn't know how to do now, but will learn soon.
   m. Describe one thing about English you don't know how to do well, but will learn this semester.
   n. Tell whose house you don't like to visit and give a reason.
   o. Name what musical instrument you don't play, but would like to learn to play.

## Verbs + Adjectives

The verbs *be, become, feel, seem, look,* or *appear* are often used to connect a subject with an adjective.

> I *am happy* in my new job.
> Sometimes people *feel sad*.
> The students *don't appear nervous* during an exam.

1. **Recognizing Verbs + Adjectives.** Listen carefully as your instructor reads the following paragraph about the moon. Underline the complete verb forms and their adjectives.

   What do we know about the moon? It looks bright in the night sky, but it doesn't have its own light. The sun shines on it for half a month; the rays are strong and would be dangerous for a human without a space suit. To someone standing on the moon's surface, everything would appear gray in the sharp light. The surface isn't smooth; there are rocks everywhere. In between the small rocks, the soil is fine and dusty. Nothing moves because there is no wind. To us the moon seems like a strange world; to those men who have explored it, it is calm and peaceful. The footsteps they left behind will remain in the soft dust for millions of years.

2. **Sentence Composing.** Write a complete sentence following the directions for each item. Use a verb + adjective for each answer. The following adjectives will help you write your sentences. The first one is done for you.

   | noisy | comfortable | splendid | busy |
   | messy | serious | tired | easy |
   | crowded | hungry | bright | relaxed |
   | careless | difficult | neat | careful |
   | friendly | blue | nervous | |

   a. Tell us how you feel on Sunday mornings?
       *I feel tired on Sunday mornings.*
   b. Describe how the school cafeteria appears at lunchtime.
   c. Tell how students seem during an exam.
   d. Tell what color the sky appears to us.
   e. Describe how you are when you meet a new person.
   f. Tell how some drivers are on the road.
   g. Explain how the exam seems when you don't know the answers.
   h. Describe how your living room looks after a party.
   i. Tell how the stores are at Christmastime.
   j. Describe how the moon appears in the night sky.
   k. Tell how the exam seems when you know all the answers.
   l. Tell how the health problems are in the world today.

m. Describe how wild animals look when they can't find food.
n. Tell how you don't feel on a long bus ride.

## Singular Possessives

> my friend's computer (the computer belonging to my friend)
> Hawaii's climate (the climate of Hawaii)
> a bird's nest (the nest of a bird)
> the doctor's office (the office of the doctor)

The apostrophe + *s ('s)* form is used to show that one person, place, or thing has or owns another noun.

1. **Sentence Completion.** Choose the correct word from the following list to fill in the blank space in each sentence. Change the noun before each blank space to the singular possessive form to show the correct relationship between the two nouns. The first one is done for you.

   | | | | | | |
   |---|---|---|---|---|---|
   | museums | boss | brain | house | desk | health |
   | progress | rays | jewelry | office | mistakes | laws |
   | explanations | | past | | | |

   a. My sister's *jewelry* is expensive.
   b. I always get nervous sitting in the doctor _____.
   c. The city _____ against smoking on buses are strict.
   d. Objects from the earth tell us about our country _____.
   e. I'm going to my friend _____ for dinner.
   f. My father _____ is president of the company.
   g. The instructor _____ are quite clear.
   h. There is a typewriter on the secretary _____.
   i. Some of the sun _____ are dangerous.
   j. Smoking is harmful to a person _____.
   k. A father is always interested in his child _____ in school.

l. Our country _____ are among the best in the world.

m. A person _____ is the center of the nervous system.

2. **Sentence Composing.** We often use the word *whose* to ask a question about possession. (Do not confuse *whose* with *who's*. The word *who's* is a contraction for *who is*.) Answer each of the following *whose* questions in a complete statement that contains a singular possessive noun. The first one is done for you.

   a. Whose job is exciting?
   *A reporter's job is exciting.*
   b. Whose job is dangerous?
   c. Whose house will you visit next weekend?
   d. Whose dog sometimes barks at night and wakes you up?
   e. Whose health is a parent interested in?
   f. Whose office does a student go to for advice in school?
   g. Whose instructions do you listen carefully to?
   h. Whose pencil or eraser do you sometimes borrow in class?
   i. Whose car does your friend sometimes drive?

3. **Proofreading.** Read the following paragraph about the usefulness of garbage or trash. Circle all the forms that should be singular possessives, and insert the apostrophe in the correct position. The first one is done for you.

   (1) Some people in New York help clean up the environment by re-using other (people's) garbage. (2) Mr. Salinas, for example, found a wooden wire holder in front of a factory building and turned it into a night table for his childs room. (3) Mrs. Conroy noticed a cooking pot on top of her neighbors garbage pile and now cheerfully uses it in her kitchen. (4) One night Mr. Minsky brought home a clay container from a trash bin to add to his wifes collection of flower pots. (5) Skip LaPlante goes through garbage cans looking for cardboard tubes, pieces of pipe, or other industrial products. (6) He uses these items to make music. (7) All of Mr. LaPlantes instruments are created from trash. (8) Going through garbage is not everyones idea of fun, but we can say that one persons garbage may be another persons treasure.

## THE COMPOSING PROCESS

1. **Developing a Paragraph.**

   *Outlining.* Making an outline of a paragraph helps the reader understand the writer's main idea and how the idea is developed with specific information details. Outlining is also important for writing your own compositions. It helps you organize your thoughts before writing a paragraph.

   An outline begins with the complete main idea sentence. Then specific information is written in brief note form.

   a. Read the following paragraph. Fill in the main idea sentence of the paragraph on the lines that follow. Then in the spaces following the main idea, fill in the specific information in short note form. The specific information items are *examples* of the main idea statement. Two of the details are done for you.

   Some people are predicting that by the year 2000 there will be many good solutions to the world's problems. People will use sun and wind power to heat homes and run factories. Farmers will be able to grow food in very dry and cold areas of the world. There will be faster and cheaper public transportation. Cars will run on electricity rather than gasoline. Then our cities will have cleaner air for a healthier population. There will be stronger laws against the use of dangerous chemicals on farm crops. Scientists will find cures for serious illnesses such as cancer and heart disease. Life may be more pleasant in the future.

   Main Idea: _____

   _____

   Details: *sun and wind power for homes and factories*

   _____

   *faster and cheaper public transportation*

   _____

   _____

   _____

   _____

   Now copy the main idea sentence from your outline on a separate sheet of paper. Without looking at the paragraph, use just your outline to complete a paragraph with your own sentences.

   b. What do you predict about the future of your city? What things will change for the better? In an outline like that in Exercise a. list several details to expand in a paragraph. Begin with a main idea statement that expresses your general opinion about the topic.

2. **Composing a Paragraph.** Every day we are faced with environmental problems in our cities. Keep a journal for one day. Write down all the problems you notice from the time you leave your house to the time you return. For example, you may notice uncovered garbage cans, noise, and air pollution. Note where in your day's travel these problems occur. Also note your physical sensations when you experience these problems.

   a. Review your journal notes with a group of classmates. Are your experiences similar or different?
   b. Think about what bothers you most about what you experienced.
   c. Choose three of your items to write about.
   d. Note these in outline form.
   e. Use the following topic to head your outline: The things That Bother Me Most.
   f. Begin your paragraph with a sentence appropriate to the topic.
   g. Develop your paragraph by being specific about the items you listed. Tell what each problem is, where it occurs, how it affects you, and the effect on your city.

   You may want to read your paragraph to your group or exchange papers with a partner for helpful suggestions. Write a second version to improve your organization and sentence structure.

3. **Sentence Combining to Form a Paragraph.** The following sentences are about Echo Lake, a resort community in California controlled by the United States Forest Service. Combine each group of sentences into one sentence. Use pronouns instead of nouns when appropriate. Use the words in parentheses to help you. Leave out unnecessary words. Write your sentences in the form of a paragraph on a separate sheet of paper.

   a. (1) Echo Lake is a vacation place.
      (2) It is in the Sierra Nevada mountains.
      (3) It is in northern California.
   b. (1) There are only 125 cabins.
      (2) They are on this lake.
      (3) The U.S. Forest Service won't permit overcrowding.   (because)
   c. (1) The cabin owners must follow rules.
      (2) The rules are strict.
      (3) The rules are to protect the environment.

**d.** **(1)** The cabin owners cannot have electricity.
   **(2)** They cannot have flush toilets.   (or)
**e.** **(1)** They cannot chop down trees.
   **(2)** This is for firewood.
   **(3)** They cannot dig away rocks to add space to their cabins.
**f.** **(1)** There is no garbage collection.
   **(2)** The people must carry their garbage out of the area.   (so)
   **(3)** This is by boat.
**g.** **(1)** The people use boats without motors.
   **(2)** These are canoes.   (such as)
   **(3)** These are rowboats.
   **(4)** Power boats are not permitted.   (because)
**h.** **(1)** It is easy to understand why.
   **(2)** The water is clean there.
   **(3)** The air is pure there.
**i.** **(1)** Echo Lake is a beautiful place.
   **(2)** It is unspoiled.
   **(3)** It is for vacationers to enjoy.

This ideal environment at Echo Lake could be spoiled easily by the use of large power boats, electricity, or flush toilets.

4. **Paragraph Topics**

   a. How can people make their city a better place in which to live? Think of the problems you wrote about in your journal and how they can be corrected. Write about what you, your friends, shopkeepers, and others do or can do to help. You may use the following items to help you in writing your paragraph:

   cover trash          sweep sidewalks
   play radio softly    plant flowers
   curb a dog

   b. We all appreciate those people in our society who offer valuable services: sanitation workers, fire fighters, postal workers, taxi drivers, and teachers. Choose two or three occupations to write about. Describe the good that results from them. Begin your paragraph with an appropriate topic sentence. Be specific in your descriptions. Think of such question words as *who, where, when,* and *how often* to generate details about your topic.

   c. Many conveniences of modern life are damaging to our health or the environment: refrigerators, air conditioners, cars, spray cans, and cleaning fluids—all use polluting chemicals. How important are these things in your life? Can you do without them? Would it be worth while to give up these items to have a healthier environment? Discuss these questions with a partner and write a paragraph in which you express your opinions about them.

## ADDITIONAL READING

### People and Computers: A Working Relationship

[1]   Can machines be as intelligent as human beings? There is a lot of discussion these days about artificial-intelligence machines and their relation to human intelligence. People in many different occupations are involved in this discussion. They want to know how artificial intelligence will improve their lives. They also want to know if "intelligent" machines can be harmful to them. They would like to know what scientists predict for their future.

[2]   Human beings are a unique species. They have more complex brains than any other beings. They have the gift of speech and can communicate their thoughts, ideas, and feelings. Human beings are interested in the past and can learn from past experiences. They study their present problems carefully and try to find the best solutions. They look to the future and plan their next activities. They invent tools and machines to help them in their work.

[3]   Can machines perform in these ways? Some computer scientists are developing machines that may think and act in some ways like human beings.

According to these scientists, artificial-intelligence machines will understand written and spoken words and the ideas related to them. They will be able to correct their own mistakes. They will look at a problem in more than one way and choose a solution. Computers will also use information to plan for the future. They may even program, or teach, other computers to be their helpers.

[4]   Recently, some scientists in California reported the development of an extraordinary computer program. It will offer services and advice like a thoughtful assistant. Imagine a zoology student in a college. She is using her computer to outline a report on certain animals. Her computer notices some key words such as *lions, tigers,* and *bears*. It will then ask the student a question: "Would you like me to do some research into recent publications on lions, tigers, and bears?" If the answer is yes, the machine will contact a research service for related material. It will be able to tell the student which facts are more important than others. It might even tell the student which facts it thinks are interesting and which ones are boring. This program's inventors don't know if a machine can perform as intelligently as a human being. But as the inventors work on this project, they learn more about a computer's capabilities.

[5]   Some artificial-intelligence machines are in use now. Predictions are that in the future more and more people will rely on them. Doctors will use them to identify more specifically a person's illness. Reporters will be able to talk to a computer and have the computer write a summary of the news. Geologists looking for oil or other minerals will use a computer to tell them where to dig. Instead of spending long hours looking up information for a case, lawyers will consult a

Intelligent human beings have invented many kinds of artificial-intelligence machines to help them in their work. Here air traffic controllers read radar screens at Kennedy Airport in New York, where 3,200 flights daily are guided in and out of the area.

computer for the information. The so-called smart machines in use today make mistakes and can't correct them. Only humans can do that. Perhaps the newer ones will have that capability.

[6]   What happens when scientists take an artificial-intelligence machine and make it move? They get a robot. Robot arms are used today in many factories. They are capable of performing a series of motions without stopping. In the future, robot machines may help doctors in delicate operations or help find minerals deep underwater. Someday, they may even work in outer space, on the moon, or on other planets.

[7]   Some scientists predict that robots of the future will do things for ordinary people. They say there will be robot gas-station attendants that will fill a tank without the driver leaving his or her seat. Robot dressmakers will construct a dress to exact measurement for a woman while she is having a cup of coffee in the dress shop. They also say that everyone will have a personal robot for the home. Imagine what a robot will do for you!

[8]   Can science and technology take us too far by programming intelligence into machines? Some people think there is a danger in this. They say that these machines will take over jobs and leave many people unemployed. Scientists think differently. They say that artificial-intelligence computers and robots will free people from difficult, dangerous, or boring work. Then people can use their abilities and time for more creative occupations. Some people see another kind of danger. They are afraid that intelligent machines will become smarter than humans and turn into evil monsters. Scientists answer this fear simply: Machines will never have the same kind of intelligence as human beings. A machine's capabilities won't ever match human capabilities. People will always be in control of machines. According to all reliable information on the subject, people should not be afraid of a future with artificial intelligence. The prediction is for a good working relationship between human beings and their computer inventions.

## DISCUSSION QUESTIONS

1.  Have you ever used a computer? From your experience or that of your friends, is it easy or difficult to learn how to use a computer? What skills are necessary for using a computer? How does a computer make life easier? How are computers useful for learning a language or doing mathematics? What are some of the games you can play on a computer?

2.  Do you think that computers can replace instructors in the classroom? Discuss the needs that students have for learning from a person rather than from a computer. How can computers help students learn? Can computers give more individual attention to students than an instructor can?

3. Discuss the movies you have seen that portray robots in action. Do you think these robot characters are a sign of the future, or are they purely fantastic? Are robots in the movies or comic books usually portrayed as having feelings? Are they good, bad, or funny characters? What characteristics of robots make them fascinating to people?

## READING COMPREHENSION

1. **Understanding the Text.**   Choose the correct answer or follow the directions.

   a. Artificial intelligence refers to

      (1) the human brain.

      (2) ordinary computers.

      (3) special computer programs.

   b. Write the sentence from Paragraph [2] that refers to the following statement: *People like to study history; they want to know about their ancestors and how they lived.*

   c. The computer program described in Paragraph [4]

      (1) is fully developed and in use now.

      (2) is being developed for future use.

      (3) is only an imaginary program in the minds of scientists.

   d. The computer described in Paragraph [4] will be like a *thoughtful assistant*. This means that it

      (1) will only be useful to zoology students.

      (2) may be useful to anybody doing research.

      (3) will only be helpful to very intelligent people.

   e. In Paragraph [4], the statement *It might even tell the student which facts it thinks are interesting and which ones are boring* shows that the computer might

      (1) offer an opinion on a subject.

      (2) state a fact about a subject.

      (3) solve a problem in zoology.

   f. According to the information in Paragraph [5], artificial-intelligence machines

      (1) will cure people's illnesses.

The main elements of some computers are tiny microprocessor chips like these on the woman's finger. They receive and interpret signals from this electronic typewriter.

- **(2)** can correct their mistakes.
- **(3)** will save time in legal cases.

g. According to scientific predictions, robots of the future
- **(1)** will be just the same as artificial-intelligence computers.
- **(2)** will be able to "act" as well as "think."
- **(3)** will only be available to professional people.

h. Which question would a robot gas-station attendant probably ask a driver in order to fill the gas tank?
- **(1)** How much did you pay for your car?
- **(2)** Did you buy this car new or used?
- **(3)** What is the make and year of your car?

i. According to the information in Paragraph [8], scientists think that
- **(1)** artificial-intelligence machines won't be a danger to society.
- **(2)** people will suffer from unemployment because of intelligent machines.

(3) artificial-intelligence machines will be more capable than human beings.

2. **Answering Information Questions.** Answer each question in a complete sentence.
   a. What do human beings invent?
   b. Are there any artificial-intelligence machines in use now?
   c. Do "smart" machines make mistakes and correct them?
   d. Where are robot arms used today?
   e. Where may robots work someday?
   f. What are some people afraid of concerning intelligent machines and people's jobs?
   g. What do scientists say concerning this fear?
   h. Who will always be in control of machines?

3. **The Reading Process: Identifying Specific Information.** Specific sentences give the details or facts in a paragraph. These sentences support the main idea of a paragraph. Details and facts explain the main idea sentence by answering the questions *why, where, how, what, who,* and *which* about the main idea. In the following exercises you will be asked for specific information about paragraphs in the reading passage. Follow the directions for each item.

   a. Paragraph [1]: People are discussing artificial-intelligence machines and their relation to human beings. What are the two things people want to know about the subject?

      (1) _____

      (2) _____

   b. Paragraph [2]: In what ways are human beings unique? List the items in brief note form. Two of the items are done for you.

      (1) *More complex brain*
      (2) _____
      (3) *interested in the past - learn from the past*
      (4) _____
      (5) _____
      (6) _____

c. Paragraph [3]: In what ways will computers think and act like human beings? List the items in brief note form. The first one is done for you.

(1) _understand written and spoken words – ideas_
(2) _____
(3) _____
(4) _____
(5) _____

d. Paragraph [4]: Choose the correct answer to complete the given item. In this paragraph, there is

(1) a detailed example of the operation of a particular computer program.
(2) a detailed description of the thoughts and ideas of computer scientists.

e. Paragraph [5]: In the future more and more people will rely on intelligent computers. Who will these people be? List them.

(1) _____  (3) _____
(2) _____  (4) _____

f. Paragraph [6]: This paragraph informs us briefly about robots today and in the future. Answer each question in brief note form.

(1) Where do robots work today? _____
(2) Who may they help in the future? _____
(3) Where may they work in the future? _____
_____

g. Paragraph [7]: This paragraph states that future robots will do things for ordinary people. Which three kinds of robots are mentioned?

(1) _____
(2) _____
(3) _____

h. Paragraph [8]: This paragraph states two fears that people have about the use of artificial-intelligence machines. It also gives the scientists' responses to these fears. Write the numbers of the sentences that tell of people's fears. Write the numbers of the sentences that tell the scientists' responses. Write the numbers on the lines.

(1) Fears: Sentences _____ and _____
(2) Responses: Sentences _____ and _____

## VOCABULARY

1. **Expanding Vocabulary.** Choose the word that means the same as the italicized word in each sentence.

   a. People *communicate* by telephone, telegram, and letters, as well as in person. When people *communicate*, they

      (1) use machinery.
      (2) exchange thoughts.
      (3) are lonely.

   b. Chemists make different kinds of *artificial* material such as plastic and nylon. Something *artificial* is always

      (1) man-made.
      (2) useful.
      (3) natural.

   c. It is sometimes difficult to find a *solution* to a math problem. When you find a *solution*, you

      (1) look in a textbook.
      (2) ask a question.
      (3) discover an answer.

   d. Human beings are *unique* among all the animals because of their greater intelligence. To be *unique* means

      (1) to be the same.
      (2) to have no equal.
      (3) to go far.

   e. Scientists need to *develop* better computer programs for air-traffic safety. To *develop* means to

      (1) fly in an airplane.
      (2) bring to an advanced state.
      (3) do an experiment.

   f. The world is faced with many *complex* economic, social, and political problems. When something is *complex*, it is

      (1) very complicated.
      (2) easy to understand.
      (3) worldwide.

g. If you have bad stomach pains, you should *consult* a doctor. When you *consult* someone, you

   (1) ask someone for advice.
   (2) agree with a person.
   (3) do someone a favor.

h. Many people are *involved* in community projects that help the elderly or help young children have a better life. To be *involved* in something means to

   (1) be uninterested in it.
   (2) be concerned about it.
   (3) be happy about it.

i. A child's language *capabilities* must be developed in school. A person's *capabilities* are things that

   (1) a person can do.
   (2) a person owns.
   (3) can be seen.

2. **Using Vocabulary.** Write a complete sentence in answer to each question. Use the italicized word in your sentence.

   a. Which is an *artificial* material, cotton or nylon?

   _____

   b. What is the best way to *communicate* with a friend who lives far away?

   _____

   c. Who do you *consult* when you have a problem in school?

   _____

   d. Who is teaching you how to *develop* a paragraph with a main idea statement and details?

   _____

   e. Are you *involved* in any science projects in your school? If so, tell which class it is in.

   _____

   f. Which animal has more humanlike *capabilities*, a dog or a monkey?

   _____

g. Whose brain is probably more *complex*, a snake's or a cat's?

_____

h. In your experience, which soft drink has a *unique* flavor?

_____

i. Which can find a quicker *solution* to a math problem, a person or a computer?

_____

3. **Word Families: Verbs Versus Nouns of Persons.** Some English nouns can be formed by adding the suffix *r, er,* or *or* to the verb. This noun form means "one who does something." Study the following lists.

| **Verb** | **Noun** |
|---|---|
| speak | speaker |
| teach | teacher |
| write | writer |
| swim | swimmer |
| translate | translator |
| instruct | instructor |
| invent | inventor |

*Sentence Completion.* Fill in the blank space in the second sentence of each pair with a noun made from the verb in the first sentence. The first one is done for you.

a. It is difficult to *climb* mountains. A mountain __*climber*__ must be in very good health.

b. My friend *runs* in the park for twenty minutes every morning. She'll be one of the _____ in a race next week.

c. I *ride* the bus to school in the morning. Thousands of _____ use public transportation.

d. My aunt will *visit* New York in July. The Metropolitan Museum of Art is a wonderful place to take a _____ from out of town.

e. Many people *borrow* books from the library. A _____ must return books within a month.

f. The students will *begin* a course in English next semester. There are special textbooks for _____ .

g. Some American artists go to Paris to *paint*. Paris is an exciting city for a _____.

h. It isn't difficult to *bake* bread. My brother is an excellent _____.

i. I'll *drive* to Mexico on my vacation. But I'll need another _____ to help me.

## PARAGRAPH TOPICS

1. What kind of job do you hope to have in the future? Write a paragraph about the kind of skills necessary for that job. Explain what you are doing to acquire those skills. Include information about the kind of place you will work in someday and the location of that place. Begin your paragraph with a sentence that states the subject and expresses your hope about it.

2. Think of some machines you have, such as a typewriter or computer, or some household appliances like a vacuum cleaner or microwave oven that make your life easier. Write a paragraph describing a few of these items. Tell when you use them and how they help you. Begin your paragraph with an appropriate main idea.

Some people believe in nonscientific methods of predicting the future, such as palmistry. What similar methods of predicting the future are familiar to you?

# UNIT 1 REVIEW

NAME _____

INSTRUCTOR _____

1. **Sentence Completion.** Choose the correct item from the columns following the paragraph to fill in each blank space in the paragraph.

   There (1) _____ extraordinary mountains on Earth called volcanoes. A volcano is (2) _____ mountain that erupts or blows up, leaving a large hole (3) _____ the top or on the side. From time to time, steam, ashes, and lava (4) _____ deep inside the earth blow out into the air. Active volcanoes can be very (5) _____ . Sometimes (6) _____ destroy whole cities. (7) _____ May 8, 1902, Mount Pelée, on the Caribbean island of Martinique, erupted (8) _____ killed thirty thousand people in the city of St. Pierre. Archeologists have discovered the (9) _____ city of Pompeii, which was buried under twenty feet of ashes two thousand years ago. Thousands of people died there, but we now (10) _____ a detailed record of their (11) _____ because the ashes preserved everything so well. People in Hawaii (12) _____ live near Mauna Loa volcano, so there isn't any (13) _____ when it (14) _____ . In fact, many people go to observe (15) _____ eruptions from a safe distance. Is there a way to predict volcanic eruptions (16) _____ ? In the future, geologists (17) _____ better ways to predict (18) _____ eruptions and so save lives.

   (1) is/are/will be
   (2) leave blank/an/a
   (3) at/to/for
   (4) on/of/from
   (5) crowded/skillful/dangerous
   (6) it/they/you
   (7) On/In/At
   (8) and/also/but
   (9) roman/Rome/Roman
   (10) has/have/will have
   (11) live/lives/alive
   (12) does/doesn't/don't
   (13) danger/dangerous/dangerously
   (14) informs/invents/erupts
   (15) Mauna Loa's/Mauna Loas/Mauna Loa
   (16) ,/?/.
   (17) develop/development/will develop
   (18) leave blank/an/a

115

2. **Word Forms.** Fill in the chart with the correct forms of the given words. (Some parts of speech may have more than one word.)

|   | Verb | Noun | Adjective | Adverb |
|---|---|---|---|---|
| a | protect | | | |
| b | produce | | | |
| c | X | intelligence | | |
| d | | | special | |
| e | explore | | | X |
| f | | observer | | X |
| g | | activities | | |
| h | compare | | | |
| i | X | | skillful | |
| j | | behavior | | X |

*Word Form Completion.* Fill in the blank space in each sentence with the correct form of the word from the same lettered item on the Word Form chart. Use verbs and nouns in their singular or plural form as necessary. For dictation with blanks, close your textbook.

a. Reptiles don't show _____ behavior toward their young ones.

b. Brazil _____ a great amount of coffee every year.

c. Scientists hope to find signs of _____ life in other parts of the universe.

d. My favorite restaurant _____ in northern Chinese cooking.

e. Christopher Columbus was an Italian _____ in the service of Spain.

f. Most babies are very _____ ; they notice everything around them.

g. I always take an _____ part in student organizations.

h. After class my friend and I study together and _____ notes.

i. Foreign students should read an American newspaper to improve their language _____ .

j. Your pet cat or dog will _____ well if you teach it properly.

3. **Developing a Paragraph**

   a. For each paragraph write a main idea sentence in the space provided.

   (1) _____
   In one part of Switzerland, the people speak Italian. In another part, they speak French. In a third part, the people speak Romansh. In the area of Switzerland near Germany, the people speak German.

   (2) _____
   It is warm in southern France most of the year. There isn't much rain. There isn't any snow near the sea. The air is always fresh. The sun usually shines all day. The evenings are cool.

   (3) _____
   Rice grows well in northern Italy. Farmers plant wheat in the central areas of the country. They also grow corn and barley. In the south, there are many fruit trees. Olive trees grow well in many parts of Italy.

   b. Combine the following sentences into longer, more interesting statements to form a paragraph about Mexico. Leave out all the unnecessary words. Rewrite your complete new paragraph on a separate sheet of paper.

   (1) I would like to visit Mexico.
   (2) There are many beautiful places there.   (because)
   (3) There are mountains.
   (4) The mountains are high.
   (5) The mountains are near the ocean.
   (6) The ocean is the Pacific.
   (7) The ocean is on the west coast of Mexico.
   (8) There is also jungle.
   (9) The jungle is in the center of Mexico.
   (10) There are ruins in the jungle.
   (11) The ruins are ancient.
   (12) The ruins are Indian.

(13) Vera Cruz is a city in Mexico.
(14) Vera Cruz is on the east coast of Mexico.
(15) Vera Cruz has a climate.
(16) The climate is tropical.
(17) There are beaches in Vera Cruz.
(18) The beaches are splendid.
(19) There are so many places in Mexico.
(20) These are places to enjoy.

c. When the following sentences are put in order, they will make up a paragraph about a couple's plans for taking an evening plane from New York to Paris. Rewrite these sentences in correct time order and paragraph form. Your first sentence will be: *Ilsa and Edward expect to have an easy and comfortable flight to Paris.*

(1) After the movie, they'll try to sleep.
(2) The plane will leave on time at 8:00 P.M.
(3) Then Edward will buy some magazines to pass the time.
(4) They will arrive at Kennedy Airport at 6:00 P.M.
(5) At about 9:00, the stewards will serve dinner.
(6) The plane will land in Paris at 8:00 A.M.
(7) They'll board the plane a half-hour before takeoff.
(8) After dinner Ilsa and Edward will watch a movie.
(9) In the morning, the captain will announce the landing.
(10) They'll be finished checking their bags by 6:30.

4. **Composing a Paragraph.** The following sentences are about you and your native country. Answer each question with a complete sentence. Write your answers in the form of a paragraph on a separate sheet of paper. Add more sentences about your homeland if you wish. Begin your paragraph with the following main idea sentence: *Here are some interesting facts about (name of country).*

   a. Where is your country? (Asia, South America, the Caribbean, or other area of the world)
   b. What is the capital city?
   c. Is the capital city near an ocean, a river, or mountains?
   d. What kind of climate does the country have? (Tell about the seasons.)
   e. What are some of the basic foods?
   f. Is there a large population or a small population? (in the cities, in the countryside)

**g.** What language(s) do the people speak?
   **h.** Where do the people go on vacation in your country?

5. **Paragraph Topics**

   **a.** In a paragraph similar to the one about Mexico, describe some of the beautiful places to visit in your native country or in the area where you are now living. Think about such natural features as mountains, bodies of water, forests, and beaches.

   **b.** Write a paragraph predicting your own future. Tell what you will do, where you will be, and so on, ten years from now. Write a main idea sentence and give several details about your future life.

# UNIT II

# OUR WORLD OF LANGUAGE

Language is one of the unique characteristics that makes human beings different from other animals. All human beings have the ability to learn language. Here, a group of North African students studies in a modern language laboratory to improve their listening comprehension and pronunciation.

# CHAPTER FOUR

# VOICES OF THE PAST

**PREREADING**

**Class Discussion.** How do you use writing in your everyday life? Think about every kind of writing you did this week. Could you have communicated on these occasions in some other way? What are some advantages of writing in everyday life? What other kinds of communication do you use in place of writing?

> *Free Write.* How do you feel about learning English as a second language? Describe some of your difficulties, disappointments, satisfactions, embarrassments, and sense of accomplishment.

**Vocabulary in Context.** The vocabulary in this exercise will appear in the reading passage. Circle the letter of the word that means the same as the italicized word in each of the following sentences.

1. Most civilizations have changed from the ancient *system* of picture writing to an alphabetic system.

    a. machine   b. process   c. discovery

2. If you have not made *sufficient* preparation for your speech, you may bore your audience.

    a. historical   b. simple   c. adequate

3. *Eventually*, as children grow up, they gain a larger vocabulary.

    a. previously   b. finally   c. quickly

4. To perform the jobs required by modern industry, a person must be *literate*.

    a. intelligent   b. able to read   c. skilled in mathematics

Throughout the long course of human history, people have used a wide variety of materials on which to record their thoughts and deeds in writing. Here a Chinese scribe forms Chinese characters with a brush and ink on fabric and an Egyptian column of limestone is carved with ancient hieroglyphics.

5. Spoken language *originated* so long ago that no one knows exactly how the first words were formed.

   **a.** disappeared   **b.** was recorded   **c.** began

6. Beautiful works of art have a *permanent* value that can be enjoyed long after their creators have died.

   **a.** never-ending   **b.** emotional   **c.** fundamental

7. Language students *probably* learn as much from each other as they do from their formal classroom instruction.

   **a.** absolutely   **b.** very likely   **c.** never

8. Shrugging, or lifting the shoulders, is a typical French *gesture* that means one does not know or care about something.

   **a.** object   **b.** realization   **c.** movement of the body

9. The instructions for putting together the radio were clear, but I still needed someone to *demonstrate* the process.

   **a.** find   **b.** repeat   **c.** show

10. The *emotion* of love is probably the most common subject of popular fiction.

    a. intelligence    b. feeling    c. bodily strength

## READING

### Communication: Is One Picture Worth a Thousand Words?

[1]   How did the first people on Earth communicate with each other? In the beginning, they didn't use words at all. They probably used signs or pointed to things that they wanted. For example, perhaps they rubbed their stomachs to show that they were hungry or held their noses to show that something had a bad odor. When they wanted to teach someone how to build a fire or prepare a new food, perhaps they used gestures or demonstrated the action. It was possible to communicate a great deal without words. However, as human culture developed, something more than gestures was needed.

[2]   Nobody knows for certain when people first began to use actual spoken words. Perhaps the first spoken words originated from grunts, moans, sighs, and other sounds of the human voice. These were probably used to signal danger or show basic feelings such as love, hate, fear, pain, or other basic emotions. We do not know exactly how these sounds grew into words, but some scientists believe that this process began about 1 million years ago. The first actual words in the human vocabulary probably named family members or necessary items such as food. They may have been short, simple sounds for things in nature that human beings saw every day, such as the sun, the moon, a tree, a stone, rain, or water.

[3]   Gestures and basic spoken words were sufficient for the simple hunter–gatherer societies that existed at the dawn of human history. When human life became more complex, however, and people began to engage in trade, develop systems of government, and create religious organizations, it became necessary to preserve ideas and information in permanent form. Thus, writing was born. The archeological evidence shows us that writing is about eight thousand years old. The first kind of writing was "picture writing." Egyptian picture writing, one of the oldest in the world, is called hieroglyphics. Hieroglyphics could communicate in a number of ways. They could mean exactly the same thing as the object shown. For example, 👤 meant *face* and 👁 meant *eye*. The hieroglyphic picture could also communicate an act related to the picture. For example, a picture of a pair of legs, 𓂻 , meant the verb *to go*. Hieroglyphics also suggested ideas and emotions. For instance, the picture of a person leaning over a cane meant *old age*. Furthermore, hieroglyphic signs could also be used for certain sounds. ⌒ , for example, was pronounced as the consonant *t*. And finally, hieroglyphics could be placed before other words as a kind of prefix. For instance, the figure ✋ in front of a word meant the feminine form of the word.

[4] The development of picture writing improved communication a great deal. People did not need to see each other to communicate. They could write their picture words on clay tablets, animal skins, or fiber and leave them for others to read when they were absent. They could communicate over long distances by writing down their thoughts and deeds and sending them by messenger to other places. Older members of the culture could write down their ideas and records of past events and pass them on to younger members even after the older people were dead.

[5] Although picture writing was certainly very useful, it did present some problems. Sometimes the roughness of the writing materials made it difficult to draw the picture signs clearly. In addition, the signs for certain objects, ideas, or emotions were sometimes confusing to the reader because they looked very similar to other picture signs. Moreover, as human thought and society became more complex, a huge picture-sign vocabulary developed. It was a difficult task to create new picture signs for new ideas and to remember all the picture signs in the vocabulary. Also, picture writing took a great deal of time to carve into stone or metal and a great deal of space on precious materials such as animal skins or fiber.

[6] About three thousand, five hundred years ago, language underwent another important change. The alphabet was invented. Picture signs changed to lines and curves called letters, each of which was associated with one sound. Letters were combined together to form words. Alphabetic writing was much easier than picture writing. Writing with an alphabet took less time and space than did writing with picture signs. The alphabetic words were easier to write than were picture signs, and more people could become literate. With the use of alphabetic writing, information could be communicated to greater numbers of people, and ideas were more quickly carried from land to land. With the creation of alphabetic writing, the ancient world had discovered a new tool for knowledge and communication. Most civilizations from India west to Europe and the Americas eventually adopted alphabetic writing. Here is how the letter *A* developed from picture writing to alphabetic writing:

Ancient Egyptian   Ancient Greek   Roman   Modern English

[7] Today, China is one of the few nations that still uses a system of picture writing. Chinese picture writing, like Egyptian hieroglyphics, began thousands of years ago with pictures that really looked like the objects they named. For example, the ancient Chinese picture sign for *mountain* was 𝅓𝅘 . As the Chinese language developed, however, the pictures became simplified and looked less like real objects. Today, the Chinese character for *mountain* is 山 . Chinese writing contains nearly fifty thousand separate signs, or characters, each one having a different meaning. To read a newspaper in Chinese, a person has to know about

three thousand characters. That means that a great deal of a Chinese child's education is spent just trying to learn the written language. For that reason, some people in modern times have tried to simplify the Chinese written language or even replace it altogether with an alphabet. If the Chinese ever do change to an alphabetic writing system, then picture writing, the oldest form of written communication, will almost entirely disappear from human culture.

**Guided Summary.** A summary communicates the main ideas of a reading passage. Complete the following sentences to make a summary. Write your new sentences on a separate sheet of paper in the form of a paragraph.

1. The main purpose of this reading is to tell us about . . .
2. Paragraph [2] describes how . . .
3. Writing developed . . .
4. Hieroglyphics, the ancient Egyptian picture writing . . .
5. Picture writing made communication easier, but . . .
6. About three thousand, five hundred years ago, . . .
7. The conclusion states that the alphabet . . .
8. Only the Chinese . . .

## DISCUSSION QUESTIONS

1. Some languages, such as Italian, are rich in gestures and hand movements. These help communication between people. In what ways do gestures and hand movements help get a message across? Describe a situation where you found talking with gestures helpful.

2. The following line is written in a form of picture writing called a rebus. It uses letters, numbers, and pictures to communicate a message. What does this message say in English?

Create a rebus to communicate the following sentence: *I am too tired to see you Sunday.*

Now that you have tried picture writing, what problems do you find with that system of communication?

## READING COMPREHENSION

**1. Understanding the Text.** Follow the directions for each item.

    **a.** Mark the following sentences *T* for *true* or *F* for *false* according to the information in the reading passage. Underline the part of the passage where you find your information.

        **(1)** People at the dawn of human history communicated in picture writing. _____

        **(2)** Gestures for communication originated before words. _____

        **(3)** Human language may be about 1 million years old. _____

        **(4)** Love and fear are emotions that developed about eight thousand years ago. _____

        **(5)** The alphabet was invented about three thousand, five hundred years ago. _____

        **(6)** Clay, animal skin, and fiber were used for writing in the ancient world. _____

        **(7)** A person must know about fifty thousand Chinese characters to read a Chinese newspaper today. _____

    **b.** Circle the letter of the correct answer or answer questions as directed.

        **(1)** Paragraph [2] speculates, or makes educated guesses, about the origin of language for which we have no *physical* evidence. Underline at least five words or expressions in this paragraph that the writer uses to show that our information on this subject is not certain or exact.

        **(2)** The word *however* in the last sentence of Paragraph [1] signals that this sentence

            **(a)** continues the thought of the previous sentence.

            **(b)** gives an example of the thought in the previous sentence.

            **(c)** reverses the thought of the previous sentence.

        **(3)** In the third sentence of Paragraph [2], the expression *such as* signals

            **(a)** a new thought.

            **(b)** examples of the previous noun.

            **(c)** a reason for the previous statement.

(4) Picture writing developed

   (a) long before people talked.
   (b) long after people used signs for words.
   (c) after alphabetic writing.

(5) In Egyptian hieroglyphics, a picture of legs meant

   (a) the feminine form of a noun.
   (b) the verb *to go*.
   (c) the "ing" form of a verb.

(6) In Paragraph [3], two signal expressions that mean the same thing are

   (a) *however/thus*.
   (b) for example/for instance.
   (c) furthermore/when.

(7) Picture writing

   (a) didn't help people to communicate.
   (b) was the only form of communication in the past.
   (c) was a difficult form of communication.

(8) Alphabetic writing was efficient because

   (a) it was invented after picture writing.
   (b) it saved time and space.
   (c) it developed from picture writing.

(9) In Paragraph [4], Sentence (4), to whom does the pronoun *their* refer?

(10) In Paragraph [4], Sentence (5), to whom does the pronoun *their* refer?

(11) In Paragraph [4], Sentence (3), what does the word *it* stand for?

(12) Underline the sentence or part of a sentence in Paragraph [5] that states the main idea of that paragraph.

(13) In Paragraph [7], Sentence (6), what does the expression *each one* refer to?

c. Rewrite the following sentences in their correct time order according to the reading passage. Your first sentence will be the first thing that happened.

(1) Picture writing is about eight thousand years old.

(2) Alphabetic writing is about three thousand, five hundred years old.

(3) The earliest language used signs, not words.

(4) The Chinese may simplify their picture writing.

(5) The first words were simple sounds for common things.

(6) Spoken human language may be about 1 million years old.

2. **Answering Information Questions.** Write the answers to the following questions in complete sentences.

   a. How did the first people on Earth communicate?
   b. About how old is human language?
   c. What are hieroglyphics?
   d. List three advantages of writing over speech.
   e. What happened to language about three thousand, five hundred years ago?
   f. Why is alphabetic language more efficient than picture writing?
   g. Which modern civilization still uses picture writing?

3. **The Reading Process: Linking Pronouns.** Pronouns are words that link, or tie, the writer's ideas together. The reader needs to know which words the pronouns are replacing.

   Read Paragraph [1] of the reading selection again. The subject of Sentence (1) is *the first people*. The next four sentences do not use the subject *the first people*. These sentences use the pronoun *they*. *They* is a plural subject pronoun that takes the place of *the first people*. Pronouns must agree in number and form with the nouns they are replacing. Review the pronoun chart in Chapter 2.

   a. Circle or respond with the correct answer.

      (1) The word *these* in Sentence (3) of Paragraph [2] takes the place of

         (a) human beings.   (b) words.   (c) sounds.

      (2) The word *they* in the last sentence of Paragraph [2] replaces

         (a) early human beings.   (b) the earliest words.   (c) stones and trees.

      (3) The pronoun *they* in Sentence (8) of Paragraph [3] stands for

         (a) Egyptians.   (b) hieroglyphics.   (c) numbers.

      (4) The pronoun *them* in Sentence (3) of Paragraph [4] replaces

         (a) people.   (b) picture words.   (c) clay tablets.

**b.** Read the following paragraphs. All the pronouns are circled. Draw an arrow from each pronoun to the noun it is replacing. (The same noun may be used for more than one pronoun.) The first one is done for you.

(1) Most of the first immigrants to America came from England. They spoke the English language. But they discovered many new plants and animals in their new land. These things didn't have English names, but they did have Native American names. The immigrants learned the Native American names. They borrowed them from the Native American languages.

(2) Noah Webster was a very important man in the development of the American language. He began his work as a schoolteacher in a poor area of New York. His students were unable to buy books because they were so expensive. So Webster wrote his first book for them. He called it *The American Spelling Book*. He wanted to make spelling easier. But his new spellings were unpopular. No one liked them.

## VOCABULARY

1. **New Words.** Pronounce these words following your instructor.

| Nouns | Verbs | Adjectives | Adverbs |
|---|---|---|---|
| gestures | originate | permanent | eventually |
| emotions | demonstrate | sufficient | probably |
| system |  | literate |  |

*Expanding Vocabulary*

**a.** Use the word in parentheses in answering each of the following questions. Write your answers in complete sentences in the space provided.

(1) Why do human beings speak to each other? (communicate) _____

_____

(2) According to this chapter's reading selection, where did hieroglyphics begin? (originated) _____

_____

**(3)** If two people do not speak the same language, how can they talk with each other? (gestures) _____

**(4)** When do you plan to get a position in your career area? (eventually) _____

**(5)** Why can't we see sound waves in the air? (invisible) _____

**b.** Write a complete sentence for each of the following phrases. Do not change the order or the form of the given phrase.

**(1)** the emotion of love _____

**(2)** the invention of the telephone _____

**(3)** demonstrated the computer _____

**2. Word Families: Negative Adjectives with *in-*, *im-*, and *un-*.** Study the following list of adjectives and their negative forms.

| Adjectives | Negative Adjectives |
|---|---|
| sufficient | insufficient |
| correct | incorrect |
| visible | invisible |
| efficient | inefficient |
| common | uncommon |
| important | unimportant |
| permanent | impermanent |
| original | unoriginal |
| usual | unusual |
| emotional | unemotional |
| related | unrelated |
| practical | impractical |
| possible | impossible |

**a.** The prefix *in-*, *un-*, or *im-* often goes in front of a word to make it negative. Choose the correct word in parentheses to fill in the blank space in each sentence.

(1) Italian, Chinese, and Russian are based on a (related, unrelated) _____ vocabulary.

(2) The English words *morning* and *night* are (related, unrelated) _____ to the German words *morgen* and *nicht*.

(3) It is (practical, impractical) _____ to carry a large desk dictionary around with you to class.

(4) No one uses hieroglyphic writing any longer. Therefore, it is difficult to get (correct, incorrect) _____ translations for every hieroglyphic sign.

(5) At night, dark clothing makes a bicyclist almost (visible, invisible) _____ .

(6) It is (usual, unusual) _____ for people today to use picture writing as their main form of communication.

(7) Stone, metal, and glass are more (permanent, impermanent) _____ writing materials than paper and silk.

(8) Children do not always have a(n) (sufficient, insufficient) _____ vocabulary to express their ideas.

(9) Students learn to type because writing long reports by hand is (efficient, inefficient) _____ .

(10) Instructors like students to write (original, unoriginal) _____ essays that contain their own individual thoughts.

b. Follow the directions for each item.

(1) Put a check (✓) next to the items that might make a teacher *unpopular*.

arrives late to class _____ knows students' names _____ marks homework carefully _____ never looks at homework _____ doesn't answer students' questions _____ helps students after class _____ gives many tests _____

(2) What kind of weather is improbable in January? What kind of clothing is impractical for traveling?

(3) In complete sentences, state two things that babies are *unable* to do.

> **Babies are unable to go to school.**

(4) In complete sentences, state whether you are *afraid* or *unafraid* of each of the following things.

| the dark | high places | airplanes | strange places |
|---|---|---|---|
| deep water | thunderstorms | | snakes |

(5) Write one sentence telling what makes you *happy* and one sentence telling what makes you *unhappy*. Use one or both of the following patterns.

> **It makes me happy to see my friends.**
> **Smiling people make me happy.**

(6) Put an *X* next to those items that are *unimportant* for learning a new language.

doing housework _____ using a dictionary _____ practicing new sounds _____ owning a dog _____ exploring space _____ reading a newspaper every day _____ wearing new clothes _____

c. Write a correct meaningful sentence for each of the following words.

(1) unimportant _____

_____

(2) sufficient _____

_____

(3) emotional _____

_____

(4) uncommon _____

_____

(5) incorrect _____

_____

**134** Unit II Our World of Language

## WRITING EXERCISES

### Simple Past Tense of *To Be*

The Simple Past tense is used to show that someone or something existed or that something happened or was finished in the past.

> **One million years ago language was simple. The vocabulary wasn't large.**

Study the Simple Past tense forms of the verb *to be*.

|  | Singular | Plural |
|---|---|---|
| First Person | I was | A writer and I were<br>We were |
| Second Person | You were | You were |
| Third Person | Writing was<br>He/She/It was | Things were<br>They were |

Notice that only the First Person and Third Person Singular forms use *was*. The negative forms are *wasn't* and *weren't*.

Chinese is the oldest continuously spoken and written language. Many modern Chinese characters are the same as those of ancient times.

## Chapter Four  Voices of the Past

1. **Sentence Completion.** Fill in the blank spaces in each sentence with the correct form of the Simple Past tense of *to be*. Use negatives where you are asked to do so. The first one is done for you.

   a. (negative) Early people _weren't_ exactly like us.
   b. But they _____ the same as we are in some ways.
   c. Water _____ important to them, as it is to us.
   d. The sun _____ something they saw every day.
   e. Their basic emotions _____ probably similar to ours.
   f. (negative) The first people _____ able to talk.
   g. Early language _____ probably sign language.
   h. (negative) It _____ easy for early people to communicate.
   i. Simple sounds _____ probably the first words.
   j. Ideas _____ probably hard to communicate.
   k. Clay _____ difficult to write on.
   l. (negative) Writing _____ invented until eight thousand years ago.
   m. Pictures _____ the first written words.

2. **Sentence Building.** Write a correct sentence by putting together a subject from Column A, a verb form from Column B, and one item from Column C. Your sentence should contain true information from the text. Write your new complete sentences on a separate sheet of paper.

   |    | A | B | C |
   |----|---|---|---|
   | a. | Early people | was | probably used for basic things. |
   | b. | It | wasn't | picture writing. |
   | c. | The first spoken words | was<br>were | probably hungry much of the time. |
   | d. | The first writing | were | easy to communicate without words. |
   | e. | Egyptian picture writing | was<br>weren't | one of the earliest writing systems. |
   | f. | ⌒ | | |
   | g. | The English | | the first people to use an alphabet. |
   |    |   | | the sign for the sound *t*. |

3. **Scrambled Sentences.** Rewrite the following mixed-up sentences so that they form correct English sentences. Remember: Look for the verb first. Then look for the subject. The subject and verb must agree in number.

   a. early    important    were    .    trees    people    to
   b. at first    the    was    human    vocabulary    small    .
   c. ideas    to communicate    .    difficult    were
   d. wasn't    .    picture writing    understand    easy    to    always
   e. alphabet    the    ?    was    to    invent    easy

## Simple Past Tense of Regular Verbs

The Simple Past tense of regular verbs adds *d* or *ed* to the base verb.

> People *used* sign language before they *developed* picture writing.

1. **List Completion.** Study the following list of regular verbs. Fill in the blank spaces with the correct forms.

| Basic Verb | Simple Past |
|---|---|
| talk | talked |
| use | used |
| rub | rubbed |
| point | pointed |
| want | _____ |
| simplify | _____ |
| _____ | communicated |
| _____ | showed |
| name | _____ |
| touch | _____ |
| _____ | developed |
| need | _____ |

| Basic Verb | Simple Past |
|---|---|
| happen | _____ |
| invent | _____ |
| _____ | originated |
| _____ | changed |
| demonstrate | _____ |

Single-syllable base verbs ending in a consonant double the final consonant before adding *ed: bat* → *batted*. The past tense of words ending in *y* changes the *y* to *i* and adds *ed: simplify* → *simplified*.

2. **Dictation.** Write the following sentences from your instructor's dictation. These things all happened in the past. All the verbs will be in the Simple Past tense.

   a. The first people on Earth used signs to communicate.
   b. They pointed to things such as rocks, trees, and animals.
   c. Picture writing developed about eight thousand years ago.
   d. People in the Middle East invented the alphabet.
   e. The alphabet changed our way of writing.
   f. The Chinese simplified their written characters in the early 1900s.

3. **Recognizing Subjects and Verbs.** Check your dictation and correct your errors. In the following Subject column put the subject of each sentence. Mark it *S* for *singular* or *P* for *plural*. In the Verb column, put the verb of each sentence.

|   | Subject | S or P | Verb |
|---|---|---|---|
| a |   |   |   |
| b |   |   |   |
| c |   |   |   |
| d |   |   |   |
| e |   |   |   |
| f |   |   |   |

Does the form of a verb in the Simple Past tense change for a singular or plural subject?

## Simple Past Tense of Irregular Verbs

Many English verbs do not form the Simple Past tense in the regular way. Study the following verb forms.

| Basic Verb | Change | Simple Past |
|---|---|---|
| begin | change vowel | began |
| do | change vowel / add consonant | did |
| see | change vowels / add consonant | saw |
| take | change vowel / double vowel | took |
| keep | change vowel / change consonant | kept |
| have | change consonant | had |
| make | change consonant | made |
| speak | change vowels | spoke |
| put | no change | put |
| understand | change vowel / double vowel | understood |

You will find a list of commonly used irregular verbs in Appendix A.

1. **Sentence Completion.** Fill in the blank spaces with the Simple Past tense of the verb in parentheses.

Two thousand years ago the Roman people (to speak) (1) _____ Latin. Their vocabulary (to be) (2) _____ large. The Romans (to need) (3) _____ numbers in addition to words. They (to invent) (4) _____ an interesting number system. They (to begin) (5) _____ with the number I. They (to make) (6) _____ numbers 2 to 10 like this: II, III, IV, V, VI, VII, VIII, IX, and X. They (to have) (7) _____ numbers for 100 and 1000. The Roman numbers (to be) (8) _____ common all over the Western world. But later the Western world (to take) (9) _____ over the number system of the Arabs. The Arabic number system (to be) (10) _____ easier to use.

2. **Sentence Composition.** Answer the following questions in complete sentences. Note the use of time words for the Simple Past tense. They may occur at the beginning or end of sentences. Use these time words in your writing. The first one is done for you.

   a. Where did you do your homework last night?
      *I did my homework in my room last night.*
   b. What did you have for dinner last night?
   c. When did you begin work yesterday?
   d. Did you watch the ball game on TV last night?
   e. Why weren't you in class yesterday?
   f. Why did you miss class this morning?
   g. What did you do last Saturday?
   h. Which movie did you see last month?
   i. What did the picture △ mean in hieroglyphics?
   j. What did human beings do first, speak or write?
   k. How much television did you watch last weekend?
   l. At what time did you come to school today?
   m. What did you do yesterday afternoon?

3. **Controlled Writing.** Rewrite the following paragraph. Change the subject *children* to *I*. Change the pronouns to first person. Change the verbs from Simple Present to Simple Past tense.

   Your first sentence will be the following: *I didn't talk when I was very young.*

   Children don't talk when they are very young. But they communicate. They make sounds in their throats. They use a lot of sign language. They point to things that they want. Children soon develop ideas. Then they begin to talk. They make simple sounds. They take words from their parents. They name things, and they invent words. That is how they learn to talk.

4. **Paragraph Writing with Simple Past Tense Verbs.** The following list gives you some ways that you can practice your English. Choose five or more items to use in a paragraph about how you practiced English yesterday. You may add items of your own. Begin your paragraph with a main idea sentence. Write complete sentences using your chosen items in paragraph form. Make

your sentences specific and interesting by using adjectives and prepositional phrases. Use the Simple Past tense of verbs.

> **Yesterday I practiced English with my friends. We listened to the English news in the morning.**

a. watch TV program(s)/listen to radio
b. read newspaper/chapter(s) in a textbook/novel
c. listen to tape recorder/lecture
d. talk with native speakers/other nonnative classmates
e. see an English movie/play
f. use a dictionary

## Simple Past Tense Negative Forms

The negative form of the Simple Past tense is *didn't* + the basic verb. Study the examples.

> **The Romans *didn't use* Arabic numbers.**
> **Writing *didn't develop* quickly.**

1. **Sentence Composing.** Use the following items to write complete sentences about what you or someone else did yesterday, last night, or this morning. Use time words, adjectives, and prepositional phrases to make your sentences more specific and interesting.

> **see a movie**
> **I saw a good movie last night.**

a. do my homework
b. begin a new book
c. make a drawing
d. use a pencil
e. need a dictionary
f. invent secret writing
g. be at home
h. change my mind
i. take a bus
j. begin a lesson
k. have an exam
l. speak to my instructor

2. **Rewriting Sentences.** Now write your sentences in the negative.

> I did my homework in my room. I didn't do my homework in my room.

## The Definite Article

The word *the* has three important uses in English.

1. *The* refers to a person or thing that has just been talked about.

> **This chapter has a reading passage.** *The passage* **is about language.**

2. *The* refers to someone or something that is the only one of its kind. Adjectives in the *most/-est* forms take *the* before them.

> ***The sun* and *the moon* were important to early human beings.
> Chinese is *the oldest* continuously written language in the world.**

3. *The* refers to someone or something specific.

> **The Japanese system of writing is similar to the Chinese.**
> (*Japanese system* **is a specific system.**)

**Article Completion.** Fill in the blank spaces with the word *the* where it is needed. Put an *X* in the blank spaces where *the* is not needed.

1. Chinese writing developed about six thousand years ago. (1) _____ ancient Chinese people never used an alphabet. They invented a form of (2) _____ picture writing. (3) _____ picture-writing words were called (4) _____ characters. (5) _____ Chinese invented many thousands of characters. Many of (6) _____ old characters are still used today.

2. Ancient Egyptians knew how to make (1) _____ ink. They used ink to write on (2) _____ flat stones. They also used ink to write on

(3) _____ flat pieces of pottery. (4) _____ flat stones and pottery pieces were not large. So (5) _____ ancient Egyptians had to invent a short form of (6) _____ picture writing. They used (7) _____ short form of picture writing for (8) _____ letters and (9) _____ business records.

3. (1) _____ English language developed from an old Germanic language. (2) _____ French language added many new words to English. Latin, (3) _____ language of the Roman people, also added many words to English. (4) _____ Spanish, Dutch, and Italian words are also part of our English vocabulary. When (5) _____ first immigrants came to America, they learned (6) _____ new Native American words. For example, (7) _____ word *tobacco* is a Native American word.

4. (1) _____ British and American English are not exactly alike. (2) _____ spelling of some words is different. For example, (3) _____ British word *tyre* is spelled *tire* in (4) _____ United States. A *truck* in (5) _____ United States is called a *lorry* in (6) _____ England. But (7) _____ biggest difference between British and American English is in pronunciation. Many Americans have (8) _____ difficulty understanding British speech.

Find some uses of the indefinite articles *a* or *an* in the preceding paragraphs. Explain why these indefinite, not definite, articles are used.

## Time Expressions

Study the following sentences that use expressions of time.

> **Language may be about *1 million years old*.**
> (number + time period + *old*)
> Some people invented the alphabet *three thousand, five hundred years ago*.
> (number + time period + *ago*)

Latin was the common language of Europe in the Middle Ages. This Latin manuscript, with its decorative capital letter, is from a religious text.

**Sentence Composing.** Answer the following questions in complete sentences. Use the appropriate time expression in your answer.

- a. How old is your father?
- b. When did you last visit your cousin?
- c. Was the United States at war ten years ago?
- d. Is writing eight thousand or eighty thousand years old?
- e. How did people communicate one hundred thousand years ago?
- f. How old is your best friend?
- g. When did you last speak to your friend?
- h. What were you doing two Sundays ago?

Study the following expressions of time. The dates in the first column can be expressed by the phrases in the second column.

| Date | Time Expression |
|---|---|
| in 1776 | in the eighteenth century |
|  | in the late 1770s |
| in 1810 | in the early 1800s |
| in 1850 | in the mid-1800s |
|  | in the midnineteenth century |

in 1958        in the late 1950s
in 1981        in the early 1980s

**Sentence Composing.** Use *in* + a specific date (as in the first column) or a time expression (as in the second column) to answer the following questions in complete sentences. (In some items the date is given to you in parentheses.)

> **When was the first Bible printed in Europe? (1455)**
> *The first Bible was printed in 1455.*
> or
> *The first Bible was printed in the mid fifteenth century.*

1. When was your grandfather born?
2. When did you begin to study English as a second language?
3. When did your family first emigrate to the United States?
4. When did the American Revolution occur?
5. When did the French Revolution take place?
6. When was the Russian Revolution?
7. When did Haiti become independent?
8. When was the hieroglyphic tablet called the Rosetta Stone found? (1799)
9. When was the first book printed in England? (1475)
10. When did Chinese writers begin to simplify their written language? (1911)

## THE COMPOSING PROCESS

1. **Developing a Unified Paragraph with Details.** A good English paragraph should contain only one main idea, or it may follow a few sentences of introduction. To develop the main idea of your paragraph, you should include a number of different details. These details must all relate to the main idea and to each other. They should follow a logical order in your paragraph.

   The following exercise will help you develop a paragraph with details in logical order. Use the questions as the basis for your written answers. Write your details in the form of a paragraph on a separate sheet of paper. Then answer the five questions that follow the lettered questions.

a. Where did you live seven years ago?
b. What language did you speak at home?
c. What language did you usually speak in school?
d. Did you learn to read and write in (name of your language)?
e. In what grade did you begin to study English?
f. Did you use English textbooks and workbooks in school?
g. Did you also listen to English radio programs and tapes?
h. Did you see English films and television programs?
i. Did you frequently use an English dictionary?
j. What kind of information did you look for in the dictionary?
k. Was your English teacher a native speaker of English?
l. Did he or she know English grammar very well?
m. Did he or she assign English paragraphs frequently or rarely?
n. Did you enjoy learning English in your school?

**Questions**

(1) Which lettered item(s) form(s) the introduction to your paragraph?
(2) Which lettered item(s) state(s) the main idea of your paragraph?
(3) Which lettered item(s) list(s) different ways of learning English?
(4) Which lettered item(s) give(s) details about using a dictionary for English study?
(5) Which lettered item(s) give(s) details about your English teacher?

2. **Sequencing Details in a Paragraph.** In a well-written paragraph, the details follow each other in logical order. All the sentences that deal with a particular item in the paragraph should go together. Time words, repeated topic words, and other kinds of signal words should tie related sentences together. This exercise will help you learn how to link sentences together so that your reader can follow your ideas without difficulty.

   Read the following sentences about the development of the English language. Number them in the correct order to form a logical paragraph. Put *M.I.* (for *main idea*) next to the main idea sentence. Look for time expressions, linking pronouns, repeated use of key words, and other signals to help you put the sentences in the correct sequence. Then answer the questions following the sentences.

   a. Many of the English words we use in science, education, and government have a Latin origin. _____

b. The English language has also borrowed words from Greek, Hindi, Arabic, and many other languages. _____

c. From about 1200 to 1500, Latin words also entered the English language. _____

d. First of all, English has a Germanic origin. _____

e. The English language owes its development to many different languages. _____

f. Many basic English words are similar to Germanic words. _____

g. Then in the late 1100s, a French king conquered England. _____

h. And finally, English has created many new words for new inventions. _____

i. French words became very common in English. _____

### Questions

(1) What is the topic of the paragraph?

(2) What are some time expressions that were helpful in putting the sentences in order?

(3) How many sentences does the writer use to discuss words of Latin origin? Of French origin? Of Germanic origin?

(4) Which word in Sentence (2) signals that this sentence is adding information to previous sentences?

3. **Composing a Paragraph.** Read the following paragraph in which an American student describes a humorous confusion in vocabulary.

A funny confusion in vocabulary happened when I was in Mexico. I was studying Spanish, but I didn't know many Spanish words yet. I was sitting in a restaurant in Mexico City, and I wanted to eat some seafood. I told the waiter I wanted to order *camiones*. I thought *camiones* was the Spanish word for *shrimp*. The waiter looked surprised and didn't understand me. I repeated my order, and kept saying I wanted to eat *camiones*. Finally, he smiled at me and said, "Oh, you mean *camerones*." *Camiones* is the Spanish word for *trucks*. *Camerones* is the Spanish word for shrimp. I laughed because I confused two similar words that meant very different things.

A humorous or embarrassing moment in your language learning may be a good basis for a unified paragraph. In small groups, relate a story you remember of a humorous or interesting mistake you made in learning to speak or write a new language. After each member of the group tells his or her story, other members may question the speaker to make sure they have a clear picture of the incident.

After each group member has told his or her story, he or she will write up the anecdote.

Exchange your story with a partner to check for the following items:

a. Is there an appropriate introduction identifying the language involved and the location of the incident?
b. Is the main idea clear?
c. Do all the details in the story relate to the main idea? If not, eliminate the unnecessary details.
d. Review the story for correct grammar.

You may wish to use the given story of the American student as a guide.

4. **Sentence Combining.** Combine the following sentences into longer, more interesting statements to form a paragraph about the development of American English. Leave out all the unnecessary words. Use adjective–noun combinations and pronouns to make your sentences flow smoothly. Use signal expressions as directed in parentheses.

Rewrite your new paragraph on a separate sheet of paper. Use correct punctuation.

a. Our English vocabulary has many words.
b. These words are from other languages.
c. Many English words originated in German.
d. These are short words.
e. These are basic words.
f. Many English words come from Latin. (Use signal for addition.)
g. These are long words.
h. These are for communicating invisible things.
i. These invisible things are ideas.
j. These invisible things are emotions. (Join Items i and j to Item h by the expression *such as*.)
k. Other words in English come from French.
l. These French words relate to fashion.
m. These French words relate to cooking.
n. These French words relate to the arts.
o. American English uses words from many languages. (Use signal for addition.)

p. These languages are immigrant.
q. *Boss* is a Dutch word. (Begin your sentence for Items q and r with the expression *For example,.*)
r. *Cookie* is a Dutch word.
s. *Canyon* is a Spanish word.
t. *Cigar* is a Spanish word.
u. *Cocoa* is a Spanish word.
v. American English owes a lot to languages.
w. These languages are many.
x. These languages are different.

5. **Paragraph Topics**

   a. You can learn a new language through many different activities. With your class, brainstorm the many different activities you can do to help you learn a new language. After you have a complete list of the various language-learning activities, group together those items that relate to the language skills of listening and speaking, reading and writing. Write a unified paragraph about learning a new language based on one or more of the groups of items. Make sure your paragraph has a clear main idea statement.

   b. Written language makes our world a more interesting place. Compose a unified paragraph in which you explain at least four different ways in which written language improves our lives or makes them more interesting.

## ADDITIONAL READING

### The Tower of Babel

[1]  The book of Genesis, in the Old Testament of the Bible, tells the story of how the nations of the world came to speak different languages. The story begins after the great flood that had covered the Earth with water as a punishment for the wickedness of human beings. Only the family of Noah, which had boarded an ark, or large boat, with the male and female animals of every species, was left alive. When the floodwaters finally went down, Noah's ark landed on a mountaintop in the part of the world we now call eastern Turkey.

[2]  After a time, the descendants of Noah multiplied and became numerous. They journeyed westward, to a place in the valley of the Euphrates River that was known as Babel, or the kingdom of Babylon. At that time, the Biblical story tells

us, these descendants of Noah all spoke the same language and thought of themselves as one people or nation. As the Bible states, "And the whole earth was of one language, and of one speech."

[3]   Now, the descendants of Noah wished to remain as one people speaking one language and to become a powerful nation. So after they settled themselves in the valley of Babylon, they decided that they would build their own city and a great tower whose top would reach up to the highest heavens. They began to build their tower to the sky, using mud bricks that they baked (instead of stone) and a mortar made of mud and water. They called this tower the Tower of Babel because *babel* was a Babylonian word meaning *gate of God*.

[4]   While these descendants of Noah were building their great tower, their Lord looked down from heaven to view its construction. The Lord realized that with one language and one national identity, these people could become very proud and powerful. Perhaps they would think that they could do anything they wanted and create anything they desired. So the Lord decided to prevent them from finishing their great Tower of Babel and their city. He confused their languages, so that everyone spoke a different tongue and no one could understand anyone else. Then the people could not communicate with each other about the construction of the city and the tower, and these works were never completed. Eventually, the descendants of Noah left the kingdom of Babylon and spread themselves all over the Earth, speaking different languages and becoming different nations of people.

[5]   Was there ever a Tower of Babel such as the biblical story describes? We cannot say for certain, but today, in the land that was ancient Babylon, about thirty such towers, called *ziggurats*, still exist. These ziggurats were artificial mountains built as sacred places for the gods to visit. (The word *ziggurat* means "to build high" in Babylonian.) Usually, they contained a great exterior staircase that led from the top of the mountain down to a temple on the ground. Ziggurats were usually built on seven levels, with each ascending level somewhat smaller than the one below. A ziggurat looked like a corkscrew-shaped pyramid.

[6]   We do not know if one of the ziggurats that exists today on the site of ancient Babylon is the biblical Tower of Babel. But the English expression "a babel of languages" remains. It means a confusion of voices and tongues. It reminds us of one ancient explanation of why the different peoples of the world all speak different languages.

## DISCUSSION QUESTIONS

**1.** What kind of buildings does your native country have for religious use? Describe their shape, decoration, and setting. What special kinds of ceremonies are such buildings used for?

2. Do all the people in your native country speak the same language? If not, what are the different languages they speak? Is one language used for official purposes? If so, which language is that? What are some problems of countries that have more than one language? What are some advantages of having one language as the official language?

## READING COMPREHENSION

1. **Summarizing Through Sentence Completion.** The following paragraph summarizes the biblical story of the Tower of Babel. Fill in the blank spaces with appropriate words and phrases to summarize the story. You may use words from the reading passage or your own vocabulary.

   The biblical story of the Tower of Babel explains why (1) _____ . It tells how the (2) _____ of Noah settled down in the ancient land of Babylon and began to build (3) _____ and (4) _____ . At this time, the people all spoke (5) _____ . When their Lord saw them building (6) _____ , he became (7) _____ . He did not want them to become too (8) _____ . So he (9) _____ . Then they couldn't (10) _____ with each other, so they never completed their buildings. From this story, we get the English expression, "a babel of languages," which means (11) _____ .

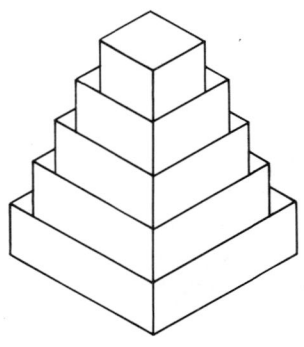

Ziggurat

2. **Using Signals of Time Order.** The first four paragraphs in the reading selection form a narrative, or story. The events of the story are told in time order. Therefore, there are many words and expressions that signal time order for the reader: *when, after, while, then, finally.*

   Underline expressions of time order in the reading selection's first four paragraphs. Be prepared to explain what they mean. Then make a time line of the main events of the story in outline form. The first step is done for you.

   *Noah's ark lands in eastern Turkey.*

3. **Answering Information Questions.** Write the answers to the following questions in complete sentences on a separate sheet of paper.
   a. Which book of the Old Testament tells the story of the Tower of Babel?
   b. Where did Noah's descendants go after the Flood?
   c. What material did the people in the story use to build their city and tower?
   d. What did the word *babel* mean in the ancient Babylonian language?
   e. Did Noah's descendants ever complete the Tower of Babel?
   f. What is a ziggurat?
   g. How many levels did a ziggurat have?
   h. How many ziggurats still exist today?

## VOCABULARY

1. **Expanding Vocabulary.** Circle the letter of all the items that mean the same thing as the italicized word in the given sentence.
   a. There are over 200 *species* of birds in the United States, each with its own song, coloration, and mating customs.

      (1) kinds   (2) diseases   (3) types   (4) educational centers
      (5) foods

   b. Many Chinese immigrants *journeyed* from California to the eastern United States in the late 1800s.

      (1) kept journals   (2) traveled   (3) assisted   (4) made a trip
      (5) celebrated

c. Parents try to *prevent* their children from injuring themselves.

   (1) think   (2) complete   (3) stop   (4) prepare   (5) keep from

d. Nonnative speakers of English may *confuse* the words "live" and "leave" because their vowel sounds are similar.

   (1) include   (2) mix up   (3) misunderstand   (4) satisfy
   (5) mistake

e. Temples are *sacred* places where gods are believed to live or visit.

   (1) frightening   (2) holy   (3) expensive   (4) spiritual
   (5) religious

f. Do the ruins of ancient temples *exist* in your native country?

   (1) occur   (2) leave   (3) excite   (4) remain   (5) disappear

g. What *explanation* does the dictionary give for the meaning of the word *babel*?

   (1) result   (2) interpretation   (3) reason   (4) celebration
   (5) communication

h. We should all be *proud* of our national or cultural identities.

   (1) be very careful   (2) feel good about   (3) think well of
   (4) become nervous about   (5) put a high value on

2. **Word Families: Parts of Speech.**   Sometimes an English word will keep the same form for its use in different parts of speech. For example, we use the verb *to journey* and the noun *journey* without changing the form of the word. In many other cases, however, the related meanings of the same word have different forms depending on their part of speech.

   In each of the items below you are given two different forms of a related word. Use the appropriate form to complete the sentences. Be prepared to explain which part of speech you are using in each answer.

   a. (pride/proud) In the biblical story of the Tower of Babel, the Lord did not want the people to become too _____. If they had too much _____ and power, perhaps they would think they were as good as their Lord.

   b. (construct(ed)/construction(s)) The descendants of Noah decided to _____ a tower and a city. These _____ were made of mud bricks and mortar. The people _____ only part of their city, however. Their Lord prevented them from completing the _____ of their tower.

c. (exist(s)/existence) Can people _____ without language? Yes, they can _____ , but their _____ is not fully human. A deaf person _____ without hearing and a mute person _____ without speaking. Blind people _____ without seeing written words. But all these people still have language.

d. (describes/description/descriptive) The biblical story _____ how Noah's descendants built the Tower of Babel out of mud bricks. The story in the Bible does not give many specific _____ details, but we get some idea of how the Tower looked. Towers of this same _____ are still found in eastern Turkey. They are called ziggurats.

e. (express/expression(s)/expressive) Many English _____ come from the Bible. For example, if you wanted to _____ something about old age, you might use the _____ "as old as Methuselah." The Bible tells us that Methuselah was a man who lived for nine hundred years. This kind of _____ language makes communicating interesting.

f. (different/difference) There are thousands of _____ languages in the world. Some of these, such as Arabic, English, or Chinese, have several _____ forms of the same tongue. For example, there is a great _____ between spoken Mandarin Chinese and Cantonese Chinese. There is some _____ between Egyptian and Moroccan Arabic. British English is only a little _____ from American English in writing, but it is quite _____ from American English in pronunciation.

## PARAGRAPH TOPICS

1. Write a story about an interesting event in your life. Your story should have a definite beginning, several specific details in time order to tell what happened to you, and a conclusion. Use time signals to help your reader follow the action of your story.

2. Write a description of an interesting religious or historical building from either your native country or your current neighborhood. Begin with a general statement that identifies the building and expresses your opinion of it. Use specific details of color, size, shape, and appearance to give your reader a clear picture of the building.

# CHAPTER FIVE

# LANGUAGE FOR LIVING

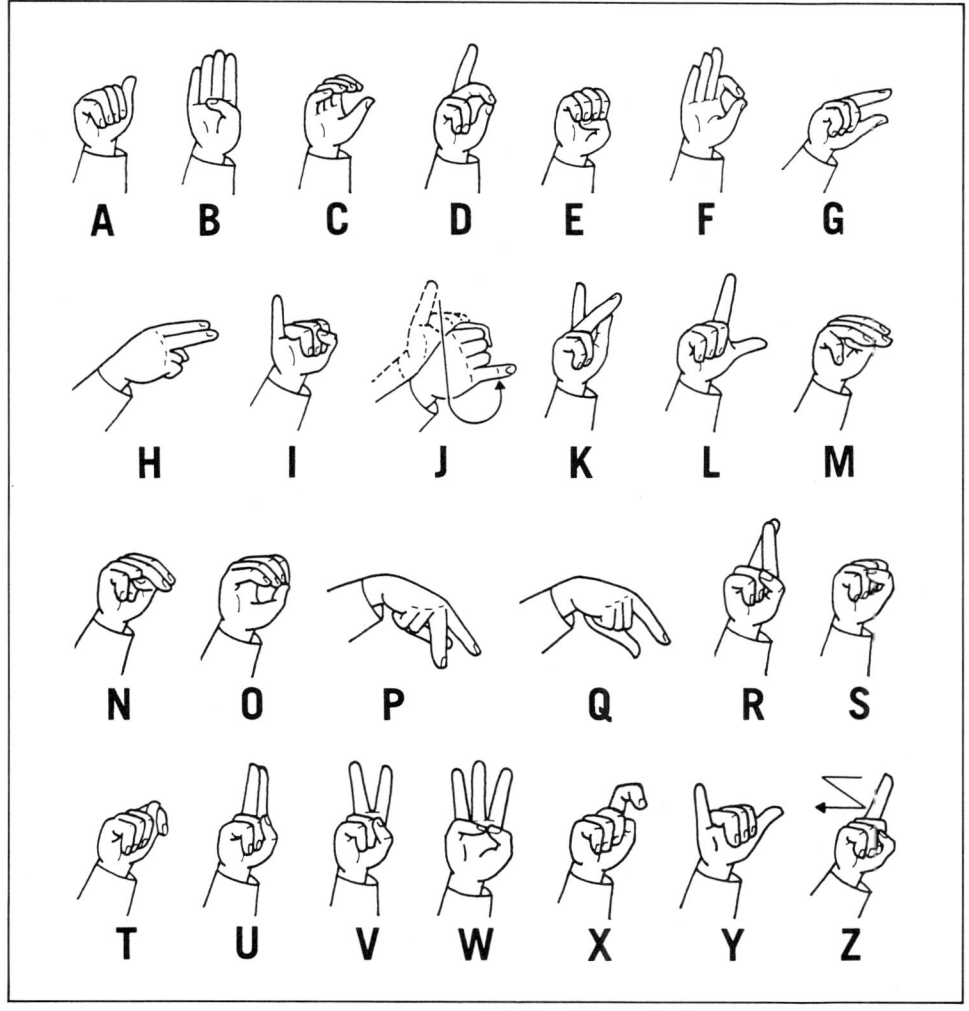

This chart of American Sign Language shows the manual method by which deaf people can communicate with each other. Some words are spelled out letter by letter while other common words have short forms.

**Unit II  Our World of Language**

## PREREADING

**Class Discussion.**  Nonverbal means of communication vary from culture to culture. What signs would you use to communicate the following information?

1. To show that you disagree with someone
2. To show that you agree with someone
3. To show anger
4. To show that you don't know something
5. To show that you want a ride from a passing vehicle
6. To show that your team just won its game

Among your classmates, do students from different cultures use the same signs as you? Discuss some of the similarities and differences.

> *Free Write.*  Some signs and signals, such as those used for driving, are universal; everyone can understand them. Do you think the world would be a better place if there were a universal language, one that everyone could speak and understand? Why? Which language might be best as a universal, or common, language? Explain your response.

**Vocabulary in Context.**  The vocabulary in this exercise will appear in the reading passage. Fill in each blank space in the paragraph with a word or expression from the following list that means the same thing as the item in parentheses.

send                    orders
ask for                 useful
rough                   carry
mix                     is reduced
stood for               able to be heard
necessary               very surprised
mainly

Most people use their voices or words to (1) (transmit) _____ their ideas, feelings, and information to someone else, but it is sometimes (2) (essential) _____ to use artificial signs or signal languages to (3) (convey) _____ messages. You would be (4) (amazed) _____ at the different kinds of voiceless languages people have created. One hundred years ago, a man named Sodre invented a musical language. He called it Solresol because the musical notes such as *so, la,* and *re* (5) (represented) _____ words. But most such artificial languages are not very (6) (effective) _____ for communication because they have only (7) (primitive) _____ vocabularies. They are used (8) (primarily) _____ to give (9) (commands) _____ or (10) to (request) _____ simple information, but not to exchange ideas. Naval or military communication often uses signals, either visible, such as a light, or (11) (audible) _____ , such as the blast of a foghorn. In some theatrical language, gestures or body movements (12) (combine) _____ with props such as a fan or scarf to communicate certain feelings or situations. As an artificial, voiceless, sign, or signal language becomes more complex, the number of people who can understand it (13) (is diminished) _____ .

## READING

### Signs and Signals: Communication without Voices

[1]  Sign and signal language is a system of communication that does not use the human voice or natural speech. Some sign language is based on a code of hand and arm gestures or movements of other parts of the body. Other sign language, called signaling, refers to the transmission of information by visible and audible signals, electrical communications through wire and radio waves, or the use of messengers and even trained animals. Some gestures and signals in sign language may convey actual ideas or directions. For example, a traffic director blows a whistle and holds up his or her hand, palm facing out, in order to make traffic stop. In contrast, other signals are symbolic; that is, they convey some idea associated with, but not the same as, themselves. In Japanese No theatre, for instance, the fluttering of a fan may stand for violent swordplay.

[2]  Sign language and signaling have many different purposes. Sign and signal language can convey information, give commands, tell stories, or communicate requests and prayers to deities, or gods, in religious ceremonies. Sign and signal language can be used for communication among special groups of people who cannot use ordinary speech, such as the deaf. Voiceless languages can also be used to communicate in special situations where people cannot see each other, where they are long distances from each other, or where it is important to commu-

In this Klana Topeng performance from West Java, Indonesian dancer Deena Burton employs arm and finger movements to represent a boastful attitude in a demon-king.

nicate only a few essential ideas quickly and secretly. Baseball coaches on the sidelines or in the dugout, for example, use signals that the other team does not understand in order to instruct their own players on the field to make certain plays.

[3]  Gestures, or movements of the body, particularly the hands, fingers, and eyes, are frequently used together with dancing, to entertain, or for religious purposes. In the Hindu religion of India and Indonesia, for example, gestures combined with dance movements have been used for over two thousand years to represent emotions, activities of daily life such as eating or drinking, common objects such as the moon or water, and living creatures. The Kathakali school of Hindu dance has a vocabulary of 500 signs, each of which represents a different word, which is sung along with the dance. In Tai Chi Chuan, a Chinese form of physical exercise, the different movements of the hands, legs, and head represent various animals such as the deer or the horse. Among Native Americans of the southwestern United States, certain gestures and body movements are used in the rainmaking dances as requests to the gods to send down rain for the crops.

[4]  Signal communication differs from theatrical or religious sign language in purpose. Signal communication is used primarily to convey useful information. Its origin is in the military, where signals are used to convey the voice of the

commanding officer. Audible signals such as the blast of a trumpet or the notes of a bugle have been used for thousands of years to control armies and signal the beginning of battles. Visible signals for military purposes, such as flags, banners, and the waving of swords in different ways, are other means by which commands have been given to armies and navies. In today's navy, for example, semaphore signaling uses two black and white flags held in different positions to represent the letters of the alphabet, numbers, and certain special signals. There is also an international flag alphabet in which different shapes and colors of each flag are used to represent the letters of the alphabet and certain special orders.

[5]  Of the various audible signaling languages used in modern times, the most familiar to the average person is the international Morse code. Many films about World War II include a scene in which a soldier or sailor is sitting at his radio transmitter tapping out the dots and dashes of the Morse code. The Morse code was first created by Samuel Morse and his assistant Alfred Vail to communicate messages on their electric telegraph machine. The Morse code consists of long and short pulses, or taps, known as dots and dashes. Each combination of dots and dashes represents a single letter of the alphabet. Because Morse and Vail spoke English, they used the letters of the English alphabet as the basis for their code. They gave the most common letters such as *E* and *T* the easiest patterns of dots and dashes. Thus, an *E* is one dot, or short tap. A *T* is one dash, or long tap. Less frequently used letters, such as *Z*, have more complicated patterns. Thus, the letter *X*, for example, is represented by one long dash, one short dot, and two long dashes. The Morse code can also be used to communicate without electricity by tapping on walls or by the use of lights.

[6]  The use of Morse code by signal lights is particularly effective in the naval service. Ships can transmit messages to each other across distances as far as five miles at night by using powerful flashlights to make the dots and dashes of the Morse code. These flashlights can transmit Morse code dots and dashes in the sunlight as well, although the distance of communication is lessened to about two miles. One of the biggest advantages of the Morse code is that the person who is sending the message can transmit any message he or she wishes. Messages are not limited to a few basic pieces of information. Furthermore, Morse code is easy to learn and effective in any language that uses an alphabet.

[7]  In Henry Wadsworth Longfellow's well-known poem *Paul Revere's Ride*, about the start of the American Revolution, we are told that the Boston silversmith Paul Revere signaled the colonists of the arrival of the British troops with flashing lights: "One if by land, and two if by sea;/And I on the opposite shore will be/ Ready to ride and spread the alarm/to every middlesex/neighboring village and farm." Today's military and civilian land, sea, and air operations have moved far beyond that primitive signaling system used in the American Revolution. With the perfection of radio, radio telephone, and advanced computer communication systems, even the Morse code has diminished in importance. Now we have signals

that can even communicate through outer space. Paul Revere and his fellow revolutionaries would have been amazed.

**Oral Cloze.** Number a column in your notebook from 1 to 10. Your instructor will read Paragraph [2] aloud to you twice. Listen very carefully. Then your instructor will read the paragraph aloud again, but he or she will leave out some words. Your instructor will say "blank" where these words are left out. Next to each number on your paper, write the word that correctly fills the blank space. Your instructor will read the paragraph with blanks to you several times. Now close your books.

> Sign language and signaling have "blank" different purposes. Sign and signal language "blank" convey information, give commands, tell stories, or "blank" requests and prayers to deities, or gods, in religious ceremonies. Sign and signal "blank" can be used for communication among special groups of people who "blank" use ordinary speech, "blank" as the deaf. Voiceless languages can "blank" be used to communicate in special situations where people cannot "blank" each other, where they are long distances "blank" each other, or where it is important to communicate only a few essential "blank" quickly and secretly. Baseball coaches on the sidelines "blank" in the dugout, for example, use signals that the other "blank" does not understand to instruct their own players on the field "blank" to make certain plays.

## DISCUSSION QUESTIONS

1. Signs, symbols, and signals that use pictures, body movements, colors, and sounds are used throughout the world to communicate information, beliefs, and instructions. What are some of these voiceless languages with which you are familiar with? What are some advantages of these means of communication?

2. Some people believe that art (music, dance, sculpture, painting, pottery, textile decoration, wood carving) is a universal language that all people can understand. Do you get pleasure from arts that belong to a culture not your own? Explain, with specific examples.

3. Learning a new code or language requires reading, study, practice, memorization, concentration, motivation (a desire to learn), and other qualities. Which are the most important? Do you think long hours of study for a short period of

time or shorter periods of study over a longer period of time is the best method for learning a new code or language? What specific methods or aspects of language learning are the most helpful to you?

## READING COMPREHENSION

1. **Understanding the Text.** Choose or write the correct answer.

    a. Which sentence uses the word *directions* as it is used in Sentence (4) of Paragraph [1]?

      (1) The four directions are north, south, east, and west.
      (2) Please give me clear directions to your house so I won't get lost.
      (3) The children ran off in different directions.

    b. The expression *in order to* in Sentence (5) of Paragraph [1] means

      (1) as a result of.
      (2) for the purpose of.
      (3) as an example of.

    c. The expression *In contrast* that begins the next to last sentence in Paragraph [1] suggests

      (1) a reason for the previous sentence.
      (2) a time relationship with the previous sentence.
      (3) a reversal of the idea in the previous sentence.

    d. Which two expressions in Paragraph [1] express the same idea?

      (1) or/and
      (2) in contrast/that is
      (3) for instance/for example

    e. In Paragraph [2], the expression *such as* introduces an example of the general term *people who cannot use ordinary speech*. What is the example? In the same paragraph, baseball coaches are given as an example. What are they an example of?

    f. In Paragraph [2], Sentence (4) adds information to Sentence (3). Which word introduces the idea of addition?

    g. In Paragraph [2], Sentence (4), to what does the word *they* refer?

    h. Paragraph [3] provides two samples, or examples, of general terms. What are these? What signal expressions of example introduce them?

    i. In Paragraph [3], what idea is illustrated by the mentions of the Kathakali school of dance, Tai Chi Chuan, and Native American raindancing?

    j. In Paragraph [4], Sentence (3), to what does the word *its* refer?

k. The main idea of Paragraph [4] is that signal languages
   (1) use trumpets or bugles to convey military commands.
   (2) have been used for over two thousand years.
   (3) are used primarily to communicate information.
   (4) are similar to religious and theatrical sign languages.
l. In Paragraph [5], what is the author's purpose in describing the film scene?
m. In Paragraph [4], semaphore flag and international flag alphabet signaling is an example of signal language that
   (1) communicates audibly and visibly.
   (2) requires the sender and the receiver to be able to see each other.
   (3) entertains as well as informs.
n. According to the information in Paragraph [5], which group of letters would have the most complex pattern of dots and dashes?
   (1) *A, E, S*
   (2) *I, M, L*
   (3) *K, X, Q*
o. In Paragraph [6],
   (1) Sentence (5) contradicts Sentence (4).
   (2) Sentence (5) gives an example of Sentence (4).
   (3) Sentence (5) expands Sentence (4).
p. In Paragraph [6], Sentence (3), the word *although* suggests
   (1) an opposition of ideas.
   (2) an addition of ideas.
   (3) an illustration of a general term.
q. In Paragraph [6], two advantages of Morse code are given. Which word signals the addition of a second advantage?
r. Paragraph [7] suggests that Paul Revere would be amazed because
   (1) Morse code has diminished in importance.
   (2) signaling language has become so technologically advanced.
   (3) the U.S. Navy is still using flashing lights to signal.

2. **Answering Information Questions.** Write the answers to the following questions in complete sentences on a separate sheet of paper.
   a. List at least three types of communication that can be used in signal or sign languages.
   b. What are two purposes of sign or signal languages?

c. Why do baseball coaches use secret hand signals to their players?
d. Give one example of an audible car, plane, or ship traffic signal.
e. Give one example of a visible car, plane, or ship signal.
f. Who first created Morse code? How are signals in Morse code formed?
g. Which branch of the military uses semaphore signaling?
h. Describe the signal that was used by Paul Revere to announce the arrival of the British troops.

3. **The Reading Process: Scanning for Specific Information.** To scan means to read a passage quickly to find specific facts. To scan for the answer to a question, you must first pick out the main words in the question.

   Answer the following questions by scanning the reading passage for facts. The main question words are italicized for you. Write the number of the paragraph and sentence where you find your answer. The first one is done for you.

   a. Is *Morse code* an *ancient or a modern* signaling system?
   *Morse code is a modern signaling system.*
   *Para. 5 Sent. 1.*

   b. What *signal* is used to *stop auto* traffic?

   c. What is the meaning of a *fluttering fan* in *Japanese No theatre*?

   d. In Chinese *Tai Chi Chuan*, what do one's *body movements* represent?

   e. For what *purpose* did systems of *signal communication originate*?

   f. What *signal system* uses *black and white flags* held in different positions to communicate?

   g. *How far* can Morse code flashlight signals transmit *at night*? During the *day*?

   h. What are the *three most modern means* of *military signal* communication?

164  Unit II  Our World of Language

## VOCABULARY

1. **New Words.** Pronounce these words following your instructor.

   | Nouns | Verbs | Adjectives | Adverbs |
   |---|---|---|---|
   | commands | combine | amazed | primarily |
   | requests | convey | audible | |
   | transmission | diminish | effective | |
   | | represent | essential | |
   | | | primitive | |

   a. *Expanding Vocabulary.* Choose the item that best explains the meaning of the italicized word.

   (1) Morse code is *primarily* a military signaling language.

   (a) recently   (b) historically   (c) mainly

   (2) Morse code flashlight signals are *effective* up to five miles at night.

   (a) useful   (b) impossible   (c) artificial

   (3) Different flags may *represent* different letters of the alphabet.

   (a) reduce   (b) design   (c) stand for

   (4) The effectiveness of flashlight signals in Morse code *diminishes* during daylight hours.

   (a) is increased   (b) is made easier   (c) is reduced

   (5) The *transmission* of a few basic commands is possible by blowing a trumpet.

   (a) celebration   (b) rejection   (c) sending

   (6) Dance movements can *combine* with gestures to entertain an audience.

   (a) confuse   (b) mix   (c) come before

   (7) Symbolic gestures can be used to *make requests* of deities, or gods.

   (a) bring rain   (b) explore ideas   (c) ask favors

   (8) With today's computer communication, earlier signaling languages appear *primitive*.

   (a) underdeveloped   (b) most important   (c) splendid

   b. *Using Vocabulary.* Read the following brief passages. Then use each of the vocabulary words in a sentence related to the topic.

   (1) In order for armies and navies to move into action quickly and to communicate with each other, they must use signaling languages.

command(s)
audible
essential

(2) People who cannot hear often have problems speaking clearly as well. Yet many hearing-impaired, or deaf, people can communicate with each other through a sign language in which different movements of the fingers represent different letters of the alphabet.

convey
amazed

2. **Word Families: Adjectives and Adverb Use.** Adjectives describe nouns or pronouns.

---

**Speech is the *primary* method of human communication.
(What kind of method? *primary* method.)**

---

Adverbs of manner tell how (in what manner) verb action is done.

---

**Human beings learn language *primarily* through imitation. (How do human beings learn language? *primarily* through imitation.)**

---

Most adverbs are formed by adding *ly* to adjectives.
Study the following list of adjectives and adverbs.

| **Adjectives** | **Adverbs** |
|---|---|
| natural | naturally |
| audible | audibly |
| visible | visibly |
| actual | actually |
| violent | violently |
| certain | certainly |
| essential | essentially |
| physical | physically |
| different | differently |
| international | internationally |
| effective | effectively |
| powerful | powerfully |
| basic | basically |
| particular | particularly |
| secret | secretly |

**a.** In the blank space write the correct form of the word in parentheses.

(1) Soldiers used Morse code (particular, particularly) _____ during World War II.

(2) There are (certain, certainly) _____ notes on the bugle that signal the ending of the day's activity.

(3) The finger movements of American Sign Language are all (different, differently) _____ from each other.

(4) Semaphore flags can only transmit (essential, essentially) _____ signals.

(5) Morse code works (basic, basically) _____ with long and short electrical impulses.

(6) Newspaper articles can be (powerful, powerfully) _____ means of influencing people's ideas.

(7) (Violent, violently) _____ behavior will not be permitted in the classroom.

**b.** Add one adverb from the list to each of the following sentences. The adverb will tell us how, or in what manner, the italicized verb action is done. The first one is done for you.

(1) Signal lights *shine* at night.

*Signal lights shine powerfully at night.*

(2) Morse code *is transmitted* by dots and dashes.

_____

(3) Flag language *communicates*, and the receiver and sender must be able to see each other.

_____

(4) Indonesian dancers *perform* movements and gestures from Spanish dancers.

_____

(5) In the days of Alexander the Great of Greece, armies *were commanded* by the sound of a trumpet.

_____

**(6)** It is a shame when members of a family *act* toward each other.
___

**(7)** Do you find it difficult to *speak* in front of an audience?
___

   **c.** Add one adjective from the list to each of the following sentences. The adjective should tell us something about the italicized noun.

      **(1)** Each dot and dash of the Morse code has a *pulse*, or tapping sound.
___

      **(2)** There are some *exercises* you should learn before trying advanced calisthenics.
___

      **(3)** In Tai Chi Chuan, the *movements* of the body represent different animals.
___

      **(4)** A baseball coach uses *signals* to communicate with his own team that the other team cannot understand.
___

      **(5)** The Kathakali school of Hindu dance has a vocabulary of 500 *words*.
___

## WRITING EXERCISES

### Present Continuous Tense

The Present Continuous tense of verbs is used to express action in progress and action that is limited in duration of time. It tells about activity that is going on now or in the present period of time. It can also communicate future intention. The Present Continuous tense is formed by *am, is,* or *are* + the *ing* ending of the main verb.

> **The soldier *is sending* Morse code signals to transmit important information.**
> **Now we *are learning* the Present Continuous tense.**

Some soldiers sit in special signaling rooms at army bases all over the country. They tap out military information in Morse code on a radio. They also listen to signals from their receivers on a special headset. Soldiers pay careful attention while they send and receive Morse code.

Study the Present Continuous tense of the verb *to wave*.

|  | **Singular** | **Plural** |
|---|---|---|
| First Person | I am waving | My friend and I are waving<br>We are waving |
| Second Person | You are waving | You are waving |
| Third Person | The sailor is waving<br>He is waving | The sailors are waving<br>They are waving |

The negative forms are *am not* (*I'm not, is not, isn't*) and *are not* (*aren't*) + the *-ing* form of the verb. Note that verbs that end in *e* drop the *e* before adding *ing*: *wave* becomes *waving*.

1. **Sentence Completion.** Complete the following sentences by putting the verb in parentheses in the Present Continuous tense.

    a. You and your classmates (communicate) _____ in English.

**b.** Perhaps you (use) _____ a tape recorder for pronunciation.

**c.** The sailor (negative: use) _____ the semaphore flags for entertainment.

**d.** and **e.** He (try) _____ to communicate the weather information to another ship, which (sail) _____ two miles away.

**f.** When armies (move) _____ into battle, they must be in touch with their commanders.

**g.** Currently, many high school and college students (study) _____ Spanish.

**h.** We hope that you (look) _____ up new words in your dictionary.

**2. Sentence Building.** Write complete sentence by matching the subjects in Column A with the related Present Continuous verb phrase in Column B. The subjects must agree in number with their verbs. Use the information from the chapter as a basis for your answers.

| | A | B |
|---|---|---|
| a. | You | is studying English with me. |
| b. | The soldier | are studying English in England. |
| c. | He | are learning Spanish. |
| d. | Currently, Chinese children | is tapping out Morse code. |
| e. | The Indonesian dancer | are learning English this term. |
| f. | One of my friends | isn't performing Tai Chi Chuan. |
| g. | We | is trying to communicate military information. |
| h. | Many foreign students | are learning a simplified form of Chinese. |
| i. | Many American high school students | are practicing Present Continuous tense. |

**3. Controlled Writing.** Look at the photograph of the soldier tapping out Morse code. The caption is written about soldiers in general, using the Simple Present tense. Rewrite the caption about the soldier in the photograph who is working on an army base in Georgia. Change the main subject to *This soldier*.

Change the verbs to Present Continuous tense to indicate action in progress. Make all necessary noun, verb, and article changes from plural to singular. To practice Present Continuous tense orally, change your paragraph about *This soldier* to *These soldiers*. Make all necessary plural changes.

## Compound Sentence Parts with *And*

The word *and* connects sentence parts that add information. These sentence parts must be related in meaning, and they must have the same form.

> A dictionary tells you the *spelling* and *meaning* of words.
>         (noun)        (noun)
> Dictionaries are *valuable* and *necessary* to students.
>                  (adjective)   (adjective)
> We hope you *are checking* spelling and *looking up* synonyms in your
>             (verb: Present Continuous)   (verb: Present Continuous)
> dictionaries.

1. **Sentence Building.** Complete the items in Column A by adding the related phrase from Column B. Each sentence will need the connecting word *and* to join its compound parts. Rewrite each complete new sentence. Remember that the sentence parts connected by *and* must be related in meaning and must have the same form. The completed sentences will form a paragraph about a well-known international dictionary.

   | | A | B |
   |---|---|---|
   | a. | *Webster's Third New International Dictionary* is the biggest | women wrote the newest *Webster's Dictionary*. |
   | b. | Two early editions appeared in 1806 | most complete dictionary of American English. |
   | c. | Thomas A. Knott | preparing future dictionaries. |
   | d. | More than 250 men | carefully. |
   | e. | Today, writers are finding new words | Paul W. Carhart were the writers of the 1934 edition. |
   | f. | Dictionary writers work slowly | an individual teacher. |
   | g. | Your dictionary is a good friend | in 1828. |

2. **Rewriting Sentences.** Study the following sentences that have compound sentence parts with *and*. On a separate sheet of paper, rewrite each sentence

using the words in parentheses to replace the italicized compound parts. Name the type of compound parts you use in each sentence.

   **a.** *French and English* are two international languages. (Spanish, Arabic)
   **b.** We *are studying and learning* English. (reading, writing)
   **c.** Many foreign students *in the United States and in England* are studying English. (Canada, Australia)
   **d.** A lot of *scientific and technical* writing is produced in English. (beautiful, interesting)
   **e.** The soldier is transmitting Morse code *slowly and carefully*. (correctly, easily)

3. **Sentence Completion.** Follow the directions in parentheses to complete each sentence. In some sets, one item is provided for you.

   **a.** There are many different ways to study and (compound verbs) _____ a new language.

   **b.** (compound noun subjects) _____ and _____ give classes in different languages.

   **c.** You can practice oral language with a phonograph and a (compound nouns) _____ .

   **d.** Television is a (an) (compound adjectives) _____ and _____ way to improve your listening skills.

   **e.** For oral practice, you should also speak the language with (compound nouns) _____ and classmates.

   **f.** For reading practice, start with simple things such as advertisements and (compound nouns) _____ .

   **g.** Then you can go on to read books and (compound nouns) _____ .

   **h.** Practice your new language at home and (compound prepositional phrases) _____ .

   **i.** Soon you will produce your new language (compound adverbs) _____ and _____ .

   **j.** Knowing English will help you to (compound verb phrases: basic form) _____ and _____ .

**172** Unit II  Our World of Language

4. **Paragraph Building.** Make two columns on a separate sheet of paper. Read the following paragraphs. Underline each set of compound sentence parts. Write the first item of the set in your left-hand column. Write the second item in your right-hand column. The first ones are done for you.

a.            French  |  Spanish

*French and Spanish* are similar to each other. French and Spanish both come from Latin. They have many similar nouns and verbs. In French and in Spanish, the verbs have many different endings and spellings. For that reason, French and Spanish verbs are difficult for some people to learn. It takes time to speak and write these languages easily and correctly.

b.            interesting  |  valuable

The big *Webster's Dictionary* tells you many interesting and valuable things about language. It has sections on history and biography. It gives you the meanings of abbreviations and signs. It tells you synonyms and antonyms of words. *Webster's Dictionary* helps both foreign students and native speakers to improve their English.

Read each paragraph several times. Then close your textbook. Using only your columns of compound parts, rebuild each paragraph sentence by sentence. Make them as similar to the original paragraphs as you can.

## Sentence Patterns with *Because*

We answer questions that ask *why* with the connecting word *because*. The word *because* joins together two thoughts. One thought tells what happens, that is, the result. The other thought gives a reason why.

> Many people are learning English because it is an international language.
> (result)                                      (reason)

1. **Sentence Combining.** In each of the following items, one sentence tells us the result, and the other sentence explains the reason. Combine the two sentences into one complete sentence using the connecting word *because*. Replace

nouns with pronouns where necessary. Rewrite each new sentence with correct punctuation and capitalization.

> (1) Many people are learning English.
> (2) English is an international language.
>
> *Many people are learning English because it is an international language.*

 a. (1) A traffic controller holds up his or her hand.
  (2) He or she wants traffic to stop.

 b. (1) There are so many different languages in the world.
  (2) It is difficult for people from different lands to communicate.

 c. (1) Baseball coaches use secret signals.
  (2) They do not want rival teams to understand their instructions.

 d. (1) I want to have better English pronunciation.
  (2) I listen to English TV programs.

 e. (1) There are many factories near the river.
  (2) The river is very polluted.

 f. (1) Most scientific writing is produced in English.
  (2) Scientists should study English.

 g. (1) Archeology takes you to many different lands.
  (2) Archeology is an interesting profession.

2. **Sentence Expansion.** Complete the following result clauses by adding a reason that explains why. Join the two sentence parts with the word *because*. Complete your new sentences in the space provided.

 a. Many people are studying Spanish _____
_____

 b. Museums are interesting places _____
_____

 c. Architects are designing new cities for the future _____
_____

d. Many immigrants come to the United States _____

e. Language changes _____

f. The air in my city is very dirty _____

g. Paris is an important city _____

h. Very little vegetation grows in the desert _____

i. It would be difficult to live on the moon _____

j. I am studying English _____

k. It is interesting to go to college _____

l. It is useful to speak two languages _____

## Plural Possessives

You have already learned how to form singular possessives in the apostrophe + *s* form. Study the following model. It shows you how to write plural possessives in the *s* + apostrophe form.

| Singular | Singular Possessive | Plural | Plural Possessive |
|---|---|---|---|
| a writer | a writer's decision (decision of a writer) | writers | writers' decisions (decisions of the writers) |

With your instructor, talk about how the plural possessive is formed with an *s* + apostrophe. We mainly use this form of the plural possessive with living things.

1. **List Completion.** Fill in the missing forms on the following list. The first one is done for you.

**Chapter Five   Language for Living**   175

a.  a friend  *a friend's* tape recorder      friends  *friends'* tape recorders
b.  _____ an immigrant's difficulty    immigrants _____ difficulties
c.  a man    a man's signal    _____    _____ signals
d.  a student    _____ work    _____    _____ work
e.  _____    a scientist's interest    scientists    _____ interests
f.  a parent    _____ love    parents    _____ love

2. **Rewriting Sentences.**  Rewrite each sentence, changing the italicized expressions to plural possessives in the *s* + apostrophe form.

> The *notebooks of the students* were filled with exercises.
> *The students' notebooks were filled with exercises.*

a.  The *problems of the immigrants* were not easily solved.
b.  The *children of my neighbors* are literate in two languages.
c.  The *assignments of my instructors* are usually clear.
d.  The *children of the immigrants* learned English quickly.
e.  At first, the *paragraphs of the students* were quite short.
f.  The *first job of the geologists* was to find fossils.
g.  The American Constitution protects the *rights of the citizens*.
h.  *Opinions of teachers* about that book were mixed.
i.  The *conditions of the workers* in the early 1900s were very bad.

Now identify the subject of each new sentence. Draw an arrow from the subject to its main verb. Do they agree in number?

3. **Proofreading.**  Some of the following sentences have errors in the formation of the possessive. Some sentences are correct. In the space provided, correct any error in the possessive. If the sentence is *correct*, write *C* in the space.

a.  Dictionaries are writers' friends. _____
b.  A writers' opinion can help you choose a good TV program. _____
c.  Childrens games often use special vocabularies. _____
d.  It is difficult to understand some professor's pronunciation. _____
e.  English teachers must carefully review their students papers. _____
f.  Babies' first words are learned in their parent's home. _____

g. The United Nation's official languages' are English and French. _____

## THE COMPOSING PROCESS

1. **Developing a Paragraph with Logical Sequence.** Read the following sentences. Put *M.I.* (for *main idea*) next to the main idea sentence. Then number the other sentences in the correct order to form a logical paragraph. Look for pronouns and other words that suggest the correct order of the sentences.

   a. They do not have to worry about weather conditions to send their messages. _____
   b. Telegraphic codes can be sent across any distance. _____
   c. Yet such codes can transmit long, complex messages. _____
   d. Telegraphic signaling codes are superior to visible codes. _____
   e. But the many advantages of telegraphic codes clearly outweigh this one disadvantage. _____
   f. The senders and receivers of telegraphic messages do not have to see each other. _____
   g. Also, telegraphic codes can be learned fairly easily. _____
   h. Telegraphic equipment is more complicated than visible signaling equipment. _____

   How many separate advantages are listed for telegraphic codes? List these in short form.

2. **Developing a Paragraph with Several Points.** One way to develop a subject for an extended paragraph is to think of two or three main points about your subject and support them with details or examples. In this way, you can be sure that your paragraph is really developing, not just repeating itself. The following exercise will help you practice this pattern of composition.

   The notes listed below describe the scene in a school cafeteria where a variety of activities is taking place. The introductory notes tell where and when the action is taking place and present the writer's general feeling about the scene.

   The notes are grouped by three main points: students alone, pairs of students, and groups of students. Each point is supported by several details that tell what these people are doing.

   Read the notes and then write the given information as a complete paragraph. You will use the Present Continuous tense for those sentences that tell what people are doing. You will use the Simple Present tense for those sentences that tell how people look, seem, or are.

<u>Lunchtime - Noon - 2:00 - College cafeteria</u>
<u>busy - crowded - lots of different activities</u>
I. <u>Students alone</u>
    <u>reading newspaper</u>
    <u>studying textbooks</u>
    <u>look serious - concentrating on work -</u>
II. <u>pairs of students</u>
    <u>a couple - holding hands; smiling at</u>
    <u>each other - seem in love - two students</u>
    <u>arguing - loud voices - waving hands around -</u>
    <u>excited</u>
III. <u>groups of students</u>
    <u>playing cards, video games, reviewing for an</u>
    <u>exam - asking each other questions - discussing answers.</u>

3. **Brainstorming, Organizing, and Drafting a Paragraph with Several Points.** With your classmates, look out the window of your classroom or go to some place where a lot of activity is taking place. Carefully observe and note down all the different activities you see. Do not worry about the order of your observations or the form of your notes at this time.

    When all your notes have been made, list all the activities on the board. Eliminate repeated items. Combine items that are similar or related.

    Review the list of activities. Think about separate clusters, or groups, as headings for the different activities; for example, you may choose such categories as (1) traffic activities (2) street construction activities, or (3) pedestrian activities. Assign each specific activity listed on the board to one of your clusters.

    Brainstorm some main idea statements for the paragraph. The main idea statement should include the place, time, and a general feeling, impression or opinion about the scene of your observation.

    Compose a paragraph based on the clusters, or groups of items on the board that interest you. You may omit items from the groups you select, or you may add details as you write. Do not worry about correct grammar at this time. Focus on making your paragraph clear and detailed.

When you have finished writing your paragraph, review it for correct verb forms. You should be using the Present Continuous tense for the activities people are doing. You should be using the Simple Present for statements about how people look, seem, or are.

Read your corrected paragraph to a partner. Make final improvements in your sentences and rewrite your paragraph if necessary.

4. **Paragraph Construction with Three Points.** Think about whether English would be a good international language. Look over the different positive and negative reasons outlined below. Each reason is developed with several details to explain it. Individually or as a class, choose *three* of the reasons to include in a paragraph about English as an international language. You may use the details given for each reason or you may add your own. Make sure your paragraph begins with a clear main idea: either for or against English as an international language. Then choose only those reasons that support your main idea.

**Grammar—Simple**

few verb endings
few rules for singular-plural
simple article use

**Pronunciation—Difficult**

many combined sounds
many foreign words
some difficult consonant combinations

**Verbs—Not Too Difficult**

simple helping verbs
regular present tense endings
not too many irregular past tenses

**Some Difficult Verb Forms**

many modals—different meanings
many tenses for different time periods
difficult question forms

**Spelling—Difficult**

many foreign words
words not spelled as they sound
many long words from Latin

**Language in Common Use**

uses common alphabet
vocabulary shared by other Romance languages—Spanish/French/Italian

**Adjectives—Simple**

almost always before noun
no plural endings

**Spoken all over World**

used for scientific writing
official language of United Nations
already second language in many nations: India, Nigeria
has beautiful literature

The gesture of a finger against the lips is a widespread signal for "keep quiet."

5. **Sentence Combining to Form a Paragraph.** Combine the following sentences into longer, more interesting statements to form a paragraph about international languages. Leave out unnecessary words. Use adjective–noun combinations, linking pronouns, plural possessives, and reason–result clauses to make your sentences flow smoothly. Follow the direction in parentheses.

    a. People have always dreamed of a language.
    b. This is a single language.
    c. This is an international language.
    d. People always want to trade with each other.
    e. The people are from different countries.
    f. People want to have exchanges.
    g. These exchanges are cultural.
    h. This is difficult.

i. People speak many different languages. (Use signal for changing a thought; use signal for reason.)
j. Currently, many people are creating languages.
k. These languages are artificial.
l. These languages are international.
m. Esperanto is one of these languages.
n. Esperanto uses many words in its vocabulary.
o. These words are from Romance languages. (Use signal to introduce examples.)
p. These words are Spanish.
q. These words are Italian.
r. These words are French.
s. Volapuk is another language.
t. This language is artificial.
u. Its vocabulary is primarily German.
v. Its vocabulary is primarily Slavic.
w. Esperanto and Volapuk do not use words.
x. These words are from Chinese.
y. These words are from Korean.
z. These words are from other languages.
aa. These languages are Asian.
bb. Other world languages do not employ words.
cc. They use signs.
dd. They use musical notes. (Use signal to introduce examples.)
ee. They use numbers.
ff. They use computer codes.
gg. A sign language might be easy to learn. (Use signal for reason.)
hh. A sign language would have a small vocabulary.
ii. A sign language would have a basic vocabulary.
jj. But could we write poetry in a language?
kk. This would be a language with only a few basic signs.

6. **Paragraph Topics**

   a. Choose some public place such as a restaurant or train station. Carefully observe this place and make notes of all the activities taking place. Review your notes to separate the activities into three logical groups, or points. Put the details for each grouping together. Compose a paragraph based on your notes that gives your reader a clear idea of the scene you have observed. Make sure you begin with a main idea statement that introduces your reader to the scene and your general opinion about it.

**b.** Every culture has gestures, or face and body movements, that communicate certain kinds of information. Brainstorm all the gestures you can think of that are used in your culture. Group your brainstormed items into gestures of the face (eye, mouth, other parts of the face) and body (hand, arm, head). Compose your paragraph based on two or more of your grouped items. You may use the subjects *People* (in my culture) or *We* plus the Simple Present tense to express the different gestures. Make sure your introduction tells the reader what culture you are describing.

## ADDITIONAL READING

### Learning to Read: Malcolm X

[1]  Malcolm X was a black civil rights activist, religious leader, writer, and speaker. He was born in Omaha, Nebraska, in 1925 and was mysteriously assassinated at a religious rally in 1965. By that time, his *Autobiography of Malcolm X* was widely known. Malcolm X was born Malcolm Little, but he took the name Malcolm X after he became a leader in the Black Muslims. This is a religious organization based on the beliefs of Islam, or the Moslem faith. The American Black Muslims have changed some of the practices of Islam to apply more specifically to the lives of black people in the United States.

[2]  Malcolm X learned about the Black Muslims while he was serving time in prison. Because he was poorly educated, he felt that he could not adequately teach his new political and religious beliefs to others. On the street, he had been able to express his thoughts and ideas in the slang of the "hustlers." When he tried to inform people about the Black Muslims, however, he found that he did not have an adequate vocabulary and communication skills for his purpose. In his own words, he "wasn't even functional."

[3]  To increase his knowledge and improve his skills, Malcolm X turned to books. But when he tried to read serious books on his own, he found he couldn't comprehend most of the words. "They might as well have been in Chinese," he wrote. And if he skipped all the words he didn't know, he would end up with very little idea of what the book was about. "I became frustrated," Malcolm wrote in his autobiography.

[4]  Malcolm X's frustration at his inability to read and write made him determined to overcome these deficiencies. "I saw that the best thing I could do was get hold of a dictionary," he tells us, "to study, to learn some words. I was lucky enough to reason also that I should try to improve my penmanship. It was sad. I couldn't even write in a straight line. It was both ideas together that moved

American sculptor John W. Rhoden's statue of ex-slave Frederick Douglass holding a book beautifully captures Malcolm X's feeling that reading is a means of liberation.

me to request a dictionary along with some tablets and pencils from the Norfolk Prison Colony school."

[5]   For the first two days, Malcolm X just skimmed through the pages of the dictionary. He tells us of his amazement at the contents of the dictionary: "I'd never realized so many words existed! I didn't know which words I needed to learn. Finally, just to start some kind of action I began copying." In his slow, careful uncertain handwriting, Malcolm X copied everything on the first page of the dictionary into a notebook. He even copied the punctuation marks. This copying took him one day. After that, he read aloud everything he had written. "Over and over, aloud, to myself, I read my own handwriting," Malcolm recalled.

[6]   Malcolm X describes how the next morning he woke up thinking about the words he had copied and read aloud the night before. He felt "immensely proud" to realize that he had written more than he had ever written before. He had even written words that he didn't know were in the world. He could even remember the meanings of most of the words he had written. "I reviewed the words whose meanings I didn't remember," he states in this section of his autobiography. "Funny

thing, from the dictionary's first page right now, that aardvark springs to my mind. The dictionary had a picture of it, a long-tailed, long-eared, burrowing African mammal, which lives off termites caught by sticking out its tongue as an anteater does for ants."

[7]   Malcolm X was so fascinated that he went on to copy the dictionary's next page and study that by reading it aloud as well. And once again, when he woke the next morning, he had the same experience. With every succeeding page he copied and read aloud, Malcolm X found he was learning and remembering more and more words. In addition, he learned about people, places, and events from history. "The dictionary is like a miniature encyclopedia," he discovered. Finally, when he finished copying the entire *A* section of the dictionary, he had filled an entire writing tablet. Then he went on to the *B*s. "That was the way I started copying what eventually became the entire dictionary."

[8]   As Malcolm X's word base broadened, he began to understand what a book was saying when he picked one up to read. It was the first time in his life that this had ever happened. "Anyone who has read a great deal can imagine the new world that opened. Let me tell you something: from then until I left that prison, in every free moment I had, if I was not reading in the library, I was reading on my bunk. . . . Months passed without my even thinking about being imprisoned. In fact, up to then, I never had been so truly free in my life."

[9]   Malcolm X was imprisoned in an institution that believed strongly in the rehabilitation of its prisoners. The prison philosophy was to prepare its inmates as well as possible for success in life on the outside after their prison terms were over. Therefore, the prison authorities were pleased at any inmate who showed an interest in books. There were many well-read inmates in Malcolm X's prison. Some of them were "practically walking encyclopedias"; they "had devoured more literature than any university would have required." These men were the prison celebrities.

[10]   In this section of his autobiography, Malcolm X reflected on what learning to read meant to him. "I knew right there in prison that reading had changed forever the course of my life," Malcolm wrote. Malcolm X describes in his book how one day an English writer telephoned him from London for an interview. The interviewer asked Malcolm X what college he had graduated from. "Books," Malcolm told him. "I told the Englishman that my *alma mater* [college from which one graduates] was books, a good library."

## DISCUSSION QUESTIONS

1. Malcolm X states that even though he was in prison, his ability to read made him free. What do you think he meant by the word *free* in this context? Do you agree with him that reading can be a form of freedom? Explain your answer. Has reading made you feel *free*? In what way(s)?

2. Malcolm X was imprisoned in an institution that believed in the rehabilitation of its prisoners. Therefore, he was encouraged to read. What do you think is the purpose of prison? In what ways can prisons rehabilitate their inmates? How can the use of a prison library help prepare a prison inmate for life outside of prison?

3. Study the following entries from the *Webster's New World Dictionary*. What order do the entries follow? What does the dictionary tell you about the entry word? What do the abbreviations mean?

   a. **ex·pert** (ek′-spērt, ik-spūrt′), *adj.* [see experience], very skillful, *n.* (ek′-spērt), one who is very skillful or well-informed in some special field.—expert′ly, *adv.*—ex·pert′ness, *n.*

   b. **pre·pare** (pri-pâr′), *v.t.* [-pared, -paring], [<L. *prae*, before + *parare*, get ready], 1. to make ready. 2. to equip or furnish. 3. to put together; as *prepare* dinner. *v.i.* 1. to make things ready. 2. to make oneself ready.

4. Some teachers think that dictionaries are *over*used by English-as-a-second-language (ESL) students. These teachers want students to try to guess the meaning of a word from its use in the sentence. They do not want their students to use the dictionary as a crutch, or something to lean on.

   How do you think a dictionary should be used in beginning ESL study? Do you think a student should look up the meaning of every unfamiliar word in a reading passage? Should a student keep lists of vocabulary words learned from the dictionary? Should students write the dictionary meaning of a word in the reading passage where the word occurs?

   What do you do if you don't understand the meaning of a word given in a dictionary?

## READING COMPREHENSION

1. **Understanding the Text.**

   a. In Paragraph [1], Malcolm X's original name is given as well as the name he took as a Black Muslim. Which word signals the contrast between the two names?

   b. In Sentence (2) of Paragraph [2], what thought relationship does the word *Because* signal: contrast? addition of ideas? reason? result? example?

   c. In Paragraph [3], when Malcolm X stated that words in books "might as well have been in Chinese," he meant that

   (1) he could read Chinese.

   (2) Chinese was a mysterious language to him.

(3) Chinese is as difficult as English.

(4) he would have liked to have known Chinese.

**d.** In Paragraph [6], Malcolm X describes the aardvark to show

(1) that aardvarks are interesting creatures.

(2) an important word he learned from the dictionary.

(3) how a dictionary is alphabetically arranged.

(4) how useful his method of studying the dictionary was.

**e.** In Paragraph [8], in the sentence *It was the first time in his life that this had ever happened*, what does the word *this* refer to?

**f.** In Sentence (6) of Paragraph [8], the use of the word *free* means that

(1) Malcolm X left prison a free man.

(2) the library books Malcolm X read were free.

(3) Malcolm X had freedom to do as he pleased in prison.

(4) Malcolm X's mind became free through his reading.

**g.** In Paragraph [9], what is the thought relationship between Sentences (2) and (3)?

(1) Sentence (3) is an example of Sentence (2).

(2) Sentence (2) is a contrast to Sentence (3).

(3) Sentence (3) is a result of Sentence (2).

(4) The two sentences relate to each other in time order.

Which word(s) signal the relationship?

**h.** In Paragraph [9], Malcolm X uses the expression *prison celebrities* to describe men who

(1) were very much respected by the other inmates.

(2) became famous outside of prison after their release.

(3) were correction officers and administrators of the prison.

(4) were Malcolm X's friends.

**i.** In Paragraph [10], it is implied that the Englishman was interviewing Malcolm X because

(1) he wanted to write an article about Malcolm X.

(2) he wanted proof of Malcolm X's college degree.

(3) he was going into prison himself.

(4) he wanted the names of some good books.

**2. Answering Information Questions.** On a separate sheet of paper, write the answers to the following questions in complete sentences.

a. Why did Malcolm X want to improve his reading and writing skills?
b. What happened when Malcolm X read a book if he skipped all the words he didn't know?
c. Why did prison authorities encourage Malcolm X to read books?
d. Why did Malcolm X think that a dictionary was like a miniature encyclopedia? What is the difference between a dictionary and an encyclopedia?
e. What were some of the benefits Malcolm X got from learning to read and write?
f. Define the word *celebrity*. Why were some of the prison inmates called *celebrities*?

## VOCABULARY

1. **Choosing the Correct Definition.** Many words in English have two or three different meanings that are not exactly the same. Sometimes, different meanings of a word are not even similar. You must read the context, or sentence surrounding the word, to understand which dictionary definition is the correct one. Use your dictionary to find two correct meanings for each of the following words. Which meaning is the one that is being used in this article?

    a. tablets (Paragraph [4])
    b. skimmed (Paragraph [5])
    c. states (Paragraph [6])
    d. bunk (Paragraph [8])
    e. terms (Paragraph [9])
    f. reflect (Paragraph [10])

2. **Expanding Vocabulary.** Each of the italicized vocabulary items from the passage on Malcolm X is followed by several common synonyms. First, read the given sentence aloud, substituting one of the synonyms for the original vocabulary word. Then write an original sentence using one of the synonyms.

    a. *beliefs:* ideas   notions   tenets   opinions
    The beliefs of the Black Muslims are based on those of Islam.
    b. *adequate:* sufficient   good enough   suitable   acceptable
    Malcolm X did not have an adequate vocabulary to express his ideas.
    c. *frustrated:* baffled   defeated   blocked   stopped
    Malcolm X felt frustrated because he could not read and write well.
    d. *amazement:* surprise   astonishment   wonder
    Malcolm X felt great amazement at the number of words in the dictionary.

e. *fascinated:* interested   delighted   attracted   charmed
   The dictionary fascinated Malcolm X so much that he went through it to the very end.

## PARAGRAPH TOPICS

1. Malcolm X had to learn to read the hard way, by himself. An education gained in school has many advantages over self-education. Write a paragraph in which you discuss some of the advantages, or benefits, of learning subjects in school rather than at home alone. You may include your own school experience to illustrate some of the benefits you mention.

2. Malcolm X states that certain men in the prison were celebrities because they had become so educated. What kinds of people usually become celebrities in the world at large? Write an extended paragraph in which you describe three celebrities with whom you are familiar. Identify the fields in which they are celebrated and the qualities for which they have become celebrities.

# CHAPTER SIX

# THE CLEVERNESS OF ANIMALS

## PREREADING

**Class Discussion.** All humans are mammals, but not all mammals are human. Humans and other mammals are alike in certain ways. For example, mammals give birth to their babies alive. Mammals take care of their young babies. They protect them by forming family units.

But humans and other mammals are also different in certain ways. Talk about some ways in which humans are different from other mammals. Your answers to the following questions will help you develop your ideas.

1. How do humans move around? How is this different from other mammals?

Gorilla

Dolphin

Donkey

2. What are some ways that humans protect themselves from cold, heat, and rain? How is this similar to or different from the way other mammals protect themselves?

3. How do humans get some of their basic foods? Do other mammals get their food in the same way?

4. How do humans communicate with each other? Name some things that other mammals do to communicate with each other.

> *Free Write.* **What pet animal have you observed in regard to its intelligence and emotions? Did this pet seem to understand and love its owner? Explain and include a specific incident to illustrate your response.**

**Vocabulary in Context.** The vocabulary in this exercise will appear in the reading passage. Read the following paragraph through once. Then read it again, paying particular attention to the italicized words. Next to each word is a blank space in parentheses. Write your own meaning for the italicized word in the blank space. Do not use a dictionary. The first one is done for you.

1. Have you ever *raised* (_brought up_) a puppy and trained it to obey your commands? If you have, you probably know that these *creatures* (_____) are quite intelligent. If you treat your pet *decently* (_____) and give it a reward when it obeys, it will want to keep on pleasing you. Dogs particularly seem to have a natural *ability* (_____) for catching objects you throw to them. You can help this natural ability *improve* (_____) by working *patiently* (_____) with your pet.

2. Some people *claim* (_____) that their pets can really understand them, just as human friends do. Certainly, if you hold out a dog biscuit to your dog, he will give you the *response* (_____) you want: he will hold out his paw. If you *attempt* (_____) to hold a conversation with your pet, however, as you would do with a human friend, you may not get the response you desire. There is plenty of *evidence*

(_____) that dogs are very intelligent, but no *experiment* (_____) has yet proved that they can communicate or understand messages on a human level. Is it *morally* (_____) right to experiment with dogs or other pets to test their level of intelligence?

## READING

### Experiments with Language Learning

[1]   Throughout the ages, humans have wanted to communicate with other species. Folktales in every culture entertain us with stories about humans who learned the language of birds or animals. In many other stories, animals speak to humans in their own language. These age-old stories are not actually true, of course, but they do show the interest we humans have in communicating with other species and the emotional bond we feel toward animals.

[2]   In the past twenty years or so, communication between our human species and other creatures has moved from the storybook to the scientific laboratory. Several experts have attempted to teach human language to apes and monkeys. One American psychologist trained his ape Sarah to make sentences on a computer. Another scientist trained an ape named Washoe to make signs for words. A group of scientists in Africa claims that vervet monkeys use a series of cries, barks, and other sounds that we might call language. Is this evidence that in the future humans and some of the higher mammals will be able to communicate with each other through language?

[3]   Some scientists claim that only humans can truly learn language. They say that language ability is born into humans and no other species. They agree that other species may have a form of communication among themselves. They know, for example, that chimpanzees can learn signs for different objects and that animals like dogs or horses can be trained to obey human gestures and words. But no other species is physically able to talk. Other animals do not have the organs to make sounds as humans do. Furthermore, no creature except the human seems to communicate on the level of *ideas*.

[4]   In the 1970s, Dr. Herbert Terrace, a New York City psychologist, conducted an important experiment in the language ability of apes. He decided to raise a young ape in his home. He would send the ape to school, and teachers would teach him sign language. Then Dr. Terrace would give different language tests to the ape. By this experiment, he would discover if apes could really learn language as humans do.

[5]   Dr. Terrace named his chimpanzee Nim Chimpsky in honor of a famous American linguist named Noam Chomsky. He sent Nim to nursery school at Columbia University. There he had special teachers who taught him signs for English

words. These teachers worked with Nim for five hours every day. They treated him lovingly and patiently, just as they would treat a human child. In four months, Nim learned the signs for 125 words. Most of these words were nouns for visible things such as *table* or *apple*. Some of these were active verbs such as *bite, jump,* or *hurry*. Nim also learned some basic colors such as *red* and *blue*. Based on this evidence, did Dr. Terrace claim that apes could learn language?

[6] After several years of training Nim Chimpsky in human communication, Dr. Terrace decided that apes cannot learn language the same way that humans do. After the first few months, Nim did not improve his vocabulary very much. Nim never created new words as human language learners do. He might use two or three words together so that they sounded like a real sentence, but then he would use the same three words in another way that did not make sense. For example, Nim might make signs that said "Nim eat apple." But then he would use the signs meaning "Eat Nim apple." These words in this order do not make sense in English. In addition, Nim never began sentences. He would only give responses to his teachers' questions. Will future experiments show that apes can learn language? Dr. Terrace doesn't think so.

[7] Other scientists working with "talking" apes disagree with Dr. Terrace's conclusions. In one experiment at the Language Research Center in Atlanta, Georgia, scientists claim that a pygmy chimpanzee named Kanzi has learned language. Kanzi communicates by using geometrical signs for words. He punches out his signs on a computer keyboard. He can ask to go to his tree house for a banana, or to play tag, or to watch a videotape. Kanzi can respond to human commands in a very humanlike way. Unlike Nim Chimpsky, Kanzi sometimes creates his own statements and adds new information to sentences. Kanzi's intelligence is certainly high, but has he really learned language in a human way? Dr. Terrace still doesn't think so. He doesn't think the evidence is strong enough to prove it. It seems as if this interesting argument about the language ability of apes will be going on for quite a while yet.

[8] Dr. Terrace's experimentation with Nim Chimpsky raises another important question regarding the similarity between apes, particularly chimpanzees, and humans. Recent studies of ape intelligence, language ability, and emotional development show that these animals, especially chimpanzees, are more advanced than most people believed. Chimpanzees, in fact, are the closest living relatives to humans. The chimpanzee reproductive system is so similar to a human's that researchers use female chimps for experiments in human birth control. Furthermore, apes have the same blood types as humans and they are the only nonhuman species that develop certain diseases such as hepatitis B. In scientific research then, chimpanzees and other apes may be used as surrogates, or stand-ins, for humans.

[9] Many scientists claim that apes, particularly chimpanzees, are absolutely necessary for research into human disease as well as human language. Yet these animals often suffer a great deal of physical and emotional pain when they are

used for experiments. Not every laboratory chimpanzee used in research is treated as well as Nim Chimpsky. Larry, for example, is a laboratory chimpanzee who has spent nearly all his life in a three-foot-square room. Larry has never climbed a tree or felt grass under his feet. He has occasionally seen other chimpanzees, but he has never touched one. Larry shows many symptoms of an emotionally disturbed human. He is close enough to a human to be useful for medical experiments. But scientists would not treat humans the way Larry is treated.

[10] If chimpanzees and other apes are so close to humans, is it morally right to treat them so badly? Is it right to deprive them of open space, fresh air, and the companionship of other members of their species? Scientists differ in their opinions about whether we should use apes in research to advance human knowledge. Some look at laboratory apes as just "test tubes," that can be used in experiments and then put away. Others, however, disagree. Roger Fouts of Central Washington University, who worked with Washoe, the first chimpanzee to learn a sign language of the deaf, has claimed that "Washoe and I are much closer [mentally] than I am to a two- or three-year-old child." Fouts believes that chimpanzees deserve the same rights to decent treatment as humans do. An even stronger view is that of Australian philosopher Peter Singer. He believes that we should not use apes in any laboratory experiments unless we would use a retarded child in the same situation. Even if chimpanzees do not have the special intelligence necessary to learn human language, they are close enough to us to raise these questions about their use in experiments. What do you think?

**Summary Completion.** A summary gives the main ideas of a passage. It also includes the most important supporting details for the ideas in the passage. In the following summary of this reading selection, some items are missing. Choose the correct item from the columns following the summary paragraph to complete each numbered blank space.

In the past few years, several scientists have done (1) _____ studies on the language abilities of apes. These scientists hope (2) _____ if apes (3) _____ language as humans do. After many experiments with his chimpanzee Nim Chimpsky, Dr. Herbert Terrace believes that he knows the truth. Apes can learn some signs (4) _____ they cannot really learn language. The language of human children grows, improves, and becomes more creative. But Nim's language (5) _____ . Many (6) _____ opinions are different from Dr. Terrace's. Some of these scientists are still (7) _____ experiments with the language ability of apes.

Apes like Nim Chimpsky are very (8) _____ in scientific research because apes are (9) _____ to human beings in important ways. But some of these animals suffer physically (10) _____ emotionally when they are used in experiments. Many people raise the question of whether we (11) _____ use apes for experiments if it causes pain to these humanlike creatures.

(1) visible/valuable/ angry/unknown
(2) discover/ to discover/ discovered/ is discovered
(3) won't learn/must learn/can learn/
(4) and/then/,/but
(5) improves/always improved/doesn't improve/never improved
(6) scientists/ scientist's/
scientists'/ scientist
(7) did/does/doing/ do
(8) useless/use/used/ useful
(9) similar to/ different from/
exactly like/ more intelligent than
(10) but/then/and/if
(11) could/would/ will/should

## DISCUSSION QUESTIONS

1. Have you ever tried to train a pet dog or bird to obey orders or do tricks? What methods did you use? Were you successful in your training? Do you think your pet really understands your language? Did you have to cause your pet any pain to teach it? Explain your responses.

2. Some people claim that we must use animals experimentally to advance human knowledge. These research animals must sometimes undergo pain in the course of these experiments. What is your opinion about using animals in scientific experiments? Would you make a difference between using higher animals such as apes, using other mammals such as dogs or rabbits, or using still less humanlike mammals such as rats or mice? Support your responses with specific reasons.

## READING COMPREHENSION

1. **Understanding the Text.** Follow the directions for each item.
    a. Mark *T* for *true* or F for *false* next to each statement. Be prepared to identify the part of the text where you find your answer.
        (1) Apes can learn signs for words. _____
        (2) In four months, Nim Chimpsky learned to speak English. _____
        (3) Nim always made correct English sentences. _____

**(4)** Dr. Terrace doesn't believe that apes have language ability. _____

**(5)** Orangutans are the closest living relatives to humans. _____

**(6)** Human beings and apes are the only mammals that can develop hepatitis B. _____

**(7)** According to the information in the passage, a rat could be a surrogate mother for a bird. _____

**(8)** The story of Larry, the laboratory chimpanzee, shows that all animals used in scientific experiments are poorly treated. _____

**(9)** The chimpanzee Washoe has the mind of a retarded child. _____

**(10)** Scientist Roger Fouts and philosopher Peter Singer have basically the same idea about using animals for laboratory research. _____

**b.** Choose the correct answer.

**(1)** Folktales about talking animals show us that

  **(a)** nonhuman creatures can really speak.

  **(b)** humans feel close to animals in certain ways.

  **(c)** laboratories are not the only places for experiments with talking animals.

**(2)** The primary purpose of Paragraphs [2] through [7] is to

  **(a)** show similarities between apes and human beings.

  **(b)** explain why Dr. Terrace is a good psychologist.

  **(c)** describe experimentation with the language ability of apes.

**(3)** According to the reading selection, what do Sarah, Washoe, Nim Chimpsky, and Kanzi have in common?

  **(a)** They were all raised in the homes of American scientists.

  **(b)** They were all taught English in nursery school.

  **(c)** They all learned to produce signs for English words.

**(4)** Check (√) any of the following statements that support the main idea of Paragraph [3]:

  **(a)** Folktales often contain human characters than can understand animal language. _____

  **(b)** Vervet monkeys have a language of cries and barks. _____

(c) Apes do not have the organs to produce human sounds. _____

(d) Dr. Terrace raised Nim Chimpsky in his home. _____

(e) Dogs and horses will obey human commands. _____

(f) Apes and monkeys cannot communicate ideas. _____

(g) Kanzi punched out his responses on a computer keyboard. _____

(5) In Paragraph [3], the pronoun *they* that begins Sentences (2) through (4) refers to

(a) some scientists.

(b) humans.

(c) language.

(6) The word *Furthermore* that begins the last Sentence of Paragraph [3] means the same as

(a) but.

(b) in addition.

(c) after.

(7) According to Paragraph [6],

(a) Nim Chimpsky always created grammatically correct sentences.

(b) Nim Chimpsky never created grammatically correct sentences.

(c) Nim Chimpsky sometimes created grammatically correct sentences.

(8) In Paragraph [7], the word "talking" is in quotations because

(a) the author has used an unusual spelling of the word.

(b) the author wants to emphasize that apes can really talk.

(c) the author doesn't believe that apes can really talk.

(9) Which expression in Paragraph [7] suggests that Nim Chimpsky and Kanzi are different from each other?

(a) It seems as if   (b) Unlike   (c) Certainly

(10) The basic meaning of Sentence (2) in Paragraph [8] is that

(a) humans are more advanced than we thought.

(b) apes are more advanced than humans.

(c) apes are more advanced than we thought.

(d) humans are more advanced than apes.

(11) In Sentence (5) of Paragraph [8], which expression introduces an example?

  (a) Furthermore
  (b) the same . . . as
  (c) such as

(12) Which set of words that appear in Paragraph [9] are all used as time expressions:

  (a) not/nearly/never
  (b) frequently/never/occasionally
  (c) for example/a great deal of/all his life

c. Follow the directions for items (1) and (2).

  (1) Check (√) the ideas that are implied, but not necessarily stated openly, in Paragraph [9]:

   (a) Chimpanzees are the only animals used in scientific experiments. _____

   (b) Some scientists treat experimental animals worse than humans. _____

   (c) Scientific research animals may be captured when they are very young. _____

   (d) Chimpanzees like to climb trees. _____

   (e) Humans are frequently used for medical experiments. _____

  (2) Put a check (√) next to each sentence that gives evidence for Dr. Terrace's belief that apes do not have real language ability.

   (a) Nim Chimpsky learned the basic colors. _____

   (b) Nim never began new sentences himself. _____

   (c) Nim didn't create new words. _____

   (d) Nim went to nursery school. _____

   (e) Nim learned over 100 words in four months. _____

   (f) Nim never added new information to sentences. _____

d. Put an O next to the statements that are opinions. Put an F next to the statements that are facts.

  (1) Stories about talking animals are the most entertaining kind of folktales. _____

(2) An ape named Sarah learned to make sentences on a computer. _____

(3) Laboratory experiments in animal language learning have used chimpanzees more than other types of apes. _____

(4) Kanzi is smarter than many humans. _____

(5) The study of language ought to include writing as well as speaking. _____

(6) Dogs do not have the physical organs for making human sounds. _____

(7) Dr. Terrace's view that apes cannot learn language is correct. _____

(8) Apes are the only mammals that have the same blood types as humans. _____

(9) Laboratory animals are often separated from other members of their species. _____

(10) Roger Fout's mentality is closer to the chimpanzee Washoe's than it is to a two-year-old child's mind. _____

2. **Answering Information Questions.** Write the answers to the following questions in complete sentences.
   a. What did an American psychologist train Sarah to do?
   b. Do other species have the physical organs to make human sounds?
   c. What did Dr. Herbert Terrace want to study?
   d. Where did Dr. Terrace raise Nim Chimpsky?
   e. How often did Nim's teachers work with him?
   f. How many signs did Nim Chimpsky learn?
   g. What do recent studies of ape intelligence show?
   h. Describe three ways in which Larry, the laboratory chimpanzee, was badly treated.
   i. Who is Roger Fout? Who is Washoe?
   j. What is a test tube? What does the word *retarded* mean when it is applied to a child?

3. **The Reading Process: Skimming for Main Ideas.** To *skim* means to read a passage quickly to get the main ideas. Every reading selection has an overall

main idea. Each paragraph also has its own main idea. A main idea tells you the subject of the passage and the writer's opinion about the subject. Sentences stating main ideas do not tell you specific details about the subject. Often the main idea sentence is the first or second sentence in a paragraph. But sometimes it is the last or next-to-last sentence.

Skim the first paragraph of the Prereading at the beginning of this chapter. The main idea is in the second sentence. It tells you the subject: humans and other mammals. It also gives you an opinion about the subject: Humans and other mammals are alike.

**a.** Skim Paragraph [1] of the reading passage. Which of its sentences expresses the main idea?

(1) The first sentence

(2) The third sentence

(3) The last sentence

**b.** Which sentence best expresses the main idea of Paragraphs [2] through [7]?

(1) Apes can learn signs for nouns, verbs, and adjectives.

(2) There is still disagreement about whether apes can learn language.

(3) Folktales and laboratory experiments both emphasize the importance of talking animals.

**c.** The following sentences give us details about some of the things Dr. Terrace did with Nim Chimpsky. Skim Paragraphs [4] through [6] to find and underline the sentence that would be a good main idea for these details.

(1) Dr. Terrace raised Nim in his home.

(2) Dr. Terrace hired special teachers for Nim.

(3) Dr. Terrace sent Nim to school.

(4) Dr. Terrace's teachers taught Nim sign language.

(5) Dr. Terrace tested Nim's vocabulary.

**d.** Skim Paragraph [6]. The main idea is

(1) the first sentence.

(2) the third sentence.

(3) the next-to-last sentence.

**e.** The main idea of Paragraph [7] is not stated in a single sentence. In the space provided, write one sentence in your own words that explains the main idea of Paragraph [7].

**f.** The basic purpose of Paragraph [8] is to explain the similarity between apes and humans. Number the sentences in that paragraph and check the three sentences that state the paragraph's main idea or basic purpose in different words.

**g.** The following sentences give us some details about Larry, the laboratory ape described in Paragraph [9]. Underline the sentence in Paragraph [9] that is a good main idea statement for these details.

  (1) Larry has lived almost his whole life in a tiny cubicle.
  (2) Larry has never climbed a tree.
  (3) Larry has only occasionally seen another chimpanzee.
  (4) Larry has never touched another chimpanzee.
  (5) Larry never goes out to play in the grass.

**h.** In your own words, state the main idea of Paragraph [10].

## VOCABULARY

**1. New Words.**   Pronounce these words following your instructor.

| Nouns | Verbs | Adjectives | Adverbs |
| --- | --- | --- | --- |
| ability | deprive (of) | decent | patiently |
| experiment | raise | | particularly |
| creatures | treat | | morally |
| evidence | improve | | |
| response | attempt | | |
| | claim | | |

**a.** *Expanding Vocabulary.*   Replace the italicized word(s) in each sentence with a word from the New Word list.

  (1) Nim gave correct *answers* to his teachers' questions, but he never *tried* to begin statements himself.
  (2) Nim's teachers *handled* him *without irritation*.
  (3) After two years, Nim's language didn't *get better*.
  (4) According to Dr. Terrace's *tests*, apes don't have the *mental skill* to learn language.
  (5) Apes, *especially* chimpanzees, are the closest biological relatives of humans.
  (6) Animals used in laboratory experiments should be given *satisfactory* living conditions.
  (7) It must be exciting to *bring up* a wild animal in your home.
  (8) We must act *ethically* in all situations that involve living creatures.

**b.** *Using Vocabulary.* Write a complete sentence that responds to each item. Try to include the word in italics.

   **(1)** What is an appropriate *response* when the telephone rings?
   **(2)** What might be a piece of *evidence* in a murder case?
   **(3)** Describe some ways in which a parent might treat a child *patiently*.
   **(4)** List some foods that make up a *decent* diet for a child.
   **(5)** Describe what happens when you *deprive* a child of a good education.

**c.** Circle the things that humans can improve:

   mountains     behavior     climate     ancestors     cooking ability

**d.** In complete sentences, tell three things that you have the ability to learn. Tell two things that snakes do not have the ability to do. Tell one thing that birds have the ability to do that humans don't.

2. **Word Families: Verb versus Noun Forms.** Study the following list of verbs and their related nouns. Note that *ion* and *ment* are common endings that change verb forms into nouns.

| **Verb** | **Noun** |
| --- | --- |
| (a) protect | protection |
| (b) communicate | communication |
| (c) conclude | conclusion |
| (d) prepare | preparation |
| (e) omit | omission |
| (f) create | creation |
| (g) develop | development |
| (h) require | requirement |
| (i) treat | treatment |
| (j) improve | improvement |

Your instructor will dictate ten sentences to you. Letter each sentence *a* to *j* in sequence. In each sentence, when your instructor says "blank" for a missing word, draw a blank line. When the dictation is finished, fill in each blank space with either the verb or the noun from the corresponding item on the list. Now close your books.

   **a.** Ape mothers _____ their babies from harm.

   **b.** How do birds _____ with each other?

   **c.** Dr. Terrace reached the _____ that apes don't learn language.

   **d.** Your instructor can't _____ you for every new word.

e. There is an _____ of two words in that sentence.
f. In every language you can _____ new words.
g. It is interesting to read about a new _____ in science.
h. Some instructors _____ two compositions a week.
i. Taking aspirin is a good _____ for a cold.
j. I hope to _____ my English this term.

## WRITING EXERCISES

### Modals + Basic Form of Verbs

A *modal* is a helping part of a verb. Modals tell about certain conditions related to the main verb. They are used to express ability, possibility, probability, or advisability. The main verb following a modal is always in the basic form with no endings for person or tense.

Study the following explanations and examples of some common modals. The frequently used negatives are in parentheses.

Can (can't): Present Ability; Possibility

> **Many mammals *can* learn simple tricks.**
> **I *can* meet you at 10:00 A.M.**

Could (couldn't): Past Ability; Possibility less certain than can (complementary clause in Simple Past tense)
Will (won't): Future Certainty

> **We *will* learn more about language in the next reading selection.**

Would (wouldn't): Future Probability; Conditional (with if clause in Simple Past tense)

> **You *would* need a lot of patience to raise an ape in your home.**
> **If you studied apes closely, you *would* learn many interesting things.**

> **Nim *could* make signs after a few lessons.**
> **I *could* meet you at 10:00 A.M. if I did my shopping first.**

May: Present or Future Possibility; Permission

> **Dr. Terrace *may* try more experiments with apes.**
> **Students *may* leave this class early.**

Might: Possibility less certain than may (complementary clause in Simple Past tense)

> **Columbia University *might* continue to support Dr. Terrace's work.**

Must: Necessity; Strong Probability (complementary clause in the Present tense)

> **Animal trainers *must* handle their subjects patiently.**
> **Kanzi *must* like the warm climate of Georgia, which is like his native Africa.**

Must not (mustn't): Prohibition

> **Scientists *mustn't* give false information in their reports.**

Should (shouldn't): Obligation or Advisability; Expectation

> **Scientists *should* communicate with others in their profession.**
> **Since you registered early, you *should* find your classes open.**

Chapter Six   The Cleverness of Animals   203

1. **Identifying Modals.**  Read the following sentences. Underline the modal with its main verb in each sentence.

   a. Apes can learn to work computers.
   b. They can learn signs for words.
   c. But they will never learn language as human beings do.
   d. Nim could answer his teachers with signs.
   e. But he couldn't begin conversations with his teachers.
   f. Other mammals besides apes can understand human orders.
   g. The police might teach a dog to discover drugs.
   h. Many people think the police should use dogs in their work.
   i. Do you think we should train dogs for this purpose?

   Do any of the verbs that follow the modals end in *s*, *ed*, or *ing*? Use your answer to state a rule about the use of modals. Now circle the subject of each combination of modal and main verb. Write an *S* for *singular* subjects and a *P* for *plural* subjects. Does the modal change form for a single or plural subject?

2. **Scrambled Sentences.**  On a separate sheet of paper, rewrite the following mixed-up sentences so that they form correct English sentences. Remember to look for the modal and its main verb first. Then look for the subject.

   a. learn      apes      .      probably      language      can't      human
   b. .      could      teachers      usually      Nim      his      understand      school      in
   c. scientists      in the future      try      experiments      .      may      other      with apes
   d. Dr. Terrace's      Nim      live      .      next year      won't      in      home
   e. would      to raise      ape      ?      an      like      at home      you

3. **Sentence Completion.**  Fill in a modal + a main verb in its basic form and whatever other words you need to create complete sentences from the items listed. Write your sentences in the space provided. The first one is done for you.

   a. Tomorrow I . . . class . . .
      *Tomorrow I can meet you after class.*
   b. When I was twelve years old, I . . .

c. (negative) Children . . . touch . . . objects . . . museums . . .

d. In the future people . . . moon . . .

e. Immigrants to the United States . . . English . . . job . . .

f. Students . . . for exams . . .

g. (negative) Nim Chimpsky . . . new words . . .

h. I . . . a letter . . .

i. Next summer . . . Haiti or Jamaica . . . vacation.

4. **Sentence Composing.** Write a complete sentence for each of the following items. Use modals in your answers.

   a. Name two things a dictionary can tell you about a word.
   b. Name two languages you would like to learn.
   c. Name two courses you might take next term.
   d. Name two things archeologists may discover in the ground.
   e. Name two cities where you might want to live in the future.
   f. Name two kinds of words Nim Chimpsky could use.

## Verbs + Infinitives

An infinitive verb is formed by *to* + the basic form of the main verb. Some verbs such as *want, like, would like, hope, expect, learn,* and *begin* are often followed by infinitives.

> **Dr. Terrace** *wanted to study* **the language ability to apes.**
> **The teachers** *began to teach* **Nim signs.**

Two verb phrases that include infinitives have special meanings. *Has* or *have to* + the base verb means *must*. *Used to* + the base verb means something that a person did in the past but doesn't do anymore.

> **Psychologists *have to* do their experiments carefully.**
> **Nim *used to* live in Dr. Terrace's apartment.**

1. **Answering Questions with Infinitives.** Write your answers to the following information questions in complete sentences. Refer back to the reading passage for your information. Use an infinitive in each sentence. Underline the verb-infinitive phrase.

    a. In the past twenty years, what have some American experts tried to do?
    b. What did an American psychologist train Sarah to do?
    c. What did another scientist train Washoe to do?
    d. What did Dr. Terrace want to discover in his experiment?
    e. Where did Dr. Terrace decide to raise Nim?
    f. Does Dr. Terrace expect to train a talking ape in the future?

2. **Sentence Completion.** Look at the photograph of the ESL class and read the caption under it. Then, on a separate sheet of paper, complete the following sentences with details from the caption or with your own ideas. Use an infinitive in each of your sentences.

Immigrants of all ages attend college in the United States. They would like to become proficient in the English language. These ESL students have to work hard to accomplish their goal.

a. These students are planning . . .
b. They expect . . .
c. They hope . . .
d. They want . . .
e. Their children want . . .
f. After finishing their course, several students will begin . . .

*Pair Dictation.* Dictate three of your sentences to your partner. Then take dictation from your partner of his or her sentences. Correct your dictations together.

3. **Sentence Composing.** Write a complete sentence for each of the following items.

   a. What two courses do you want to take next term?
   b. Where would you like to go on vacation next summer?
   c. Why are you learning to speak English?
   d. Do you know how to run a computer?
   e. Name two things your parents used to do for you when you were a child.
   f. At what age did you begin to walk?
   g. What salary do you expect to earn on your first full-time job?
   h. Where do you plan to live next year?
   i. What do you hope to learn in this class?

## Changing the Direction of a Thought: The Use of *But*

*But* is used to change the direction of a thought or to present a contrasting idea. In academic English the word *but* is used in the middle of a sentence between the two contrasting ideas. A comma goes before the word *but*. Sometimes in newspapers or magazines the word *but* is used to begin a new contrasting sentence.

> Nim Chimpsky learned over one hundred signs, *but* he never really learned language.
> Nim Chimpsky learned over one hundred signs. *But* he never really learned language.

Note that when *but* is used in the middle of a sentence, a comma goes before it.

1. **Sentence Rewriting.** Rewrite each of the following pairs of sentences using , *but* or *But*.
    a. (1) Human speech is probably about 1 million years old.
       (2) Writing is much newer.
    b. (1) The earliest writing was picture writing.
       (2) Today most languages use an alphabet.
    c. (1) There are thousands of languages in the world.
       (2) The United Nations uses only two official languages.
    d. (1) It is difficult to learn a second language.
       (2) Many people do.
    e. (1) Latin was a world language in the past.
       (2) Today very few people can speak it.
    f. (1) There is no world language today.
       (2) There may be one in the future.
    g. (1) Nim learned signs for words.
       (2) He never created new words himself.
    h. (1) Children's sentences grow longer all the time.
       (2) Nim's sentences had three words at the most.
    i. (1) The babies of mammals are born alive.
       (2) Bird babies are born from eggs.
    j. (1) Nim was not a human child.
       (2) He attended a nursery school with special teachers.
    k. (1) At first Dr. Terrace thought apes could learn language.
       (2) Then he discovered that they cannot.
    l. (1) Human beings walk on two legs.
       (2) Most other mammals walk on four legs.

2. **Sentence Expansion.** Change the direction of the thought in each of the following sentences by adding , *but* + a new contrasting thought. Rewrite each new sentence. You may want to use the words in parentheses to guide you.

> **Millions of people speak Chinese. (few, Welsh)**
> *Millions of people speak Chinese, but few speak Welsh.*

a. American English writing is very similar to British English writing. (pronunciation, different)
b. I would like to live in Paris. (expensive)
c. A pocket dictionary doesn't have every word. (easy, school)
d. Dogs can be trained to do many tricks. (rabbits)
e. I would like to go bowling. (must study)
f. I would like to visit Egypt. (far away)
g. English articles are simple. (verbs, difficult)
h. I am not learning French. (studying, English)
i. There are many planets in our solar system. (one sun)
j. I would like to see a movie tonight. (must study)

3. **Sentence Completion.** Read the following sentences carefully. Decide whether *and* or *but* is the correct connecting word to use in the blank space. Write in your answer using correct punctuation.

   a. Archeologists often find pottery in the earth, _____ they don't usually find gold.
   b. Overpopulation is one serious problem, _____ water pollution is another.
   c. There is only one moon circling the Earth, _____ there are many moons around Jupiter.
   d. Chinese writing uses characters, _____ English uses an alphabet.
   e. Millions of people speak Hindi, _____ it is not an official language of the United Nations.
   f. Canadians speak English, _____ Australians do too.

4. **Sentence Composing.** Respond to the following items in complete written sentences. Use , *but* in each sentence.

   a. Name one kind of food you eat a lot of and one kind you rarely eat.

b. Tell one sport you enjoy and one sport you don't like to play.
c. Tell one language you can speak and one language you can't speak.
d. Tell one pleasant thing about your native city and one unpleasant thing.
e. Describe one interesting thing about studying English and one boring thing about it.

## Punctuation: Series of Parallel Items

A series of parallel items is a group of three or more words that do the same kind of work in a sentence. A sentence may have a series of nouns, adjectives, verbs, or adverbs. Each item in a series is followed by a comma. The word *and* goes before the last item in the series. All the items in a series must have the same form.

> ***Nim Chimpsky, Sarah, and Washoe*** all developed small vocabularies.
>    (series of proper nouns)
> Nim's teachers were *patient, able, and kind.*
>    (series of adjectives)
> Nim *slept, ate, and played* at Dr. Terrace's home.
>    (series of verbs: Simple Past)

1. **Sentence Combining.** On a separate sheet of paper, combine each group of sentences into one complete sentence. Leave out unnecessary words. Add correct punctuation, and make whatever other small changes are needed. Rewrite each new sentence. The first one is done for you.

   a. (1) Nim was angry when he was left alone.
      (2) Nim was afraid when he was left alone.
      (3) Nim was unhappy when he was left alone.
      
      *Nim was angry, afraid, and unhappy when he was left alone.*

   b. (1) Immigrants brought their native cultures to the United States.
      (2) Immigrants brought their native customs to the United States.
      (3) Immigrants brought their native languages to the United States.

   c. (1) Some British words differ from American words in spelling.

(2) Some British words differ from American words in pronunciation.
(3) Some British words differ from American words in usage.

d. (1) The big *Webster's Dictionary* would be an interesting gift for a friend.
(2) The big *Webster's Dictionary* would be a valuable gift for a friend.
(3) The big *Webster's Dictionary* would be a useful gift for a friend.

e. (1) Nim Chimpsky liked to look at magazines.
(2) Nim Chimpsky liked to play with pencils.
(3) Nim Chimpsky liked to learn new signs.

f. (1) Archeologists find toys in the earth.
(2) Archeologists find pots in the earth.
(3) Archeologists find gold in the earth.

g. (1) The sun is part of our universe.
(2) The moon is part of our universe.
(3) The planets are part of our universe.

h. (1) A map shows us the location of rivers.
(2) A map shows us the location of seas.
(3) A map shows us the location of oceans.

i. (1) Astronauts need special suits for space travel.
(2) Astronauts need special shoes for space travel.
(3) Astronauts need special food for space travel.

j. (1) People in England speak English.
(2) People in Australia speak English.
(3) People in Canada speak English.

k. (1) With a world language, people could communicate easily.
(2) With a world language, people could trade easily.
(3) With a world language, people could travel easily.

2. **Sentence Composing.** Follow the directions for each item.

a. Use a series of parallel adjectives to describe how a main street in your native city looks.

b. Use a series of verbs to state what you usually do after your English class.

c. Use a series of nouns to name three sports or games you like to play.

d. Use a series of proper nouns to tell what special holidays people in your native culture celebrate.

3. **Proofreading.** There is one error in the use of parallel items in a series in each of the following sentences. On the line provided correct the error in each sentence.

   a. My friends enjoy swimming, running, and to play tennis in the summer. _____

   b. Maria, George, Pierre sit near me in English class. _____

   c. You can keep a pocket dictionary in your pocket your schoolbag, or your handbag. _____

   d. In our English class we listen to new sounds, learning new words, and write compositions. _____

   e. An intelligent and patient and kind teacher will try to answer students' questions about language. _____

## THE COMPOSING PROCESS

1. **Sequencing Ideas in a Paragraph.** Put *M.I.* (*main idea*) next to the sentence that states the main idea of the paragraph. Then number the sentences in the appropriate order to form a good paragraph. Look for pronouns, time signals, and other such words to help you find the correct order. On a separate sheet of paper, rewrite the sentences in correct order, *skipping a line between each one*.

   a. He sent him to a special nursery school. _____

   b. Nim enjoyed his days at nursery school because of these activities. _____

   c. Dr. Terrace created a very human environment for Nim Chimpsky. _____

   d. When Nim learned a new sign, his teachers gave him a treat. _____

   e. They taught Nim signs for English words. _____

   f. It had a lot of pictures and magazines in it. _____

   g. The teachers were well trained to work with Nim. _____

   h. The schoolroom was bright and colorful. _____

   *Expanding the Paragraph.* Review your completed paragraph. You will see that the first few sentences following the main idea talk about Nim's nursery school and what is special about it. The next lines talk about the teachers. Then the paragraph tells us about what Nim learned. If you wanted to make this

These Norwegian children are learning their lessons in a bright, cheerful classroom. The children's colorful paintings decorate the classroom walls.

paragraph more complete, you could add details or examples for each of these points. For example, after the fourth sentence (ending with "in it") you could add another detail to show why the schoolroom was "bright and colorful." After the fifth sentence (ending with "with Nim") you could add some information about how the teachers worked with Nim that would show their training. After the sixth sentence (ending with "English words") you could give an example of some words that Nim learned. Write these additional details in your own paragraph. Notice how they *develop* your paragraph so that the reader gets a fuller picture of your subject.

2. **Composing a Paragraph.** The following lists in Columns A and B describe two different types of language classrooms. You may add items to either list by brainstorming.

Review list A. Make up a main idea statement that would apply to the items in that list. Review list B. Make up a main idea statement that would apply to items in that column. Then complete the following informal outline by choosing either list A or B for your topic and adding appropriate details from the chosen list or from your own imagination for each of the given points. One is done for you.

## Chapter Six  The Cleverness of Animals

**A (Ms. Jones's class)**
- classroom looks bright/cheerful
- teacher reads stories to children
- teacher corrects mistakes patiently
- many books/maps/magazines
- children sometimes create own stories/dialogues
- children sometimes get treat for good work
- children often talk about ideas/feelings/interests
- children sometimes work with each other
- some useful textbooks/dictionaries in class
- children experiment with new words/sounds/symbols

**B (Mr. Smith's class)**
- classroom looks dull/uninteresting
- teacher never reads stories to children
- teacher corrects mistakes impatiently
- few books/maps/magazines
- children never create own stories/dialogues
- children rarely get a treat for good work
- children rarely talk about ideas/feelings/interests
- children always work alone
- no useful textbooks/dictionaries in class
- children never experiment with new words/sounds/symbols

**Informal Outline**

(main idea): _____

classroom and equipment: *Many books/maps/magazines* _____

_____

teacher: _____

_____

activities: _____

_____

When you have finished your outline, compose a complete paragraph based on your notes. Use complete sentences and correct paragraph form. Review your writing for grammatical errors.

3. **Sentence Combining to Form a Paragraph.** Combine the following sentences into longer, more interesting statements to form a paragraph about Kanzi, the pygmy chimpanzee. Leave out unnecessary words. Use adjectives, pronouns, signal expressions, and other types of connectives to make your paragraph flow smoothly. Rewrite your new paragraph on a separate sheet of paper. Use correct punctuation.

   a. Kanzi is a chimpanzee.
   b. Kanzi is a pygmy.
   c. Kanzi is a four-year-old.
   d. Kanzi lives at the Language Research Center.
   e. This is in Atlanta, Georgia.
   f. Kanzi has an area to roam around there.
   g. This area is large.
   h. This area is grassy.
   i. In this area there is a tree house for Kanzi.
   j. In this area there is a trailer for Kanzi.
   k. In this area there is a path for Kanzi.
   l. This path is special.
   m. This path is to the woods.
   n. Kanzi likes to play like a child.
   o. The child is human.
   p. Kanzi has the motor skills of a boy.
   q. Kanzi has the interests of a boy.
   r. Kanzi has the spirit of a boy.
   s. This boy is a seven- or eight-year-old.
   t. Kanzi has eight teachers.
   u. The teachers show Kanzi signs.
   v. The signs are on a keyboard.
   w. The keyboard is on a computer.
   x. Kanzi watches signs on television. (Use signal word for addition.)
   y. There is a television program.
   z. It is special.
   aa. It is for the research animals.
   bb. It shows a bunny.
   cc. The bunny is a giant.
   dd. The bunny talks to the research animals.
   ee. The bunny demonstrates certain signs for the research animals.

**ff.** The bunny entertains the research animals.
**gg.** The show is not just for fun. (Use signal for reversing a thought.)
**hh.** The show is a way.
**ii.** The way is pleasant.
**jj.** The way is to teach Kanzi English.

4. **Paragraph Topics**

   **a.** Training a child for the future is an important responsibility. With your class, brainstorm the qualities or characteristics you think a child should possess. Cluster, or group, the brainstormed items into two or three major points. Write a paragraph based on your selected groups of items.

   **b.** A higher education is one of the chief ways in which we can prepare ourselves for the future. What are some ways in which your college is preparing you for a better future? What are some things your college might, could, or should do to improve the education of its students?

## ADDITIONAL READING

### "Rabbit and Antelope": A Timeless Tale

Folk tales, especially those that include talking animals, have universal appeal. Such narratives have been used for thousands of years to communicate important human beliefs, feelings, and ideas about nature. In many different cultures and at many different times in history, folktales have been used as a disguise for political or social beliefs that people could not express openly for fear of punishment. In this African folktale, we find some universal themes that communicate across cultural boundaries.

    For many months, there had been a drought and no rain had fallen. All the animals were suffering because there was no water and the weather was terribly hot. Those animals who had not dug their own wells were extremely thirsty. Finally, Rabbit went to Antelope and said, "Friend Antelope, because of this long drought I am very thirsty. I have no well, and neither do you. Will you cooperate with me to dig a deep well? Then we can both have water to drink."

    "Indeed I will," said Antelope. "Let us eat first to gain some strength, and then I will help you dig our well."

    "I have a better idea," said Rabbit. "Let us hide our food and save it for later. We will be very hungry after we have dug our well."

    The antelope agreed and gave Rabbit the food to hide. Then Rabbit and Antelope together began to dig their well. They both worked very hard, and the hole got deeper and deeper.

After several hours of digging, Rabbit said to Antelope, "I hear my wife calling me. She has just given birth to a baby rabbit, and I must go home to name it."

"I can't hear anyone calling," said Antelope. "But if you want to go home, you may."

Rabbit bounded away and ran back to the village where he took some of the food he had hidden and ate it. Then he ran back to the well and began digging again.

"What did you name your baby?" asked Antelope.

"I called him 'Not Done,' " replied Rabbit.

"What a strange name," thought Antelope, as he went on digging the well.

Some hours later, Rabbit again interrupted the digging. "I hear my wife calling again," said Rabbit. "She is having another baby, and I must go home to name it."

"I can't hear anything," said Antelope, but he allowed Rabbit once more to leave the well and go home to his wife. Rabbit ran back to the village and took some more food from the hiding place and ate it. Then he went back to the well and resumed digging alongside of Antelope.

"What did you name the second baby?" asked Antelope.

"I named him 'Half Done,' " said Rabbit.

"That's a strange name, too," said Antelope, but he made no further comment and continued to dig the well.

Once more, after several hours, Rabbit told Antelope that he heard his wife calling him to come home and name their third baby. "I don't hear anyone calling you," said Antelope, but Rabbit insisted he had to go home. Off he went to the village, where he took the remaining food from its hiding place and ate it all. Then he ran back to the well.

"What did you name this baby?" asked Antelope.

"We named him 'All Done,' " said Rabbit, and once again Antelope was puzzled by the strange name.

Finally, at the end of the day, when the sun was setting, Antelope turned to Rabbit and said, "I have worked all day, Friend Rabbit, and now I am very hungry. Go to the village and get our food." Antelope sat down to rest and awaited Rabbit's return.

Rabbit went back to the village but returned very quickly. He did not have any food with him. "Friend Antelope," he said, "there is no food in our hiding place. I think Cat ate it." Antelope was displeased because he had to go to bed tired and hungry, but what could he do?

The next day Antelope realized that Rabbit had deceived him. "You did not go home to name your children," he accused Rabbit. "You went back to the village to steal my food. Therefore, I will not allow you drink from the well." Each night Antelope tried to guard the well, but he was so tired that every night, after midnight, he fell asleep. Then Rabbit would sneak to the well and drink its water.

Finally one day, a little bird, which stayed awake all night and saw what Rabbit was doing, told Antelope, "Do you know that every night, when you fall asleep, Rabbit comes to drink the water from your well?"

Antelope was so angry he decided to trick Rabbit as Rabbit had tricked him. Antelope carved a rabbit out of wood and covered the wooden rabbit with a sticky gum. Then he propped the wooden rabbit up beside the well. That night, when Rabbit came along to drink the water, he saw another rabbit at the well.

"What are you doing here?" Rabbit demanded of the wooden rabbit. "This is my well!" But the wooden rabbit said not a word.

Friend Rabbit became so angry at the wooden rabbit's silence that he beat him with his fist. "Answer me," Rabbit cried, but the wooden rabbit remained silent, and Rabbit's fist was stuck in the gum on the wooden rabbit's face. Try as he might, he could not free his fist.

"If you don't answer me, I'll kick you," shouted Rabbit. But the wooden rabbit remained silent as before. When Friend Rabbit kicked the wooden animal with one foot, that foot stuck in the gummy mixture and Rabbit could

Highly intelligent animals such as this Labrador Retriever, a guide dog for the blind, can be trained to perform services for human beings. Discuss other animals who have been trained to help in the activities of human life.

not get it free. Then Rabbit kicked the wooden animal with his other foot, and that too, stuck in the gummy mixture.

"You answer me, you thief of my water," cried Rabbit, "or I'll hit you with my head." And Rabbit became so angry at the wooden animal's silence that he butted him with his head. But his head stuck to the wooden animal's body and he could not free it no matter how hard he tried.

Rabbit cried and shouted and tried to get away from the wooden rabbit, but he could not do so. His shouting awoke all the other animals who came running to the well. When they saw Rabbit's predicament, and how ridiculous he looked stuck to the wooden rabbit, they laughed until the tears ran down their cheeks. Then they carried him to the village, where they showed him to Antelope, who laughed the hardest of all.

## DISCUSSION QUESTIONS

1. Folktales about talking animals often communicate basic ideas about human nature underneath their humorous surface. The animals in this tale, for instance, suggest different personality types of people in human society. Discuss the characters of Rabbit and Antelope as examples of human nature. What qualities do they each show that are similar to those of humans?

2. In many folktales, small, weak, and powerless figures such as Rabbit often have to deceive larger and more powerful creatures in order to survive. Have you ever been in a situation where you had to use your brains to outwit someone stronger or more powerful than you? Why were you successful or unsuccessful in this attempt?

3. This story illustrates the English saying that "He laughs best who laughs last." What do you think this proverb means? How does the story of Rabbit and Antelope illustrate this idea? Do you have a similar saying in your language and culture? Explain.

## READING COMPREHENSION

1. Write *T* for *true* or *F* for *false* next to each item according to the information that is stated or implied in the African folktale. Be prepared to explain your answers with reference to the text.

    a. This tale is set in a moderate climate with many rivers and forests. _____

    b. None of the animals had dug their wells before the drought came. _____

    c. Rabbit hid his and Antelope's food in a nearby settlement. _____

d. Antelope could not stay awake all through the night to guard his well. _____

e. Antelope built a wooden rabbit to keep him company throughout the night. _____

f. Rabbit's wife gave birth to three baby rabbits. _____

g. Rabbit beat the wooden rabbit because it had stolen his food. _____

h. The other animals laughed at Rabbit because he was stuck in the gum covering the wooden rabbit. _____

i. Antelope was satisfied at his punishment of Rabbit. _____

j. Tears ran down the cheeks of the other animals because they were sad about the suffering from the drought. _____

2. **Answering Information Questions.** Write the answers to the following questions in complete sentences on a separate sheet of paper.

   a. Why did Rabbit want to dig a well?
   b. Whom did Rabbit accuse of eating all the hidden food?
   c. Why did Rabbit say that his wife was having babies?
   d. Why did Rabbit tell Antelope that his babies were named 'Not Done,' 'Half Done,' and 'All Done'?
   e. With what did Antelope cover the wooden rabbit he built?
   f. Why did Rabbit beat the wooden rabbit at the well?
   g. Why did the other animals laugh at Rabbit?

## VOCABULARY

1. **Expanding Vocabulary.** There is an italicized word in each of the following sentences. Without using your dictionary, try to write a word or phrase that means the same as the italicized word in the context of the sentence. Then check your dictionary for accuracy.

   a. Folktales about talking animals have had a *universal* attraction for over two thousand years.
   b. Sometimes people try to *disguise* their true feelings in front of strangers.
   c. Desert areas often suffer severe *droughts* that last many years.
   d. If students *cooperate* with each other, they may improve their oral language skills.

e. A phone call from the college president *interrupted* the meeting.
f. Many mothers *resume* their careers when their children are in school.
g. It is best not to *deceive* yourself about the level of your language abilities.
h. Students sometimes get themselves into terrible *predicaments* by overspending their budgets.
i. Rabbit looked *ridiculous* stuck to the gummy wooden rabbit.

2. **Word Families**

   a. **Negative prefix *dis*.** The prefix *dis* attached to a word or word stem often means *not* or *the absence of* a quality. Column A gives you some base words whose negatives are formed by adding *dis*. Complete Column B by writing the negative word in full. Then choose five of the negatives and use them in complete original sentences.

   | A: Base Word Form | B: Negatives with *dis* |
   |---|---|
   | pleased (adjective) | |
   | use (noun) | |
   | content (adjective) | |
   | like (verb) | |
   | agree (verb) | |
   | agreement (noun) | |
   | allow (verb) | |
   | appearance (noun) | |
   | appear (verb) | |
   | ability (noun) | |

   b. Adverbs can be used to describe the degree or extent to which an adjective (descriptive word) is true. Most adverbs are formed by adding *ly* to the adjective form.

   > **Rabbit was *terribly thirsty*.**
   >         (adverb) (adjective)

   Write the adverb form of each adjective given. Then use the adverb with the given adjective + noun combination in an original sentence.

| Adjective | Adverb | Adjective + Noun Combination |
|---|---|---|
| extreme | extremely | intelligent student |

*Lee is an extremely intelligent student.*

| | | |
|---|---|---|
| fair | | cold weather |
| real | | splendid building |
| basic | | well-built automobile |
| careful | | developed plan |
| artificial | | preserved food |
| beautiful | | performed concert |

## PARAGRAPH TOPICS

1. One of the reasons we enjoy folktales is because they use humor to teach a lesson. Try to think of a joke or humorous story that people in your culture tell to teach a lesson or illustrate a point about human nature and write it up for your classmates to share.

2. In this tale, Rabbit gives his children names that have special meaning. What kinds of names have special meaning in your culture or language? What are some of the most popular names? Why? Are children named after certain people, events, or qualities? Write a paragraph that informs your reader about the selection of names in your culture.

NAME _____

INSTRUCTOR _____

# UNIT II REVIEW

1. **Sentence Completion.** Choose the correct item from the columns following the paragraph to fill in each blank space in the paragraph.

   Since very (1) _____ times the different people of the world have spoken (2) _____ different languages. International communication has often been difficult (3) _____ people have not understood the languages of others. Many men (4) _____ women have developed systems for a universal language (5) _____ different language groups communicate. For example, (6) _____ French scientist Descartes thought that a symbolic language (7) _____ be useful. One hundred years ago a man named Sodre (8) _____ a musical language. He called (9) _____ Solresol because it (10) _____ musical notes such as *so, la,* (11) _____ *re*. These artificial languages have some (12) _____ : They have simple vocabularies and grammars. (13) _____ they have never developed large numbers of speakers. In fact, most of them have never gone further than their (14) _____ front doors. Yet currently, many people (15) _____ on a universal language.

   (1) numerical/
       ancient/literate/
       official
   (2) a/an/the/
       leave blank
   (3) and/but/
       because/then
   (4) but/and/,/also
   (5) to helps/
       is helping/
       to help/help
   (6) the/a/an/
       leave blank
   (7) can/will/may/
       would
   (8) is inventing/
       invents/
       invented/
       inventor
   (9) her/him/their/it
   (10) uses/used/
        is using/to use
   (11) leave blank/./,/
        and
   (12) opinions/
        emotions/
        immigrants/
        advantages
   (13) And/But/
        Because/Then
   (14) inventors/
        inventors'/
        inventor/
        inventor's
   (15) work/
        are working/
        worked/
        is working

223

## Unit II  Our World of Language

2. **Word Forms.**  Fill in the chart with the correct forms of the given words. (Some parts of speech may have more than one word.)

|   | Verb | Noun | Adjective | Adverb |
|---|---|---|---|---|
| a | communicate |  |  | X |
| b |  |  | various |  |
| c | develop |  |  |  |
| d | X |  | native |  |
| e |  | immigrants |  | X |
| f | create |  |  |  |
| g | prepare |  |  | X |
| h |  | symbols |  |  |
| i | decide |  |  |  |
| j | invent |  |  |  |

*Word Form Completion.*  Fill in the blank space in each sentence with the correct form of the word from the same lettered item on the Word Form chart. Use verbs and nouns in their singular or plural form as necessary. For dictation with blanks, close your textbook.

a. There should be good _____ between parents and children.

b. We should study a _____ of subjects in college.

c. I would like to _____ my oral skills in French.

d. My grandfather was a _____ of Poland.

e. Many people _____ to the United States each year.

f. Artists, musicians, and sculptors are _____ people.

g. Men and women must have good _____ for their careers.

h. A red light _____ the word *stop*.

i. Have you reached a _____ about continuing your college education?

j. The ballpoint pen is a useful _____ .

3. **Paragraph Composition.** Write a paragraph that uses five to eight of the words from the Word Forms chart. Select one of the following topics to write about or make up one of your own.

   A Useful Invention
   An Important Decision
   A Beautiful Creation

4. **Article Review.** Study the following chart of article use. Then review the paragraphs below the chart. Next to each article and some nouns in the paragraphs is a blank space. The reason for the use or absence of that particular article is given on one of the lines on the chart. Put the number of the appropriate line from the chart in the blank space next to each article. The first one is done for you.

|    | Article | Countable or Uncountable | Singular or Plural | Definite or Indefinite |
|----|---------|--------------------------|---------------------|------------------------|
| 1. | an/an   | countable                | singular            | indefinite             |
| 2. | X       | countable                | plural              | indefinite             |
| 3. | the     | countable                | singular            | definite               |
| 4. | the     | countable                | plural              | definite               |
| 5. | X       | uncountable              | singular            | indefinite             |
| 6. | the     | uncountable              | singular            | definite               |

a. The (1) __3__ English language developed from an (2) _____ old German language. The (3) _____ French language added many new words to English. (4) _____ Spanish, Dutch, and Italian words are also part of our English vocabulary. When the (5) _____ first immigrants came to America, they learned (6) _____ new Native American words. For example, the (7) _____ word *tobacco* is a (8) _____ Native American word.

b. The (1) _____ British and American versions of English are not exactly alike. The (2) _____ spelling of some words is different. For example, the (3) _____ British word *tyre* is spelled *tire* in the (4) _____ United States. A (5) _____ truck in the United States is called a (6) _____ lorry in England. But the (7) _____ biggest difference between (8) _____ British and American language is in pronunciation. Many Americans have (9) _____ difficulty in understanding British speech.

5. **Verb Completion.** Choose an appropriate verb from the list to fill each blank space. Put each verb in the simple past tense. You may use a verb more than once or not at all.

   | | |
   |---|---|
   | become | begin |
   | be | mean |
   | have | put |
   | want | write |
   | receive | use |
   | move | get |

   William McGuffey had an important place in the development of American English. He (1) _____ born in western Pennsylvania in 1800. Then his parents (2) _____ further west to Ohio. His area (3) _____ few schools. So McGuffey (4) _____ _____ his own teacher. He (5) _____ to teach school himself when he (6) _____ thirteen years old. But he (7) _____ to go to college. So he (8) _____ _____ his free time to study. After eight years of part-time study, he (9) _____ his degree. McGuffey (10) _____ _____ very interested in the public schools. He (11) _____ many reading books for young children. McGuffey (12) _____ to teach children good behavior in his books. So he (13) _____ in many little stories about how children should behave. McGuffey's readers (14) _____ the most popular schoolbooks in America.

6. **Developing a Paragraph.** In the following paragraph, a student describes an occasion when she had to make a speech. Use the guide to corrections following the paragraph to improve this piece of writing.

(1) In Chinese culture for special occasions we have a banquet. (2) Everyone meets at a restaurant and has a meal. (3) Then someone gives a speech. (4) One time my family chose me to make the speech. (5) I prepare a speech. (6) It was a good speech. (7) I practiced it many times in front of the glass. (8) But I couldn't eat dinner. (9) I was so nervous about my speech. (10) We had delicious soups and fish. (11) I stood up to speech, but I forgot every word. (12) Then I remembered the first line. (13) After that it was easy for me to complete my speech.

    **a.** Which sentences are the introduction? How do they make the paragraph more interesting?
    **b.** Which sentence is the main idea sentence?
    **c.** Sentence (1) would be improved by adding the adverb of frequency that means "most of the time." Sentence (3) would be improved by adding the adverb of frequency that means "a lot of the time." Where would you put these adverbs?
    **d.** In Sentence (5), the verb is the wrong tense.
    **e.** Try combining Sentences (5) and (6) into one new sentence. Is that an improvement?
    **f.** In Sentence (7), one noun must be made plural. What is a better word for *glass* in that sentence?
    **g.** Combine Sentences (8) and (9) by adding a connecting word of reason.
    **h.** In Sentence (11), a word is in the wrong form.
    **i.** Should any sentence in the paragraph be left out? Explain your answer.

**7. Paragraph Topics**

    **a.** Write about an occasion when you had to make a speech in front of a class or some other group of people. How did you prepare for this? How did you feel about it? Was it a successful speech? Why or why not?
    **b.** If you have friends or relatives who live far away, do you prefer to communicate by letter, by telephone, or by tape recorder? Write a paragraph in which you give some reasons for your preference.

# UNIT III

# OUR SOCIAL WORLD

The development of strong friendships and family ties in youth contributes to good social relationships in later life.

# CHAPTER SEVEN

# WOMEN OF THE AMERICAN PAST

**PREREADING**

**Strip Story.** Listen to your instructor read the story "Molly Pitcher, An American Patriot." Then as a class, or in groups, copy each of the following sentences onto a separate strip of paper. Put the strips in the proper order to tell the story of Molly Pitcher. Use pronouns, time expressions, and other words as clues for sentence order. When the strips are correctly arranged, number them in sequence. Then read the story aloud from the strips.

Molly Pitcher was a heroine of the Battle of Monmouth in the American Revolution.

At camp she was useful in washing clothes, cooking, and keeping the camp clean.

Finally, the battle was over and the Americans had won.

Then, on July 28, 1778, the American army marched out to fight the British army in the Battle of Monmouth.

Much of the credit for this victory belongs to Molly Pitcher, a brave and quick-thinking American woman.

Molly dropped her pitcher and took over her husband's cannon.

During the hard war years of 1777 and 1778, Mary joined her husband in the army camp at Valley Forge.

The heat was so great that day that the soldiers became terribly thirsty.

She fired round after round of shot at the British with it.

Suddenly, during the battle, Molly's husband fainted from heatstroke.

So Mary Ludwig followed the soldiers into battle with a pitcher of water for them to drink.

Mary Ludwig was a heroine of the Battle of Monmouth in the American Revolutionary War.

That's why the soldiers gave her the nickname "Molly Pitcher."

She was married to John Hayes, who was a gunner in the American Revolutionary army.

Each time the pitcher was emptied, Mary would run back to a nearby stream to fill it.

---

*Free Write.* There is an ancient Chinese proverb that says, "Women hold up half the sky." What do you think this means? Do you think this proverb is true? If so, write about a woman you know who holds up half the sky. If not, explain why.

---

**Vocabulary in Context.** The words in this exercise will appear in the reading passage. Circle the word(s) in the second sentence of each pair that mean(s) the same as the italicized word in the first sentence. The first one is done for you.

1. Historians are now writing books that describe the *role* of women in creating the American nation. Most old history books mainly describe the (part) that men took in events of the past.

2. When new *territories* opened up in the American West, the women went along with the men to settle there. In those regions, both men and women suffered hardships.

3. Women *labored* beside their husbands. They worked hard clearing the land and building homes in wild places.

4. It took a great deal of *courage* for families to settle in those lonely areas. Those people were called pioneers, and the story of their bravery is well known.

5. Pioneer women had to be strong in *spirit* even if they weren't strong physically. A good mental attitude was necessary to live in the wilderness.

6. Slave women taken from Africa *survived* hardships and loneliness. Native American women, once called Indians, lived through terrible times when their men were killed in battle with the pioneers.

7. Hundreds of thousands of immigrants came to America from Europe and Asia in the nineteenth century, looking for a more *successful* existence. Many of them were women who wanted a more favorable life for their families.

8. Immigrant women were often *weary* from hard work in big city factories. Even though they were tired most of the time, they tried to care for their husbands and their children, too.

9. The Statue of Liberty in New York Harbor is a monument in *honor* of all the people who came to America and helped build our nation. Each group deserves respect for the traditions it has given to this land.

10. The stories of women and men of the American past *enrich* our lives today. The contributions of the past add value to the present.

## READING

### Harriet Tubman: The Moses of Her People

[1] In the development of the United States, many groups of women played an important role. Native American women traveled with the earliest explorers. They guided the men through deep forests and across wide rivers, helping them to find a way to the West. Black women from Africa labored as slaves in the fields and homes of the American South. Although they were not allowed to become educated, slave women used their native skills and intelligence as healers and midwives to help both black and white families. In the 1800s, the West opened up and pioneer women made difficult journeys with their families to find new homes. Pioneer women suffered many hardships, and they had to be very strong in body and spirit to survive. In the nineteenth and twentieth centuries, many immigrant

women made the long journey across the oceans to settle in America. They, too, had the strength and ability to face difficult times in a strange, new homeland.

[2] Some people may think of women as the "weaker sex," but the history of women in America proves that they are mistaken. We don't have the names of all the individual women who showed themselves equal to men in strength of body and spirit. But the stories of some are told in books. The life story of Harriet Tubman, an active leader of escaping slaves, is especially well known. Her story is an example of all the women who played an important role in creating the American nation.

[3] Harriet Tubman was born in the southern state of Maryland in 1820. Her parents were slaves and worked on a plantation. When Harriet was only seven years old, she was taking care of a house and a baby on a nearby plantation. Her mistress was harsh and cruel. Every hour that Harriet worked for this mean woman, she dreamed of freedom.

[4] As a teenager, Harriet was sent out in the fields to labor under the hot sun all day long. While she worked, she continued to dream of freedom. She listened to stories of slaves who had escaped to the North. One day Harriet learned that she was going to be sold. When she heard this, she knew that she had to escape immediately. She could not even say good-bye to her parents because it was too dangerous. That night she walked off the plantation and followed the North Star to freedom. She was hungry, lonely, and frightened. Nevertheless, she forced herself onward and didn't stop until she was out of slave territory.

[5] When Harriet Tubman reached Pennsylvania, she was free. But she couldn't forget the others who were still living in slavery. She then joined a secret organization called the Underground Railroad. This organization helped slaves to escape from their masters and to find homes in the free states of the North. As an active member, and later as the leader of the Underground Railroad, Harriet Tubman made frequent trips back to the South, and was successful in bringing out more than three hundred slaves. She even succeeded in leading her aged parents to safety. When there were problems for the runaway slaves in the northern states, she guided them into Canada. For all her extraordinary deeds of courage, Harriet Tubman received high praise from many famous men. John Brown, a well-known leader of the antislavery movement, referred to her as "one of the best and bravest persons on the continent."

[6] Harriet Tubman was not only a courageous woman but a clever one as well. On one of her trips back South, she was sitting in the waiting room of a railroad station in Maryland. The door was straight ahead of her, and she could see everyone who entered. Suddenly, a man walked in and looked around the room slowly. She immediately knew that the man was a slave catcher looking for a runaway slave. She had to think quickly. There was a book on the bench beside her. She picked it up and held it on her lap as if she were reading it. When the slave catcher looked at Harriet, he saw her with the book. He knew that slaves were never allowed to learn to read, so he thought that she was a northern black person,

During the Civil War, Harriet Tubman served as a nurse, laundress, and spy for the northern army.

not a runaway southern slave. Although Harriet Tubman had many such frightening experiences, she remained free through her cleverness and intelligence.

[7]   As the leader of the Underground Railroad, Harriet Tubman was known for her strict discipline. When some of her followers became weary or frightened, she encouraged them with kindness. Sometimes, however, she had to be more forceful, and she would point a loaded gun at them. For the most part, the people under her leadership were proud to obey her rules of conduct. They even called her "General" Tubman. She was strict with herself as well, no matter what kind of work she had to do. During the American Civil War, she served first as a nurse and laundress for the northern army, and later as a spy. She went to South Carolina and helped to get information that the North used successfully in a battle against the army of the South.

[8]   In 1865, when the Civil War was over, all the slaves gained their freedom. Harriet Tubman's journeys were over, but her fame remained. People honored her as "the Moses of her people." Just as the ancient Hebrew Moses led his people out of the desert to freedom, Harriet Tubman guided many of her people to safety in the North. Her life, like those of all the courageous women of the past, instructs us and enriches our own lives today.

**Summary Completion.** Fill in each blank space with the appropriate word from the columns following the paragraph.

Women have played an (1) _____ role in the development (2) _____ the United States. Native American (3) _____, slave women, pioneer women, (4) _____ immigrant women have all (5) _____ to build this country. Harriet Tubman's (6) _____ is an example of (7) _____ brave spirit of many (8) _____ women of the past. As a leader of the Underground Railroad, Harriet Tubman guided many slaves to (9) _____ in the North. She placed herself in many dangers, but because of her cleverness, she (10) _____ never caught. She was strict with her followers and with (11) _____ also. During the Civil War she served with the northern army (12) _____ a nurse, laundress, and spy. (13) _____ the war was over, the slaves were all free, and Harriet Tubman was honored for all her courageous deeds.

(1) ordinary/ dangerous/ important/ unhappy
(2) from/of/to/with
(3) men/children/ owners/women
(4) but/often/and/ again
(5) decided/helped/ brought/ developed
(6) slavery/owner/ life/cruelty
(7) a/leave blank/ the/an
(8) America/the United States/ country/ American
(9) bravery/masters/ safety/problems
(10) was/wasn't/is/ didn't
(11) them/her/ themselves/ herself
(12) for/to/as/leave blank
(13) At/When/If/Just

## DISCUSSION QUESTIONS

1. For many of us, it is natural to help people in trouble. Discuss the times you have helped someone solve a particular problem.
   There are times, however, that people are afraid to help others. Discuss the kinds of situations when it might be dangerous to go to someone's assistance. What can an observer do when a crime is being committed? How can we assist others in a dangerous situation? Should people become involved or stay far away? What about the case of an accident or a fire?

2. In your opinion is it unusual for women to do dangerous jobs and become heroines? Are women different from men in spirit? What do you think about women in government and as peaceful leaders? Are they as capable as men in politics? Do you know of any women who have served in government? What do you think about women in the military? Have there been heroines in your country's history?

## READING COMPREHENSION

1. **Understanding the Text.**

    a. Write *T* if the sentence is *True*, and *F* if the sentence is *False*. If the reading passage does not give information about the sentence, write *N.I.* (*no information*).

    (1) Native American women helped to open the way to the West. _____

    (2) Slaves in the American South knew something about medicines. _____

    (3) Women who traveled to the West often did not survive childbirth. _____

    (4) Harriet Tubman was a freeborn black woman. _____

    (5) Harriet was the first person to escape from a plantation. _____

    (6) Harriet returned to Maryland to free her parents. _____

    (7) Harriet's husband was a free black man named John Tubman. _____

    (8) John Brown thought highly of Harriet Tubman. _____

    (9) Harriet Tubman became a general in the northern army. _____

    b. Choose the correct answer, or follow the directions indicated.

    (1) Paragraph [1] tells something about the various groups of women who helped in the development of the United States. List the groups mentioned.

    (a) _____ (c) _____

    (b) _____ (d) _____

    (2) The author uses Harriet Tubman's life mainly

    (a) as a way of telling some of the history of the American South.

    (b) as an example of a courageous and capable American woman.

    (c) to describe the work of the Underground Railroad.

(3) The author writes that Harriet was *only* seven years old when she began to work. The word *only* suggests that the author thinks

   (a) seven years old is a good age to start working.

   (b) seven years old is too young to start working.

   (c) seven years old is the usual age to start working.

(4) We are told that Harriet Tubman's mistress was harsh and cruel. Check (√) the items that show this woman was harsh and cruel.

   (a) She whipped Harriet often. _____

   (b) She bought Harriet new dresses. _____

   (c) She nearly starved Harriet. _____

   (d) She paid Harriet only six cents a day. _____

(5) In a complete sentence, tell why Harriet couldn't say anything to her parents about her plans to escape from the plantation.

   _____

   _____

(6) The word *Nevertheless* in the last sentence of Paragraph [4] introduces

   (a) a reason why Harriet was frightened, lonely, and hungry.

   (b) an action that contrasts with Harriet's feelings.

   (c) another emotion that Harriet was feeling.

(7) The Underground Railroad was

   (a) a real railroad that took people from Maryland to Canada.

   (b) was started by Harriet Tubman when she reached Pennsylvania.

   (c) an organization of people who led slaves out of the South.

(8) In Paragraph [5], the author writes: She *even* succeeded in leading her aged parents to safety. The word *even* is used to show

   (a) that it was unusual for old people to make an escape from slavery.

   (b) that there was nothing extraordinary about this action.

   (c) that Harriet was lonely and wanted her parents with her.

(9) The last sentence in Paragraph [5] tells us that Harriet Tubman was "one of the best and bravest persons on the continent." This part of the sentence is in quotation marks because

   (a) the author thinks it is very important.

   (b) John Brown spoke or wrote those exact words.

   (c) Harriet Tubman didn't believe those words.

(10) John Brown was a well-known leader of the antislavery movement. This means that he

    (a) owned a great number of slaves.

    (b) preferred slave labor to free labor.

    (c) was against the practice of slavery.

(11) Choose the item that states the topic of Paragraph [6].

    (a) Harriet's clever trick to avoid a slave catcher

    (b) Harriet's trip back to Maryland

    (c) Harriet's inability to read

(12) In Paragraph [7], the author's main purpose is to describe

    (a) Harriet's participation in the Civil War.

    (b) Harriet's ability to discipline herself as well as her followers.

    (c) Harriet's knowledge of weapons.

(13) The description of Harriet Tubman in Paragraph [7] proves that

    (a) she was as good as a man in action.

    (b) she wasn't well liked or respected by her followers.

    (c) she only did work that a man usually does.

2. **Answering Information Questions.** On a separate sheet of paper, answer each question in a complete statement.

    a. Where and when was Harriet Tubman born?

    b. What was she doing when she was seven years old?

    c. Was her mistress kind and gentle or harsh and cruel?

    d. What did she dream about while she worked?

    e. How did she feel as she walked North?

    f. What organization did Harriet Tubman join when she reached Pennsylvania?

    g. How many slaves was she successful in bringing out?

    h. Where did she guide the slaves when there was trouble in the North?

    i. What did John Brown say about Harriet Tubman? (Use your own words.)

    j. What did Harriet Tubman do with the book in the railroad station?

    k. What would she do sometimes when she had to be forceful with her followers?

    l. What jobs did she have during the Civil War?

    m. What happened to the slaves when the Civil War was over?

    n. How did people honor Harriet Tubman?

3. **The Reading Process: Recognizing Signals of Contrast.** When English writers want to contradict, or state something opposite to what they have just said, they usually use signal words of contrast. These words let the reader know that the writer is going to present two pieces of contradictory, contrasting, or opposite information.

Study this list of signal words of contrast.

| , but | in contrast, | although |
| however, | in contrast to _____, | unlike _____, |
| on the other hand, | nevertheless, | |

Read the following paragraphs, and underline the signals of contrast in each.

a. Harriet Beecher Stowe was another woman named Harriet who fought against slavery. Unlike Harriet Tubman, however, Harriet Beecher Stowe was a free, white, well-educated woman from an old New England family. Harriet Tubman's relatives were poor slaves who could not help her in her work. But Harriet Beecher Stowe's family included a husband who was a professor and a brother who was a famous minister and writer. Harriet Tubman could not read or write; in contrast, Harriet Beecher Stowe was a professional writer. Her book against slavery, *Uncle Tom's Cabin*, awakened many people to the evils of slavery. These two Harriets had very different positions in life. Nevertheless, they both shared a powerful hatred of the system of slavery and had the courage to fight against it.

Now make two lists of the different, contrasting qualities of Harriet Beecher Stowe and Harriet Tubman.

b. In contrast to India and England, the United States government has never had a female leader. The wives of some American presidents have been important and well known in their own right, but none has ever been elected to office herself. The United States has had a few women senators and representatives in Congress. No woman, however, has ever been a vice president. Although the United States presidency has always been occupied by a male in the past, perhaps in the future we will see a woman occupying that position.

Mark *T* if the statement is *True*. Mark *F* if it is *False*.

(1) India, England, and the United States have all had female leaders. ___

(2) No American president's wife has ever been elected to office. ___

(3) American women have been senators and members of Congress. ___

(4) The United States has had a woman vice president. ___

(5) The president of the United States will always be a male. ___

## VOCABULARY

**1. New Words.** Pronounce these words following your instructor.

| Verbs | Nouns | Adjectives | Adverbs |
|---|---|---|---|
| enrich | courage | successful | |
| honor | spirit | weary | |
| labor | role | | |
| survive | territory | | |
| | discipline | | |

a. *Expanding Vocabulary.* Fill in the blank space with a word from the list.

(1) Farm women often _____ in the fields with their husbands.

(2) Today women play an important _____ in the American work force.

(3) The closeness of grandparents can _____ a child's life.

(4) Working people often feel _____ after a long, hard day on the job.

(5) Teachers try to keep strict _____ in the classroom so that children get the most out of their education.

(6) It takes great _____ to leave one's country and emigrate to a strange, new land.

(7) Immigrants have to be strong in body and _____ to undertake life in a new country.

(8) Many pioneer women didn't _____ childbirth because there was no medical help in the areas where they traveled.

(9) Most children are taught to _____ their parents' wishes.

(10) Wild animals have their own _____ and often fight to keep it for themselves.

(11) It takes a lot of hard work to be _____ in school, business, or life in general.

**b.** *Using Vocabulary.* Write a complete sentence in answer to each question. Use the italicized word in your sentence.

(1) When people *labor* all day, what do they need to do after work?

_____

(2) Which of the following *enriches* your life? reading literature, going to museums, attending concerts, listening to stories of the past.

_____

(3) What famous person in the history of your native land showed great *courage* in body and *spirit*?

_____

(4) In which school or grade did your teachers demand strict *discipline*?

_____

(5) Is it necessary to have a lot of money to feel *successful* in life?

_____

(6) If you were an actor, would you prefer to play the *role* of a good person or a mean person?

_____

(7) Can a person *survive* on water alone?

_____

(8) What do you do when you feel *weary*?

_____

(9) How do people usually feel when they enter a strange *territory*?

_____

(10) Why should children *honor* older people?

_____

**2. Word Families: Related Word Forms.** The stem, or root, of a word is often found in other related words. The related words may have different forms, prefixes, or suffixes from the stem word. But the meanings of all the words in a word family will have some relationship to each other. Recognizing the root of a word in other words will help you to increase your vocabulary. Study the word lists for each of the following paragraphs. Fill in the blank spaces in the paragraphs with the correct word from the list.

a.  **verb:** honor     **adjective:** honorable, honest, dishonorable, dishonest
    **noun:** honor, honesty, dishonesty, dishonor     **adverb:** honorably, honestly, dishonorably, dishonestly

Slavery was a (an) (1) _____ practice. Men and women who work deserve an (a) (2) _____ day's pay for their labor. Many Americans of the past (3) _____ wished to end slavery. They worked hard to erase the (4) _____ of slavery from the land. We (5) _____ such people as Harriet Tubman for their work against slavery.

b.  **verb:** labor     **adjective:** laborious, laboring
    **noun:** labor, laborer, laboriousness, laboratory     **adverb:** laboriously
    **related phrases:** child labor, labor unions, slave labor

(1) _____ men and women of the past had few rights and little protection. They (2) _____ many hours for very little money. There were no laws against (3) _____ , so children as young as seven often worked in mines and factories. But then (4) _____ in factories began to join together in (5) _____ _____ . They finally got better pay and working conditions.

These female astronomy students of one hundred years ago were very unusual. Most women in the past did not have an education beyond grade school. Discuss the advantages of higher education today.

c. **verb:** succeed  **adjective:** successful, unsuccessful
   **noun:** success  **adverb:** successfully, unsuccessfully

Students have to work hard to (1) _____ in school. If they complete their courses (2) _____ , they can usually find good jobs. Sometimes college graduates want to start a business of their own, but this is risky. Even though they work hard, the business may be (3) _____ . (4) _____ in business often depends on luck. Nevertheless, education can be the key to a (5) _____ career.

## WRITING EXERCISES

### Past Continuous Tense

The Past Continuous tense describes ongoing, continuous action during a limited time in the past. Actions in the Past Continuous are sometimes interrupted by another action in the Simple Past tense. The Past Continuous tense is formed by *was* or *were* + the *ing* form of the main verb.

> **Last night I *was reading* an interesting book about Harriet Tubman.**
> **While I *was reading* last night, the doorbell rang.**

Study the Past Continuous tense of the verb *move*.

|  | **Singular** | **Plural** |
|---|---|---|
| First person | I was moving | My friend and I were moving<br>We were moving |
| Second person | You were moving | You were moving |
| Third person | Harriet was moving<br>He/She/It was moving | Harriet and her family were moving<br>They were moving |

The negative forms are *was not* (*wasn't*) and *were not* (*weren't*) + the *ing* form of the main verb.

1. **Recognizing Past Continuous Tense.** Listen carefully as your instructor reads the following paragraph. Underline each verb in the Past Continuous tense. (The paragraph is part of a letter written by a grandmother to her

granddaughter about a winter hike through the mountains of northern California.)

The snow was falling steadily. We knew we had to walk quickly to reach the road three miles away. Both of us were carrying heavy packs, which were soon wet with snow. Tree branches were hanging down over our path, and our progress was slow. Because the lake was frozen, we decided to walk on it instead of the narrow path. But as we were moving across the lake, we felt cracks and soft spots in the ice. The ice wasn't completely frozen near the edge. Also, the wind was blowing in our faces, and the snow was blinding us. So we returned to the path. After several hard, weary hours, we finally reached the road.

2. **Sentence Completion.** Read each situation. Then complete the given items, using a verb in the Past Continuous tense. Use as many words as you need to make an interesting sentence.

   a. You were late to your English class yesterday. Tell what was happening when you entered the room.

      (1) The teacher _____.

      (2) Most of the students _____.

      (3) A few of them _____.

      (4) One of the students _____.

   a. Mr. Baker came home at 6:00 P.M. yesterday. Describe what the various members of his family were doing when he came in.

      (1) His wife _____.

      (2) His teenage daughter _____.

      (3) His two-year-old son _____.

      (4) His dog _____.

   c. You were on the bus early this morning. Tell what the other passengers were doing while you were riding.

      (1) The man next to me _____.

      (2) A woman across the aisle _____.

      (3) Two schoolboys _____.

      (4) A young mother _____.

   d. There was a fire in an apartment building in your neighborhood last week. Describe what was going on when you got to the scene.

      (1) Several fire fighters _____.

(2) One fire fighter _____.

(3) A woman on the third floor _____.

(4) The people on the street _____.

## Use of Past Continuous Tense and Simple Past Tense

The Past Continuous tense is frequently used in conjunction with the Simple Past tense. In telling a story about the past, we usually use the Past Continuous tense to set the scene or stop the action to describe what was going on. Often this tense is found at the beginning of the story or as background to a change in action. The Simple Past tense is used for actions that move the story forward. The actions in the Simple Past tense are the focus, or main events, of the story.

1. **Recognizing Past Continuous and Simple Past Tense.** Read the following paragraph about the assassination of Abraham Lincoln, the president who declared the slaves free after the Civil War. Underline the verbs in the Past Continuous tense. Circle the verbs in the Simple Past tense. Then with your class, discuss the use of the two tenses in the story.

   On the night of April 14, 1865, President Lincoln was sitting in Ford's Theater with his wife and some friends. They were watching a play called *Our American Cousin*. Suddenly, a man appeared in the President's box. He held a knife in one hand and a gun in the other. He pointed the gun at Lincoln's head and fired once. Lincoln fell forward. His head was bleeding slightly. Several people rushed to his side and tried to help. They decided to take him to a house across the street. As they were carrying Lincoln out, the Surgeon General arrived and tried to revive the wounded man, but it was no use. Lincoln died early the following morning.

2. **Paragraph Completion.** The following paragraph is about the capture and death of John Wilkes Booth, the man who assassinated President Lincoln. Fill in the blank spaces with the Past Continuous tense for those actions that describe or set the scene. Fill in the blank spaces with the Simple Past tense for those actions that move the story forward. Use the verbs in parentheses.

   On the night of April 25, 1865, John Wilkes Booth (hide) (1) _____ in a barn near Fredericksburg, Virginia. Suddenly, some soldiers (appear)

(2) _____ outside the barn. They (know) (3) _____ that Booth (hide) (4) _____ inside. One of the soldiers (go) (5) _____ just inside the door. Booth (walk) (6) _____ back and forth in the barn. He (shout) (7) _____ about fighting for his freedom. The soldier (wait, negative) (8) _____. He (take) (9) _____ his pistol and (shoot) (10) _____ the assassin. Booth (die) (11) _____ two hours later.

## Complex Sentences with *When* and *While*

A clause is a sentence part that has a subject and a complete main verb. Complex sentences always include an independent clause and a dependent clause. A dependent clause cannot stand by itself as a sentence. Dependent clauses must be joined to independent, or main, clauses.

*When* and *while* are time words that begin dependent clauses. Dependent clauses with *when* and *while* must join independent clauses to form a complete sentence.

A *when* and *while* clause may appear as the first part of a complex sentence or as the last part. When a *when* or *while* clause begins the sentence, it is followed by a comma.

> **When the Civil War was over, all the slaves gained their freedom.**
>     (dependent clause)        (independent clause)
> **I read the chapter about Harriet Tubman while I was riding on the bus.**
>     (independent clause)        (dependent clause)

*When* tells us about two kinds of time periods: (1) a long period of time during which many different actions take place

> **When Harriet Tubman was a slave, she was always dreaming of freedom.**

and (2) a point of time when two actions take place together or immediately following each other (at that time).

> **When Harriet heard she was to be sold, she planned her escape.**

*While* tells us about actions that take place during the same time period. *While* often introduces clauses using continuous tenses.

> **While Harriet was walking to freedom in the North, she thought sadly about her family.**

1. **Identifying Dependent Clauses.** Underline the dependent clause in each of the following sentences.
   a. While I was studying last night, I heard some strange noises.
   b. Immigrants often feel lonely when they first arrive in their new country.
   c. College students may enjoy listening to music while they are studying.
   d. I can't concentrate on my work when the television set is on.
   e. When my daughter first read about Harriet Tubman, she became very interested in her.
   f. Some students were rewriting their papers in class while others were doing grammar exercises.

   Now your instructor will dictate sentences **a** through **f**. Pay special attention to verb tense and punctuation.

2. **Sentence Completion with *When* and *While*.** The two clauses in complex sentences with *when* or *while* must have the same or related verb tenses. Study the following examples of common pairs of verb tenses in *when* and *while* sentences. Then complete the exercise that follows the charts.

**Simple Present**              **Simple Present and Future**

> **When students *enjoy* a certain history book, they often *recommend* it to others.**
> **When we *finish* this chapter, we *will continue* with the next.**

**Present Continuous**          **Simple Present and Present Continuous**

> **My sister *is working* while her children *attend* school.**
> **Some students *are studying* English as a second language while others *are learning* French.**

**Simple Past**                                     **Simple Past**

> When pioneer women *moved* west, they *suffered* many hardships.

**Past Continuous**                        **Simple Past and Past Continuous**

> While Harriet Tubman *was living* in Philadelphia, she *thought* a lot about her family.
> Once, some slave catchers *were watching* Harriet while she *was sitting* in a railway station.

**Simple Past and Past Continuous**        **Could and Would**

> When Harriet *planned* her escape, she *couldn't tell* her family.
> While pioneer families *were moving* west, their children *couldn't attend* school.

Choose the clause that correctly completes the given clause. Write the correct clause in the space provided.

a. Pioneer families suffered many hardships _____

    (1) when they move west.

    (2) when they moved west.

    (3) when they are moving west.

b. _____ when they arrive in their new homeland.

    (1) Immigrants faced difficult problems

    (2) Immigrants were facing difficult problems

    (3) Immigrants face difficult problems

c. I'll apply for a job _____

    (1) while I graduate from this school.

    (2) when I graduate from this school.

    (3) when I will graduate from this school.

d. I like to listen to the radio _____

    (1) while I'm doing my homework.

    (2) when I did my homework.

(3) when I was doing my homework.

e. _____ when I first came to this country.

   (1) I couldn't speak English well
   (2) I can't speak English well
   (3) I won't speak English well

f. _____ the women were working as nurses and laundresses.

   (1) While the men are fighting in the war,
   (2) When the men fight in the war,
   (3) While the men were fighting in the war,

g. When I left my house this morning, _____

   (1) the sun was shining.
   (2) the sun is shining.
   (3) the sun shines.

h. _____ when I got to the station.

   (1) The train was just leaving
   (2) The train is just leaving
   (3) The train will just be leaving

3. **Sentence Combining.** Combine each pair of sentences into one complete sentence with a dependent clause and an independent clause. Use *when* or *while* to combine them. Rewrite your complete new sentences.

---

**I was in New York. I decided to visit some historic places.**

*When I was in New York, I decided to visit some historic places.*

**We were waiting for the tour bus. We read our guidebook.**

*While we were waiting for the tour bus, we read our guidebook.*

---

   a. We were in Washington, D.C. We went to the Lincoln exhibits at Ford's Theater.

b. We got there. The place wasn't open yet.

c. We were waiting for it to open. We read about the exhibits in our guidebook.

d. We were reading. Several other people arrived.

e. The doors finally opened. We bought tickets and walked to the first exhibit.

f. We were looking at photographs of Lincoln. A guide came in and gave us some information about Lincoln's life.

g. It is always interesting to visit historic places. You travel to different areas of the country.

4. **Sentence Composing.** Compose a complete sentence using the given words. Make sure that the verbs you use are correctly related to the verbs given.

   a. When the weather gets warmer, _____.

   b. Someone _____ while I was swimming at the beach last week.

   c. When I don't understand a particular word in the reading passage, _____ _____.

   d. While I was doing my homework, _____.

   e. I couldn't walk or talk when _____.

   f. _____ everyone was sleeping.

   g. My friend wouldn't give me the answers when _____ _____ .

   h. Last night, while I was reading, _____.

   i. Many students _____ while the instructor _____.

5. **Punctuation of Complex Sentences.** Some of the following sentences are correctly punctuated. In others there are mistakes. Write a *C* in the blank space if the sentence is *correct*. If it is not correct, make whatever punctuation and capitalization changes are necessary.

   a. Women's lives became easier, when electricity became common. _____

   b. Harriet Tubman risked her life for others when she led slaves to freedom. _____

c. When Franklin Roosevelt was president of the United States. His wife Eleanor was a great help to him. _____

d. Eleanor Roosevelt was very shy when, she was a child. _____

e. When Harriet Beecher Stowe wrote *Uncle Tom's Cabin*. She sent a copy to Abraham Lincoln. _____

f. When European explorers came to America, Native American women sometimes acted as their guides. _____

g. Women did not have the right to vote. When the United States was a young country. _____

h. When immigrant women worked in the factories, they earned very low wages. _____

## Comparison of Adjectives

Read the following paragraph carefully. Pay special attention to the italicized adjectives.

Life was much *harder* for American women in 1880 than it is now. In the *earlier* period, there were *fewer* of the household appliances such as vacuum cleaners and refrigerators that make life *easier* today. The *newer, richer* houses of the 1880s had indoor plumbing, but the *older, poorer* homes did not. Some things were *cheaper* 100 years ago, but men earned much *lower* salaries, and married women usually did not go out to work to earn extra money. In the 1880s, housewives were usually *busier* than they are today because families were *larger*. Today modern women have *fewer* children and *better* medical care than women had 100 years ago. Modern women are *healthier* than their great-grandmothers were, and modern women live *longer* lives. Modern women have *wider* opportunities for education and careers than their great-grandmothers had. Do you think modern women are *happier* than women were 100 years ago?

The italicized adjectives in the paragraph are in the comparative form. The comparative form is used when *two* things are being compared. Most adjectives in English form the comparative as follows.

*One-Syllable Adjectives.* Adjectives of one syllable add *er* or *r* to the simple form: *old ⟶ older; large ⟶ larger.*

*Two-Syllable Adjectives Ending in* y. Two-syllable adjectives that end in *y* drop the *y* and add *ier: easy ⟶ easier; busy ⟶ busier.*

*Most Other Two-Syllable and Three-Syllable Adjectives.* Two-syllable adjectives that do not end in *y* (or in *ow* or *er*) and three-syllable adjectives keep their simple form, but take the comparative word *more* in front of them: *modern ⟶ more modern: fragile ⟶ more fragile.*

1. **Answering Information Questions.** Write the answers to the following questions in complete sentences, using information from the paragraph. Each sentence will contain an adjective in the comparative form.

    a. Was life easier or harder for women 100 years ago?
    b. Were there more or fewer household appliances 100 years ago?
    c. Which kinds of houses had indoor plumbing 100 years ago?
    d. Did men earn higher or lower wages 100 years ago than they do today?
    e. Why were women of the 1880s busier than modern women are?
    f. Why are modern women healthier than women were in the 1880s?

2. **List Completion.** Complete the following list of adjectives in their simple and comparative forms.

    | Simple | Comparative |
    |---|---|
    | early | earlier |
    | long | _____ |
    | happy | _____ |
    | large | _____ |
    | _____ | healthier |
    | expensive | _____ |
    | _____ | more popular |
    | ambitious | _____ |
    | fragile | _____ |
    | _____ | stranger |
    | busy | _____ |
    | much | _____ |
    | _____ | fewer |

3. **Sentence Composing**

    a. Look at the following pairs of subjects. Write sentences comparing the two subjects and using adjectives in the comparative form. Use the adjec-

Women of the past had harder lives than women do today, but the old proverb may still be true: "Men may work from sun to sun, but women's work is never done."

tives from Exercise 2 or the additional adjectives that follow the subjects. Remember to use the word *than*.

> My uncle is *more emotional* than my father.
> Housewives in the past were *busier* than housewives today.

### Subjects

(1) my sister/I
(2) ancient history/modern history
(3) my native country/the United States
(4) glass/wood
(5) women/men
(6) wool/cotton
(7) English/my native language
(8) gold/silver
(9) a large city/a small town
(10) life in the past/life today

### Adjectives

| | | | | |
|---|---|---|---|---|
| difficult | thick | emotional | beautiful | independent |
| lazy | shiny | expensive | quiet | boring |
| warm | quiet | fragile | hard | interesting |
| easy | crowded | cheap | big | careless |

b. Look at the list of different types of work. Compare these jobs by using the following adjectives in their comparative forms. Follow the sentence pattern in the example.

> Construction work is more dangerous than dentistry.

### Types of Work

| | | |
|---|---|---|
| construction work | taxi driving | dentistry |
| police work | engineering | airplane piloting |
| truck driving | newspaper reporting | athletic coaching |
| accounting | television broadcasting | politics |

### Adjectives

| | | | |
|---|---|---|---|
| boring | interesting | well-paid | exciting |
| active | hard | enjoyable | noisy |
| dangerous | easy | useful | lonely |
| creative | important | dull | difficult |

## Superlative Form of Adjectives

The superlative form of adjectives is used when three or more things are being compared. The patterns for the superlative are the same as for the comparative forms of adjectives, but

*er* is replaced by *est*: older ⟶ oldest; poorer ⟶ poorest
*ier* is replaced by *iest*: busier ⟶ busiest; healthier ⟶ healthiest.
*more* is replaced by *most*: more modern ⟶ most modern; more expensive ⟶ most expensive.

1. **List Completion.** Complete the following list of adjectives in the superlative form. Use *the* before each one.

| Simple | Superlative |
|---|---|
| bright | _____ |
| practical | _____ |
| brave | _____ |
| crowded | _____ |

dry                    _____
comfortable            _____
difficult              _____
serious                _____
cold                   _____
creative               _____
quiet                  _____
great                  _____
talkative              _____
good                   _____

2. **Sentence Building.** On a separate sheet of paper, write a complete sentence using the words in each set. Add an appropriate adjective in the superlative from the list in Exercise 1. Use a different adjective in each sentence. The last part of each sentence will have a prepositional phrase with *in* or *of*.

> **Mary       person       all my friends**
> *Mary is the quietest person of all my friends.*
> **poverty    one of    problems    world**
> *Poverty is one of the most serious problems in the world.*

a. sun          object          sky
b. pollution    one of          problems         our cities
c. Carlos       student         my English class
d. math         subject         all my courses
e. library      place           my neighborhood
f. the Statue of Liberty    one of    monuments    world
g. sofa         piece of furniture    my apartment
h. New York     city            the United States
i. the North and South Poles    areas    world
j. vacuum cleaner    appliance    my house
k. Sahara Desert     one of       places      world

l. Pablo Picasso    probably    artist    twentieth century
m. Harriet Tubman    one of    and    women    American history
   (write two adjectives)

3. **Paragraph Completion.** Read this paragraph over once. Then fill in the blank spaces by using the directions in the Key following the paragraph. The first one is done for you.

Emily Dickinson (1830–1886) is one of America's (1) *most famous* poets. As a child she was (2) _____ than most of her friends, but not very different from them. In school she was (3) _____ in writing, but she also studied (4) _____ subjects such as chemistry and physiology. When she was about twenty-five, she had an (5) _____ love affair. After this she became (6) _____ and (7) _____ to people outside her own family than she had been before. It was at this time that Dickinson wrote some of her (8) _____ poetry. Although the language of her poetry appears (9) _____, her thoughts are (10) _____ to understand than they appear at first. Emily Dickinson is still one of America's (11) _____ and (12) _____ poets 100 years after her death.

**Key**

(1) superlative form of *famous*
(2) comparative form of *bright*
(3) superlative form of *interested*
(4) comparative form of *unusual*
(5) simple form of adjective meaning "not happy"
(6) comparative form of *shy*
(7) comparative form of *unfriendly*
(8) superlative form of *beautiful*
(9) simple form of *simpler*
(10) comparative form of *difficult*
(11) superlative form of *respected*
(12) superlative form of *popular*

## THE COMPOSING PROCESS

**1. Developing a Paragraph of Contrast.**

   a. From the numbered sets following the paragraph, choose the appropriate signal for the same numbered blank space in the paragraph.

   Emily Dickinson and Fay Chiang are different kinds of American poets. Dickinson lived (1) _____ wrote 100 years ago. (2) _____ Fay Chiang is a modern poet, alive and writing today. Dickinson was a shy, solitary person. (3) _____ she was writing, she almost never left her house. Fay Chiang, (4) _____ is an activist who works in an Asian-American artists' community in New York's Chinatown. Chiang (5) _____ works with writers of other minority groups. (6) _____ Dickinson and Chiang are very different kinds of American women, they both express similarly powerful emotions through their poems.

   (1) but/and/then
   (2) Also/In contrast,/While
   (3) Leave blank/But/While
   (4) and/however,/in addition,
   (5) leave blank/on the other hand/also
   (6) When/Although/And

   b. Study the preceding paragraph carefully. Label all the sentences that tell about the *two* poets A–B. Label the sentences only about Emily Dickinson A. Label the sentences only about Fay Chiang B. Study how the paragraph develops the contrast between the two women by giving us details about one, then about the other, in alternating sentences.

   c. Some paragraphs that contrast two subjects are developed in a different way. They do not give details about one thing or person and then another in alternating sentences. Some paragraphs are developed in a series of sentences about one complete subject and then in a series of sentences about the contrasting subject. This kind of paragraph will have two distinct parts. It is often called the block form.

   Read the following paragraph. Then answer the questions that follow it.

   (1) In modern society, women are busy with their responsibilities whether they are full-time homemakers or they work outside the home. (2) Full-time homemakers don't have paying jobs, but they work long

hours. (3) Their primary job is taking care of their children, especially their young ones. (4) These mothers spend a good deal of their time cooking, cleaning, shopping, and doing laundry for their families. (5) Even when their children are old enough to go to school, these mothers remain at home. (6) They feel it is important to be there when their children come home from school because it creates a safe environment. (7) In contrast to these homemakers, some mothers work in offices or factories or have careers in business or the professions. (8) In addition to their jobs, these women must arrange for the care of their children. (9) They may have to hire baby-sitters or place their children in day-care centers. (10) Unlike homemakers, they often have to get someone to clean the house because they don't have the time to do it themselves, or they are too tired. (11) Working mothers always have a lot of things to think about while on the job. (12) For example, they may worry about a child getting sick while they are at work. (13) Although it is a difficult situation, many working mothers enjoy the challenge of having a job and a family.

Answer the questions in short note form.

(1) Which sentence states the main idea of the paragraph? _____

(2) What two groups of people are being compared? _____
and _____

(3) Which sentences describe the first subject? _____

(4) Which sentence begins the description of the second group? _____

(5) What expression is used to signal the contrasting group? _____
_____

(6) Which sentences describe the contrasting group? _____

2. **Composing a Paragraph of Contrast.** As a class, brainstorm different types of work or occupations with which you are familiar. Your instructor will list all of these on the board. Combine related items and eliminate repetitions.

Choose two occupations about which you want to write. (You may want to break one occupation listed into two different categories, such as dividing *police officer* into *city police officer* and *private security guard*.)

Your purpose will be to compose a paragraph that contrasts the two occupations you have chosen. Some bases for contrast may be the following: physical strength required, salary, education required, potential danger, contact with the public.

Begin your paragraph with a main idea statement that clearly identifies your topic and states an important overall difference between the two occupations. Here are some examples:

Being a secretary is a more interesting job for most women than being a nurse (or the reverse).

Practical nurses and registered nurses have different requirements and responsibilities.

Doctors and nurses both work in hospitals, but people treat them very differently.

3. **Sentence Combining to Form a Paragraph.** The following paragraph about a student's immigrant family has been broken up into short, simple sentences. On a separate sheet of paper, combine the sentences into longer, more interesting statements. Use connectors, signal words, and pronouns where necessary. Leave out unnecessary words, but do not omit any of the important ideas or details. Rewrite your complete new paragraph.

   a. My grandmother was short.
   b. My grandmother was fragile-looking.
   c. My grandmother was proud of her appearance.
   d. My grandmother was a seamstress.
   e. My grandmother sewed dresses.
   f. The dresses were for other people.
   g. My grandmother had a sewing machine.
   h. The sewing machine was in a house.
   i. The house belonged to us.
   j. My grandmother was always at the sewing machine.
   k. That was every day.
   l. My grandmother got a lot of work.
   m. My grandmother sewed very fast.
   n. My grandmother sewed very neatly.
   o. My grandmother's skills were excellent.
   p. My grandmother took care of the housework.
   q. My grandmother took care of me all day.
   r. That was when I was small.
   s. Both my parents worked.
   t. My grandmother played games with me.
   u. The games were interesting.
   v. That was after the housework was finished.
   w. My grandmother made dolls for me.
   x. The dolls were from pieces of material.
   y. I will always have memories.

z. The memories are beautiful.
aa. The memories are of my grandmother.

4. **Paragraph Topics**

   a. Write a paragraph in which you contrast two different people whom you know well. Try to use adjectives in the comparative form about your two subjects. Begin with a main idea sentence that identifies your subjects.

   b. Write a paragraph in which you compare or contrast your native city and the city in which you are now living. Choose such points to talk about as the cleanliness; degree of noise, traffic, or crowdedness; number of parks or recreational areas; or safety. Begin with a main idea statement that introduces the topic and identifies the two cities you will be describing.

## ADDITIONAL READING

### Mary Wilkins Freeman: The Revolt of Mother

The American writer Mary Wilkins Freeman was born in Massachusetts in 1852 and died in New Jersey in 1930. Her best short stories are concerned with New England village life. Her characters show a strong sense of pride even though they live a hard life with few material comforts. The following story is an adaptation of Mrs. Freeman's tale of a New England farm family in the late 1800s. It tells how a difficult problem was solved thanks to the determination of the mother.

"Father!"

"What is it?"

"What are those men digging in the field for?"

"I wish you'd go into the house, Mother, and attend to your own affairs," the man answered as he saddled his horse.

"I'm not going in till you tell me," said she. She stood waiting in front of the barn door.

The man glanced at his wife. She looked as immovable to him as one of the rocks in his field. "They're digging a cellar, if you've got to know."

"A cellar for what?"

"A barn."

"A barn? You're going to build another barn where we were going to have a house?"

The man said nothing. He hitched the horse to a wagon and rode off. The woman crossed the yard and entered the house, a tiny shelter compared with the great barn and other buildings on the property.

Nanny Penn greeted her mother, "What are they digging for, Mother? Did Father tell you?"

"They're digging a cellar for a new barn."

"Oh, Mother, another barn?"

"That's what he says."

Sammy, the young son of the family, stood in the kitchen, seeming not to pay attention to the conversation.

"Sammy, did you know Father was going to build a new barn?" his sister asked.

Sammy hesitated and then said, "Yes, I suppose I did."

"How long have you known it?" asked his mother.

"About three months, I guess. Didn't think it would do any good to tell you," replied the boy.

Mrs. Penn looked sternly at her son and asked, "Is father going to buy more cows?"

"I suppose he is. Four, I guess." The boy put on his cap, took an old arithmetic book from a shelf and left for school.

While Mrs. Penn washed the dishes, Nanny wiped. "Mother," she said, "Don't you think it's too bad Father's going to build that new barn, much as we need a decent house to live in?"

Her mother scrubbed a dish fiercely. "You haven't found out we're women-folks, Nanny," said she. "One of these days, you'll find out how men think women-folks are supposed to be. Then you'll know that we know only what men-folks think we do. Men-folks think we should consider them in with Providence, and not complain of what they do any more than we should complain about the weather."

"I don't think George is anything like that," Nanny replied. Her face, pretty as a flower, turned red, as if she were going to cry.

"Wait till you marry him. I guess George is no better than other men. You shouldn't judge your father, though. He can't help it, because he doesn't look at things just the way we do. And we've been pretty comfortable here. Father keeps the house in good repair."

"I wish we had a parlor," said Nanny.

"George can come here to see you in this nice clean kitchen. You shouldn't complain. You have a good father and a good home."

"I'm not complaining," said Nanny taking up her sewing. She was to be married in the fall and was working on her wedding dress. She sewed industriously while her mother did the housework.

Mrs. Penn was an expert housekeeper. The house, small as a box, was never dusty. She cooked and baked and no dirt ever showed when she finished. Today she was going to bake mince pies, which her husband liked better than any other kind. While she worked, she could see the sight that irritated her deeply—the digging of the cellar of the new barn. Forty years ago her husband had promised her their new house would stand in that place. She continued to roll out the pie crust. However deep her resentment she held against her husband, she would never fail in her untiring attention to him.

The pies were done for lunch. Everyone ate quickly, without much conversation. Sammy went back to school, and Nanny went to the store to buy some more thread for her wedding dress. Mr. Penn went into the yard to unload some wood from the wagon.

"Father, I want to see you just a minute," Mrs. Penn called from the door.

"I've got to unload this wood now, Mother."

"Father, come here." Mrs. Penn stood in the doorway like a queen; she held her head as if it bore a crown. Her husband went in.

"I want to know what you're building that new barn for. It can't be you think you need another barn?" Mrs. Penn said.

"I don't have anything to say about it, Mother, and I'm not going to say anything."

"Now Father, look here. I'm going to talk real plain to you. I never have since we were married, but I'm going to now." Mrs. Penn stood before her husband and one by one she spoke about all the things that were wrong with the house they lived in: no carpet on the floor, wallpaper peeling and dirty; the kitchen, the only room in which to sit, work, and eat, and where Nanny's wedding would take place. She showed him the tiny room where they slept, only large enough for a bed and a dresser. She pointed upstairs, where the children slept in two unfinished rooms, not as good a place as the horse's stall.

Mrs. Penn continued, "Now Father, forty years ago you promised me a new house over there in the field. You've been making more money, and I've been saving it for you. You've built sheds and cow-houses and one barn and now another. You're keeping your animals better than your own flesh and blood. I want to know if you think it's right."

"I have nothing to say. I've got to unload that wood. I can't stand here talking all day." Mr. Penn went out.

With red eyes, Mrs. Penn took a roll of cloth, spread it out on the kitchen table and started to cut out some shirts for her husband.

Nanny came back with her thread and sat down to do her needlework. Suddenly she looked up, her face and neck all red. "Mother," she said, "I've been thinking—I don't see how we're going to have any wedding in this room."

"Maybe we can have some new paper on the walls; I can put it on."

"We might have the wedding in the new barn," said Nanny with gentle irritation. "Why Mother, what makes you look so?"

Mrs. Penn was staring at Nanny with a curious expression. She turned again to her work. "Nothing," she said.

All through the spring months she heard nothing but the noise of saws and hammers. The new barn grew fast. It was a fine building for this little village. Men came on Sundays to admire it. Mrs. Penn did not speak of it. Mr. Penn did not mention it to her, but he seemed hurt by her silence.

"It's a strange thing how Mother feels about the new barn," he said to Sammy one day. Sammy didn't reply.

The barn was all ready for use by the third week in July. Just then Mr. Penn decided to go off to Vermont to buy a new horse. He would be gone for four days. "When the new cows come, Sammy can drive them into the new barn," he told his wife. "I'll be back by Saturday."

Mrs. Penn prepared clean clothes for her husband, a package of pie and cheese, and saw him off. "Do be careful, Father," she said. She had a strange expression in her eyes.

As soon as he was out of sight, Mrs. Penn began to pack the dishes into a basket. Her children watched. "What are you going to do, Mother?" inquired Nanny in a timid voice.

"You'll see what I'm going to do," replied Mrs. Penn.

During the next few hours a feat was performed by this simple New England mother, equal to the deed of a brave soldier. With the help of her children, she moved all their little household goods into the new barn. By late afternoon, the little house was completely empty. The new barn, designed for the comfort of animals, was more than comfortable for humans. Mrs. Penn saw its possibilities: the stalls for the cows would be better bedrooms than those in the house; the harness room would make a kitchen of her dreams; the great middle space would make a parlor fit for a palace. Upstairs there was as much room as down. With partitions and windows, what a house would there be!

Before the next morning, the news of the move spread in the village. Men and women talked about Mrs. Penn. Some thought she was insane; some thought she had a lawless spirit.

Friday the minister went to see her. "There's no use talking, Mr. Hersey," she said. "I believe I'm doing what's right, just as I think it was right for our forefathers to come over from the old country because they didn't have what belonged to them. I've got my own mind and my own feet, and I'm going to think my own thoughts and go my own way." The minister went away.

The new cows arrived, and Sammy led them into the old barn.

On Saturday Mrs. Penn prepared a special dinner for Mr. Penn's return. The children waited nervously, but with a sense of excitement.

"There he is," Sammy announced looking out of the barn window.

Mr. Penn was leading his new horse into the yard. When he went to the house door, he found it locked. In a dazed fashion, he crossed the yard to the new barn. The doors rolled back, and he saw his family.

Mr. Penn stared at the group. "What on earth are you all down here for?" he said. "What's the matter over at the house?"

"We've come to live here, Father," Sammy said bravely.

Mr. Penn sniffed the air. "What is it? Smells like cooking. What on earth does this mean, Mother?"

"Come in here, Father," said Mrs. Penn. She led the way into the kitchen area. "Now Father, you needn't be scared. I'm not crazy. There isn't anything to be upset over. But we've come here to live, and we're going to live here. We've got just as good a right here as new horses and cows. The house wasn't fit to live in any longer. I've done my duty by you for forty years, and I'm going to do it now; but I'm going to live here. You've got to put in some windows and partitions; and you'll have to buy some furniture."

"Why Mother!" the man gasped.

"You'd better get washed, and then we'll have supper."

Farm families like that in "The Revolt of Mother" had a strong sense of pride even though they lived hard lives with little material comfort.

>All through the meal, Mr. Penn stopped eating at intervals and stared at his wife, but he ate well. After supper he went out and sat on a step. When the supper dishes were cleared away, Mrs. Penn went out to him. The night was peaceful; the air was cool and calm and sweet.
>
>Mrs. Penn touched her husband on his thin shoulder. "Father!"
>
>His shoulders shook. He was weeping.
>
>"Don't do so, Father" she said.
>
>"I'll put up the partitions, and everything you want, Mother."
>
>Mrs. Penn put her apron up to her face; she was overcome by her own victory.
>
>Mr. Penn was like a fortress whose walls came down the moment the right tools were used. "Why, Mother," he said. "I had no idea you had your heart so set on it, as all this comes to."

## DISCUSSION QUESTIONS

1. In a family, should there be one authority figure, or should important decisions be made cooperatively? Is an obedient wife better for a man than one who acts or thinks independently? What type of household is best for children? Should children share in decision making?

2. People everywhere are expected to behave according to the rules of their society. If a person behaves somewhat differently (not including criminal behavior), neighbors may gossip and form negative opinions about the person. What kinds of behavior can cause bad opinions? Are these opinions sometimes mistaken? Are you concerned about other people's opinion of you?

3. Some people say that men and women are different in how they think about things, large and small. Do you agree? Are there differences in the way men and women think about marriage, children, jobs, housing, or social life with friends or relatives? Explain.

## READING COMPREHENSION

1. **Understanding the Text.** Follow the directions for each item.

    a. If the statement is *true*, write *T*. If the statement is *false*, write *F*. If the story does not give information about the sentence, write *N.I.* (*no information*). Underline the part of the passage where you find your true or false answers.

    (1) This story takes place in the western part of the United States. _____

    (2) Mr. Penn's house is small and uncomfortable. _____

    (3) Mrs. Penn keeps her house in perfect order. _____

    (4) Mr. and Mrs. Penn are forty-years-old. _____

    (5) Sammy Penn is a schoolboy. _____

    (6) Nanny sews dresses for a living. _____

    (7) Nanny will live with her parents after her marriage. _____

    (8) Mr. Penn goes to Vermont to buy some cows. _____

    (9) Eventually the old house will be torn down. _____

    b. Circle the letter of the correct answer.

    (1) Mr. Penn wants a new barn because

    (a) he made a promise to his wife.
    (b) he is going to add more animals to his farm.
    (c) the old barn is in a bad state of repair.

    (2) Mrs. Penn resents her husband because

    (a) he doesn't pay attention to the real needs of his family.
    (b) he doesn't earn enough money to build a new house.
    (c) he doesn't help her with the housework.

(3) Nanny is unhappy about her situation because

   (a) she has to work too hard in the house.
   (b) her wedding will have to take place in the kitchen.
   (c) she can't entertain her girlfriends properly.

(4) Mrs. Penn tries to

   (a) turn Nanny against her father.
   (b) influence Nanny against getting married.
   (c) explain to Nanny the good things about her father.

(5) When Mrs. Penn says, ". . . we know only what men-folks think we know," she means that

   (a) men are naturally superior to women in intelligence.
   (b) men refuse to see women as having independent minds.
   (c) men like women to think and act independently.

(6) When Mrs. Penn talks about the need for a new house, Mr. Penn

   (a) shows no understanding of the problem.
   (b) says he will try to solve the problem.
   (c) walks out before she finishes talking.

(7) For forty years, Mrs. Penn

   (a) has done little to care for the needs of her husband.
   (b) has been dissatisfied as a housekeeper and mother.
   (c) has given in completely to her husband's wishes.

(8) While Mr. Penn is away, Mother "revolts." This means that

   (a) Mrs. Penn is finally able to control her children.
   (b) Mrs. Penn fixes up the house with new wallpaper and new carpets.
   (c) Mrs. Penn changes her life by taking matters in her own hands.

(9) After the move into the barn, Mrs. Penn plans

   (a) to make it into a beautiful, comfortable home.
   (b) to share it with the farm animals.
   (c) to live there until a new house is built.

(10) The village people talk about Mrs. Penn disapprovingly because

   (a) she has gone against her husband's wishes.
   (b) she wants a better house than the one she has.
   (c) she doesn't take good care of the farm while Mr. Penn is away.

(11) At the end of the story, Mr. Penn weeps because

　(a) his family moved without telling him.

　(b) he is unhappy about living in a barn.

　(c) he finally understands his wife's needs and feelings.

(12) The author of this story is trying to show us that in her time and place

　(a) women were usually unreasonable in their demands.

　(b) it was difficult for a woman to revolt against her husband's unreasonable actions.

　(c) men expected women to be equal partners with them in deciding important matters.

2. **Answering Information Questions.** Write the answers to the following questions in complete sentences.

　a. How many barns were on the property at the beginning of the story?
　b. What kind of house did the Penn family live in?
　c. Where was Nanny's wedding supposed to take place?
　d. Why did Mr. Penn go to Vermont?
　e. What did Mrs. Penn do as soon as her husband left?
　f. Who came to visit Mrs. Penn while Mr. Penn was away?
　g. How long was Mr. Penn gone from the house?
　h. How did Mr. Penn feel when he found his house door locked?
　i. Did Mr. Penn accept or reject the new living arrangements?

3. **The Reading Process: Figures of Speech.** Authors sometimes use figures of speech to express thoughts in a vivid way to the reader. A figure of speech is often a phrase comparing one person or thing to another person or thing. These phrases give the reader a better picture of the subject in question. Recognizing and understanding these expressions will add to your enjoyment of reading. Read the following sentences paying particular attention to the italicized words. Then follow the directions for each item.

　a. Nanny's *face* was *like a flower.*
　Write a sentence in which you use adjectives to describe a face like a flower.

　---

　b. *Mrs. Penn stood* in the doorway *like a queen with a crown on her head.*
　Write a sentence in which you use adjectives to describe just how Mrs. Penn stood.

　---

c. Mrs. Penn tells Nanny that *women shouldn't complain about men just as they shouldn't complain about the weather.*
Write a sentence that explains why men and the weather are similar.

_____

d. The *house* was *like a box.*
Write a sentence in which you explain the conditions of such a house.

_____

e. By moving her household goods into the barn, *Mrs. Penn performed a feat equal to the deed of a brave soldier.*
Write a sentence in which you explain why Mrs. Penn's action and a soldier's action are similar.

_____

_____

f. The middle space of the new barn would make *a parlor fit for a palace.*
Write a sentence in which you describe what this parlor will look like when it is finished.

_____

_____

g. At the end of the story the author writes: *Mr. Penn* was *like a fortress* whose *walls came down* the moment *the right tools were used.*
Write a sentence in which you explain how Mr. Penn is like a fortress. Then write a sentence explaining the tools that Mrs. Penn used to break down Mr. Penn's resistance.

_____

_____

## VOCABULARY

1. **Expanding Vocabulary.** Choose the item that is a synonym for the italicized word in each sentence.

   a. Sammy *hesitated* before he answered the question.

      **(1)** waited  **(2)** laughed  **(3)** coughed

   b. Mrs. Penn scrubbed the dish *fiercely.*

      **(1)** gently  **(2)** with intensity  **(3)** in a slow manner

c. The sight of the men digging in the field *irritated* her.
      **(1)** greatly annoyed   **(2)** calmed   **(3)** satisfied
   d. She felt deep *resentment* toward her husband, but never failed in her attention to him.
      **(1)** emotion   **(2)** displeasure   **(3)** admiration
   e. Nanny asked in a *timid* voice, "What are you going to do, Mother?"
      **(1)** forceful   **(2)** smooth   **(3)** fearful
   f. This simple New England mother performed a *feat* by moving her family into the barn.
      **(1)** extraordinary act   **(2)** ceremony   **(3)** easy job
   g. When Mr. Penn found the house door locked, he walked across the yard in a *dazed* fashion.
      **(1)** confused   **(2)** weary   **(3)** brave
   h. All through the meal, Mr. Penn stopped eating at *intervals* and stared at his wife.
      **(1)** immediately   **(2)** altogether   **(3)** from time to time
   i. Mr. Penn said he would put up *partitions* in the barn.
      **(1)** windows   **(2)** room dividers   **(3)** kitchen cabinets

2. **Using Vocabulary.** Answer the following questions in a complete sentence. Use the word in parentheses in your answer.
   a. How would you describe a student who is afraid to ask a question? (timid)

   b. What would you use to divide a large, open space in an office? (partitions)

   c. If you lie in the sun too long, how might you feel? (dazed)

   d. How would a mother bear look at you if you approached her cubs? (fiercely)

   e. How would you feel toward your friend if he or she talked about you behind your back? (resentment)

**270** Unit III Our Social World

    **f.** What would you do before you crossed a busy street against the light? (hesitate)

_____

    **g.** What could harsh chemicals do to a person's skin? (irritate)

_____

    **h.** A fire fighter goes into a burning building and saves five lives. How would you describe this courageous act? (feat)

_____

**3. Word Families: Recognizing Word Stems.** Many of our words are formed from a common root or stem. These stems are usually formed from Greek or Latin words. We add prefixes and suffixes to the stem and change the form, but the meanings of all the words in a word family will have some relationship to each other. Recognizing the root or stem of a word will help you to increase your vocabulary. Study the following list.

| Stem | Meaning | Example |
|---|---|---|
| duc | lead | e*duc*ate, con*duc*tor, intro*duce* |
| clud, clus | close, shut | se*clude*, in*clude*, con*clus*ion |
| spect | look, watch | re*spect*, *spect*ator, in*spect*ion |
| scrib, script | write | de*scrib*e, pre*script*ion |
| nat | born, birth | pre*nat*al, *nat*ural, *nat*ive |
| vis | see | *vis*ion, super*vis*or, in*vis*ible |
| mot | move | *mot*or, pro*mot*ion |
| dict | say, tell | pre*dict*, contra*dict*, *dict*ation |
| fin | end, complete | in*fin*ite, *fin*al, *fin*ish |
| part | separate, divide | de*part*, *part*ition, *part*icular |
| press | put, push | de*press*, *press*ure, ex*press*ion |

*Choosing Definitions.* Fill in the blank space with a word from the Example column that would make the sentence correct. The italicized words will help you make the correct choice.

    **a.** If you can't *see* without glasses, you have poor _____ .

    **b.** The _____ of an orchestra is the one who *leads* all the musicians together as a group.

    **c.** A _____ over*sees* the work of many people.

**d.** When a person *moves* up to a better job, we say that he or she receives a _____ .

**e.** To *say* the opposite of something that was stated before is to _____ the original statement.

**f.** When a doctor *writes* down symbols for your medicine, he or she is giving you a _____ .

**g.** Some scientists say that the universe is *without end*; it is _____ in space and time.

**h.** When just a little water *pushes* through a faucet, we say that the _____ is low.

**i.** At the *close* of a story, we find out the author's _____ .

**j.** _____ care is important if babies are to be *born* healthy.

**k.** When you *look* into something closely, you make an _____ of it.

**l.** In a college catalog, there is usually a *separate* list for each course of study; students can then choose the _____ program they prefer.

## PARAGRAPH TOPICS

1. A nice, comfortable home can make a person feel good. Think of the different types of housing in addition to those listed:

   single-family house in the suburbs    _____

   high-rise apartment in the city       _____

   seaside cottage                       _____

   Choose the type of house that interests you. It may be a place you have now or a typical house in your native country. It may belong to a friend or relative, or it may be your dream house of the future.

   Now list all the features of that house that are important to you. Group items that may be related. Think about which items you want to describe in a paragraph. You may want to include all the features in your list, or you may choose only one or two because of their primary importance to you. Write your paragraph describing this place, its location, and its special features. Tell why these features are important or necessary in your particular case. Begin with a main idea sentence that expresses your viewpoint about your subject.

2. On a farm, there are wide open spaces for children to play in, explore, and exercise their bodies as well as their minds. Where in the city can young children do these things? What recreational activities do you or would you recommend for children you know? Do you ever accompany a child to parks, gyms, museums, theaters, ball games, circuses and festivals, or take him or her fishing or to the beach? Write a paragraph describing some exciting activities for the young in your area or nearby. Include information about yourself if you participate in these activities.

# CHAPTER EIGHT

# WORKING RELATIONSHIPS: OLD AND NEW

## PREREADING

**Class Discussion.** The following poem was written in China over a thousand years ago by a young groom to his bride.

> A feast being spread in spring-time,
> With a cup of new wine and a joyous song.
> I repeat my salutation and offer my three wishes:
> First, may you have a long life;
> Second, may I have good health;
> Third, may we live as the swallows on the beam,
> Happily together all the year round.

What might the bride's wishes be? What would living happily together mean to you in today's world? Do you think that your own ideas of happiness might be different from those of the Chinese poet? If a couple you know are getting married, what kind of message would you compose for them?

> *Free Write.* What type of man or woman do you consider to be the ideal mate? What qualities do you want this person to have? Have you found your ideal mate? Explain.

**Vocabulary in Context.** The vocabulary in this exercise will appear in the reading passage. Circle or underline the word(s) in the second sentence of each pair that is(are) a synonym for the italicized word in the first sentence. The first one is done for you.

1. In the poetry of the Middle Ages, a popular subject was the *romantic love* between a married woman and a young knight. The deep feelings between these two people did not involve a sexual relationship.

2. You may *conquer* most of your difficulties with English composition by continual practice. You can control your writing problems, for example, by carefully editing your papers.

3. In a court of law, judges are not supposed to let *personal* feelings influence their judgment. The evidence is the most important thing, not the judges' individual emotions.

4. The bank will make an *arrangement* for you to pay your telephone bill by mail. This system can save you time.

5. We all need to *strengthen* our muscles and bones. If you exercise three or four times a week, you will increase the power of those body elements.

6. If you live in a small town, your *reputation* is very important. People know each other well, and if you don't have a good name in the community, you will find it hard to do business or socialize with others.

7. There is no *benefit* to staying up all night to study for an exam. What advantage do you gain by coming to class so tired you can't even remember all you have studied?

8. In some societies, *loyalty* among family members is the most important feeling. A person must show faithfulness to his or her relatives even if he or she does not like them as individuals.

9. It is difficult to teach children *cooperation*. When children are used to doing something in their own way, they may feel unhappy about working with others and giving in on some points.

10. When you practice a second language, you will find that the ability to speak fluently comes *gradually*. You won't be able to pronounce some words correctly at first; it will be a step-by-step process as you master one sound after another.

11. Certain movies are not *suitable* for children because they contain too much violence. Should newspaper ads include information on the appropriate films for various age groups?

# READING

## Love and Marriage: Different Cultures—Different Ideals

[1] If you listen to American music, watch American television or movies, or read American magazines, you will probably agree that the most popular subject of these forms of entertainment is love. Romantic love always finds an audience in the United States. Falling in love, solving the problems of love, and achieving the happy ending—the big wedding—are subjects of interest to the adult as well as the teenage public. Millions of Americans celebrate Valentine's Day with special cards and gifts that announce their love to their mates, their friends, their co-workers, and their families. Popular songs tell us that "all the world loves a lover." A popular saying is "Love conquers all." Numerous columns in magazines and newspapers offer advice to the lovelorn, those with difficulties of the heart. To most Americans, romantic love is central to a happy life.

[2] Not only do Americans believe in romantic love, but they also believe that it is the best basis for marriage. Despite the high divorce rate in the United States, young men and women continue to marry on the basis of romantic love. Americans consider marriage a private arrangement between the two people involved. Young Americans feel free to choose their own marriage partners from

After American couples marry, they generally build a new life apart from relatives, based on love and personal happiness.

any social, economic, or religious background. The man or woman may have strong ties with parents, brothers, or sisters, but when he or she falls in love, the strongest feelings are supposed to be for the loved one. When an American couple marries, they generally plan to live apart from both sets of parents and build their own independent family structure. The goal of the young couple is to be each other's best friends and to increase the personal happiness of themselves and their children.

[3] Marriage, however, isn't always a matter of personal need for love and happiness. In most societies of the world, marriage is an important way to strengthen the main family line by uniting it with another family of the same social, economic, or religious background. In these societies, there are many rules about whom a person can or cannot marry. Parents have a strong interest in seeing that their children continue the family's good reputation and position in society. They also want their children to have a good life. So sons and daughters are not free to choose their mates. By arranging marriages, parents can control the choice of a new member for the benefit of the children, the whole family, and the class to which they belong.

[4] In India, for example, the ideal household includes the parents, the sons, and the sons' wives and children. In this type of arrangement, the strength of the family lies in the respect, loyalty, and cooperation among the children and between the children and their parents. If a son is too interested in his wife, or if the wife is too independent or uncooperative, he or she may cause trouble by breaking the unity of respect and loyalty within the family. A good wife is one who is a good daughter-in-law. She is modest and obedient. She gradually breaks the ties with her own family and becomes completely interested in her husband's. In India many parents arrange a marriage for a son with the right kind of woman.

This bride and groom from the Indian subcontinent have an arranged marriage. Beautiful wedding jewelry and special clothing is part of the marriage ceremony.

[5] Romesh Roy is the son of a successful businessman in Bombay, India. He is a college graduate and thinks of himself as a modern young man. His parents are afraid that he is too independent and might choose his own bride. So while Romesh is busy with his career, Mr. and Mrs. Roy are both looking for a suitable young woman for him to marry. They would like a young woman whose family has a slightly lower position in society than their own so that her family will treat the Roys with more respect. But they want a young woman whose family will offer a good marriage gift. They prefer a pretty woman, and one who is not too tall for their son. She should be well educated but home loving. Her parents must not expect to see much of her once she is married. The ideal wife for Romesh will be the ideal daughter-in-law for the Roy family.

[6] The Roys know many families with marriageable daughters. However, it isn't easy to arrange a good match. One of the young women is too plain. Another one is attractive, but she is taller than Romesh. Still another is too "forward" and "thinks too much of herself." My Roy knows a suitable daughter of a business partner. But her parents don't want Romesh for a son-in-law; they are looking for a wealthier family than the Roys for their daughter. Mr. and Mrs. Roy may have to

Arranged marriages are the rule in the small villages and towns of Latin American countries, as well as throughout Asia and Africa. The marriage couple (center) in this photograph had their introduction to each other, their courtship, and their wedding arranged according to traditional customs of their region.

wait a few years before they can make the best arrangement for the benefit of everyone concerned.

[7]   Eventually, Romesh will meet a woman suitable for both him and his parents. He will see her at least once or twice before they marry. The families will exchange gifts of money or jewelry, and then there will be a great wedding ceremony. The couple will live together with Romesh's parents and younger sisters and brothers. The bride will be obedient and cooperative. Because Mr. and Mrs. Roy are kind people, she will be well treated and comfortable in her new environment. Romesh's wife will provide company for Mrs. Roy and help in the management of the household. When Mr. and Mrs. Roy are away on vacation, she will take care of her husband's little sisters and brothers. Someday she will have her own children. When her son is grown, she too will look for a suitable bride for him.

**Summary Completion.**   Fill in the blank spaces with a word or phrase that is correct in both form and meaning. You may use the exact words from the text or others of your own that communicate the same ideas.

Probably the most common subject of American popular music, films, and magazine columns is (1) _____. Americans believe that (2) _____, solving the problems of love and achieving the "happy ending"—(3) _____—are central to a happy life. Americans also believe that romantic love is the (4) _____ for marriage. Even though the United States has a high (5) _____, young Americans continue to marry on the basis of their personal feelings of "love." Young American married couples try to (6) _____ from their families and build an independent family structure of their own.

In other parts of the world, however, (7) _____ not the basis for marriage. Marriage in India, for example, involves the (8) _____ of both the woman and the man. The parents of the young people will try to arrange (9) _____ based on the economic, educational, and social background of both families. In these kinds of arranged marriages, the young couple will probably live (10) _____ of either the bride or the groom.

## DISCUSSION QUESTIONS

1. What is the usual age of marriage for women in your native culture? For men? Is the usual basis for marriage romantic love and free choice by the woman and man? Or are marriages usually arranged by the parents? If marriages are arranged, how are the arrangements completed?

2. What part do the wife's parents play in the life of a newly married couple in your native culture? What part do the husband's parents play? Do married couples usually live with one partner's parents? What are some benefits and some negative points about this arrangement?

3. Do you think a couple can be happy if the man and the woman are from two different educational backgrounds? Explain your answer with specific reasons. What if the couple are from two different religious backgrounds or two different financial situations? Give specific problems that might result. Can you think of some ways in which these problems can be solved?

## READING COMPREHENSION

1. **Understanding the Text.** Follow the directions for each item.

    a. Mark the following sentences *T* for *true* or *F* for *false* according to the information in the reading passage. Underline the part of the passage where you find your information.

    (1) In some societies sons and daughters are not free to choose their own marriage partners. _____

    (2) In India the ideal household includes married daughters. _____

    (3) An Indian father also takes part in arranging a marriage. _____

    (4) The marriage gift is one of the considerations in arranging a marriage. _____

    (5) Romesh Roy will not see his bride before he marries. _____

    b. Circle the letter of the correct answer.

    (1) Paragraphs [1] and [2]

        (a) are both concerned with marriage in the United States.
        (b) offer contrasting views of marriage.
        (c) tell us that love is the most important thing in most marriages.

(2) The main idea of Paragraph [1] is that

   (a) the music of American teenagers deals mostly with love.
   (b) romantic love is a subject of interest to most Americans.
   (c) Valentine's Day is the most popular American holiday.

(3) Sentence (1) of Paragraph [2] includes the phrase *not only . . . but also*. This phrase is used to

   (a) show a reason–result thought.
   (b) reverse the direction of a thought.
   (c) give forceful emphasis to a thought.

(4) Sentence (2) of Paragraph [2] suggests that

   (a) marriages based on romantic love often end in divorce.
   (b) the writer believes that romantic love is a good basis for marriage.
   (c) the divorce rate in the United States is related to the age at which Americans marry.

(5) In the next-to-last sentence of Paragraph [2], the pronoun *their* in the phrase *build their own independent family* refers to

   (a) parents.
   (b) an American married couple.
   (c) brothers and sisters.

(6) In Paragraph [3], the word *however* in the first sentence signals

   (a) a time sequence.
   (b) a reason for a statement.
   (c) a reversal of a previous thought.

(7) In most societies of the world,

   (a) marriage is a private arrangement between two people.
   (b) married couples break the ties with their families.
   (c) there are many rules about whom a person can or cannot marry.

(8) The information in Paragraph [3]

   (a) gives specific details for Paragraph [2].
   (b) is an example of Paragraph [1].
   (c) introduces a new topic to the reading passage.

(9) The information in Paragraph [4] suggests that the main family line in India

   (a) is broken by marriage.
   (b) is continued through the males in the family.
   (c) is controlled by the daughters-in-law.

(10) In Paragraph [5], the author suggests that the Roys want their son's marriage

   (a) to be in the tradition of Indian culture.
   (b) to be different from their own marriage.
   (c) to be a real love match.

(11) Mr. and Mrs. Roy are looking for a daughter-in-law who is

   (a) short, well-educated, and independent
   (b) plain, tall, and obedient.
   (c) pretty, home loving, and cooperative.

(12) In India, a girl's parents

   (a) must accept any offer of a husband for their daughter.
   (b) can reject a man as unsuitable for their daughter.
   (c) may prefer their daughter to remain unmarried.

(13) In Paragraph [7], indicate the best place for the following sentence: The groom will wear a business suit, but the bride will wear traditional Indian dress and jewelry.

   (a) after the first sentence.
   (b) after the second sentence.
   (c) after the third sentence.

(14) In Paragraph [7], the author suggests that

   (a) Romesh's bride will be the ideal Indian daughter-in-law.
   (b) Romesh will help in the management of the household.
   (c) Romesh's parents will be away a lot of the time.

2. **Answering Information Questions.** Write the answers to the following questions in complete sentences.

   a. How do Americans celebrate Valentine's Day?
   b. What kind of personal freedom do young Americans have in choosing their mates?

c. Do married couples in the United States generally live with or apart from relatives?
d. In most societies, how does marriage strengthen the main family line?
e. Who are the members of the ideal Indian family?
f. What can happen if an Indian wife is too independent or uncooperative?
g. Does an Indian wife strengthen or break the ties with her own family?
h. What are the Roys afraid Romesh might do?
i. What will the families do before Romesh's wedding ceremony?
j. Who will take care of Romesh's sisters and brothers when their parents are away?
k. What will Romesh's wife do when her son is grown?

3. **The Reading Process: Paraphrasing.** Writers may express the same ideas in different ways. A paraphrase is another, usually simpler, way of saying something. Follow the directions for each item.

   a. The following sentences are paraphrases of some of the ideas in Paragraphs [1], [2], and [3]. In the blank space next to each sentence, write the paragraph and sentence number of the original sentence. The first one is done for you.

   (1) The love between a married couple is stronger than the ties they may have with their own relatives. _Para. 2_  _Sent. 5_

   (2) Married couples live their own lives in new surroundings. _____ _____

   (3) Parents feel strongly that their children should carry on the family's good name. _____ _____

   (4) Young people in certain cultures aren't free to marry whomever they wish. _____ _____

   (5) Arranged marriages offer advantages to family members and their social class. _____ _____

   b. In each group of four sentences, put a check (√) next to the two sentences that mean the same thing.

   (1) (a) An Indian wife will add to the wealth of her husband's family with gifts given by her parents when she marries. _____

   (b) In India the groom's family offers a small gift to the bride's family before the wedding ceremony. _____

(c) Money and jewelry are common types of marriage gifts in India. _____

(d) A bride's parents contribute money or jewelry to their daughter's new family unit as a marriage gift. _____

(2) (a) The divorce rate is increasing around the world. _____

(b) Some "love matches" end in divorce. _____

(c) Even if you marry for love, the marriage may not last. _____

(d) Love may grow deeply between a couple in an arranged marriage. _____

(3) (a) The Roys think that their son's future bride should be clever and bright. _____

(b) The Roys are looking for an obedient, modest wife for their son. _____

(c) The Roys want their son's bride to have a nice appearance. _____

(d) The Roys are interested in the physical characteristics of a bride-to-be for their son. _____

(4) (a) In the United States, the majority of marriages are "love matches." _____

(b) In most societies, "love matches" are rare. _____

(c) People in the United States generally marry at a later age than they did fifty years ago. _____

(d) "Love matches" are in the minority among the marriage customs of the world. _____

(5) (a) Some Indian sons act independently and marry women of their own choosing. _____

(b) Some Indian sons leave their parents' home to find jobs in other countries. _____

(c) Not all Indian sons marry women chosen by their parents. _____

(d) Indian sons working in other countries often return home to get married. _____

# Unit III  Our Social World

## VOCABULARY

1. **New Words.**  Pronounce these words following your instructor.

   | Nouns | Verbs | Adjectives | Adverbs |
   |---|---|---|---|
   | reputation | conquer | romantic | gradually |
   | arrangement | strengthen | personal | |
   | benefit | | | |
   | loyalty | | | |
   | cooperation | | | |

   a. *Choosing Synonyms.*  In the blank space in Column A, write the letter of the synonym from Column B.

   | A | B |
   |---|---|
   | conquer _____ | a. appropriate |
   | personal _____ | b. little by little |
   | strengthen _____ | c. have authority over |
   | suitable _____ | d. an advantageous thing |
   | reputation _____ | e. deeply loving |
   | arrangement _____ | f. individual |
   | benefit _____ | g. splendid |
   | loyalty _____ | h. position in the community |
   | cooperation _____ | i. make stronger |
   | gradually _____ | j. faithfulness |
   | romantic _____ | k. working together |
   | | l. win over |
   | | m. method |
   | | n. success |

   b. *Using Vocabulary.*  Follow the directions for each item.

   (1) Circle the items that can only be done *gradually*.

   grow old                become proficient in English
   swallow a pill          run for the bus
   buy a newspaper         learn to walk (as a baby)

**(2)** Circle the words that are related to the word *strengthen*:

strong  strongly
stretch  strangle
lengthen  strength

**(3)** Circle the number of the sentence that would correctly follow the given sentence.

*Cooperation* is very important in planning a family vacation.

   **(a)** Everyone should do what he or she wants.

   **(b)** If you go to Europe, you'll have a good time.

   **(c)** Parents and children should talk about the places they want to see together.

**(4)** Circle the items that could be considered *benefits* of living in a large city.

bad air  museums  public transportation
lots of cars  small apartments  job opportunities
variety of schools  crowded streets  personal freedom

**(5)** Complete the following sentence by circling the appropriate phrases. You can *strengthen* your body by

playing tennis.  eating sweets.
smoking cigarettes.  going to the movies.
eating proper foods.  taking dance lessons.

**(6)** Check (√) the sentences that use the word *reputation* correctly.

   **(a)** An honest businessperson will earn a good reputation. _____

   **(b)** To learn history you need a good reputation for names and dates. _____

   **(c)** I filled out two copies of a reputation for a driver's license. _____

   **(d)** Some politicians have a reputation for dishonesty. _____

2. **Word Families: Noun Formation.** Nouns in English sometimes end in *ness*, *ty (ity)*, *ship*, *ence (ance)*, and *ment*. Study the following list of sample nouns with these endings.

kindness  loyalty  friendship  experience  arrangement
happiness  majority  partnership  importance  treatment

Follow the directions for each item. Write your answers in the space provided.

**a.** The verbs *arrange* and *treat* add *ment* to become nouns. Make nouns of the following verbs in the same way.

manage _____   develop _____

govern _____   agree _____

**b.** What nouns ending in *ness* are the opposite of

kindness _____

happiness _____

**c.** What noun ending in *ness* can be formed from the adjective *lonely*? _____ What noun ending in *ness* can be formed from the antonym of the adjective *messy*? _____

**d.** What noun ending in *ty* or in *ity* means the opposite of dishonesty? _____ _____ impossibility? _____

**e.** The noun *majority* means more than 50 percent of something. What is the noun ending in *ity* that means less than 50 percent of something?

_____

**f.** The suffix *ship* means "the condition of being" or "the skill of." Write the noun forms ending in *ship* for each of the following conditions or skills.

the skill of a leader _____

the condition of being a citizen _____

the condition of being a member _____

**g.** _____ is the adjective form of the noun *intelligence*.

*Independent* is the adjective form of the noun _____ .

## WRITING EXERCISES

### Simple Present Tense Conditionals

The word *if* is the sign of a conditional statement. An *if* clause tells us that certain conditions must be true, or must happen before something else takes place. The *if* clause states the condition. The other clause in the sentence states the result. The result clause contains a modal + a main verb.

> **Children will be helpful to you if you teach them to be cooperative.**
>       (result)                                  (condition)
>
> **If an Indian man marries a woman of his own choice, his parents may be hurt.**
>                            (condition)
>       (result)

Note that when the *if* clause begins the sentence, it is followed by a comma. When the *if* clause is the second clause, there is no comma.

When the main verb of an *if* clause is in the Present tense, the most common modals in the result clause are these: *can, may, must, should,* and *will*. This type of conditional expresses the idea of possibility.

> **If a woman chooses a suitable mate, she may enjoy a happy life.**

1. **Sentence Completion.** Complete each of the following conditional statements with a second clause containing a modal + a main verb. You may use negatives. Use pronouns carefully. Rewrite your complete new sentences.

   a. If an Indian mother finds a suitable woman for her son . . .
   b. If a bride wants to be a good daughter-in-law . . .
   c. If children watch too much television . . .
   d. If you don't know the meaning of a word . . .
   e. If my friend from India visits me . . .
   f. If parents of small children want to go out in the evening . . .

2. **Sentence Building.** There are two items in each set. Make the first item into an *if* clause. Use the verb in the Simple Present tense. Make the second item into a result clause. Use an appropriate modal with the verb in the second clause. Add appropriate subjects and whatever other words are necessary to make a complete sentence. The first one is done for you.

   a. have enough credits, graduate

   *If I have enough credits, I will graduate next year.*

   b. study hard, pass courses
   c. have money, visit Greece

d. don't feel well, stay
e. borrow books, return
f. eat too much, do exercises
g. don't cooperate, cause trouble
h. read newspapers, increase vocabulary
i. work long hours, feel tired
j. play active sports, wear suitable clothing
k. watch their mothers, learn to cook
l. do well in school, continue education
m. practice conversation, improve English

3. **Sentence Composing.** Write a complete conditional sentence for each of the following items.

   a. Tell what item you will wear or carry if it rains tomorrow.
   b. Tell one thing that may happen if we elect a woman president.
   c. Describe one thing you will do next summer if you have the money.
   d. Tell one thing you should do if you are preparing for an exam.
   e. Name one thing you must do if you want to improve your English.
   f. State what you should do if you see an accident.
   g. Tell one thing children can do if they want to help their parents.
   h. Name one thing you may buy if you earn enough money.
   i. Tell what a person must have if he or she wants to drive a car.
   j. Tell how the instructor will feel if everyone passes the course.

## Expressing Conditions Contrary to Fact

We use the Simple Past tense in the *if* clause to express a present condition that is contrary to fact, or unreal. The most common modals in the result clause are these: *could, might, would*. These modals express the idea of improbability.

> If we *had* clean air, we *would live* a healthier life.

This example expresses the *present* fact that we *don't have* clean air; therefore, the result is improbable.

1. **Sentence Completion.** Circle the number of the result clause that best completes the given conditional clause.

   **a.** If I studied harder,
   - **(1)** I can succeed.
   - **(2)** I could succeed.
   - **(3)** I will succeed.

   **b.** If I didn't know any English,
   - **(1)** I wouldn't enjoy American movies.
   - **(2)** I can't enjoy American movies.
   - **(3)** I won't enjoy American movies.

   **c.** If I took a trip to India,
   - **(1)** I find out more about the marriage customs.
   - **(2)** I can find out more about the marriage customs.
   - **(3)** I would find out more about the marriage customs.

   **d.** If women had good jobs
   - **(1)** they might get married at a later age.
   - **(2)** they shouldn't get married at a later age.
   - **(3)** they must get married at a later age.

   **e.** If American parents wanted to arrange a marriage for a son,
   - **(1)** the son can't cooperate.
   - **(2)** the son might not cooperate.
   - **(3)** the son shouldn't cooperate.

   **f.** If little girls shared more sports activities with little boys,
   - **(1)** real friendships might develop.
   - **(2)** real friendships will develop.
   - **(3)** real friendships can't develop.

   **g.** If you took a pilot's job,
   - **(1)** you can't see your family very often.
   - **(2)** you shouldn't see your family very often.
   - **(3)** you couldn't see your family very often.

   **h.** If parents had jobs that required them to travel,
   - **(1)** they would need excellent child care.
   - **(2)** they need excellent child care.
   - **(3)** they must need excellent child care.

i.  If there were more good day-care centers,

   **(1)** more mothers may work.
   **(2)** more mothers will work.
   **(3)** more mothers would work.

j.  If I wanted to be a construction worker,

   **(1)** I need a lot of strength.
   **(2)** I would need a lot of strength.
   **(3)** I will need a lot of strength.

2. **Sentence Composing.** Write a complete conditional sentence to answer each of the following questions.

   a. If you became mayor of your city, what would you do to improve public transportation?
   b. If you were the manager of a professional baseball team, would you hire a woman player?
   c. If you had a daughter, what gift might you give her for her seventh birthday?
   d. If your friend gave birth to a boy, what gift would you give the baby?
   e. If your parents needed help around the house, what chores might you do for them?
   f. If a person liked working with children, what job might he or she enjoy doing?
   g. If you called a wrong telephone number by mistake, what expression could you use?
   h. If you won one thousand dollars in the lottery, how would you spend it?
   i. If there were going to be one world language, which language would you prefer?
   j. If scientists found life on another planet, would you go to live there?
   k. If you traveled to Egypt, what language would you need to know?
   l. If you lost your wallet, what would you do?

3. **Sentence Completion.** Fill in the blank space with either a conditional clause or a result clause to complete the following statements. Pay special attention to the tense sequence and modal use. The first one is done for you.

   a. *If I had children,* I would teach them to cooperate with each other.
   b. You can observe many stars _____.
   c. If you want to see a lot of Roman art, _____.

d. _____ if I traveled a lot.
e. _____ you shouldn't smoke.
f. You could pass this course _____.

## Useful Expressions with *The*

When you want to talk about a part of a larger group, you may use the expression *one (two, some, many, most, all) of the* + a plural noun.

> ***Many of the students*** **in this class speak Spanish.**

Note that the subject of the sentence is the word before the preposition *of*. In this example, the subject is *many*.

When you use the superlative form of an adjective, you put *the* before it.

> **The Ganges is *the longest* river in India.**
> **Mrs. Indira Gandhi, once prime minister, is one of *the most famous* women in India's history.**

1. **Answering Information Questions.** Write the answers to each of the following questions in complete sentences.

    a. Who are two of the tallest members of your family?
    b. What is one of the newspapers you read often?
    c. Who is one of the kindest people you know?
    d. Who are some of the most famous women in your native country?
    e. Who are some of the students who sit next to you?
    f. Who has the hardest job in your family?
    g. Who is the most studious person in your family?
    h. What are most of the students in your class doing now?
    i. What is the most interesting course you are taking this term?
    j. What is one of the most difficult features of English?
    k. Where are most of the stores in your neighborhood?
    l. What is the warmest article of clothing you own?
    m. What is the easiest way to get to school?
    n. Who is one of your most loyal friends?

o. Who is the most cooperative member of your family?
p. When is the best time of the year for you?
q. Where are most of the students at lunchtime?
r. What are some of the foods that you like best?

2. **Pair Dictation.** Dictate three of your best sentences from Exercise 1 to your partner. Then take dictation from your partner.

3. **Sentence Building.** On a separate sheet of paper, write a complete sentence using the words in each set. Add as many words as you need to make a correct sentence. Do not change the form or the order of the words. The first one is done for you.

   a. many of    books    library    old
   *Many of the books in the library are old.*
   b. One    windows    classroom    open
   c. Most of    students    school    part-time
   d. All of    stores    neighborhood    closed    Sunday
   e. Three of    people    class    Chinese
   f. Some of    stars    universe    visible    night
   g. One    chairs    living room    broken
   h. Some of    exercises    book    difficult

4. **Article Completion.** The following wedding announcement is typical of those we find in the Sunday edition of many American newspapers. Fill in the blank spaces with the correct article: *a, an,* or *the*. If no article is needed, mark *X* in the space. (Review Chapter One, Singular and Plural Nouns; Chapter Four, the Definite Article; and Appendix A: Articles.)

   (1) _____ marriage of Gilda Harvey, (2) _____ only daughter of (3) _____ Mr. and Mrs. George Harvey, to Eric Johnson, (4) _____ son of Mr. and Mrs. Alan Johnson, took place yesterday at (5) _____ Bronxville Field Club. (6) _____ Reverend James Pace, (7) _____ Episcopal priest, performed (8) _____ ceremony. Diana Robinson was (9) _____ bride's matron of honor and William Hadley was (10) _____ best man.

   Mrs. Johnson, (11) _____ graduate of New York City Technical College, is (12) _____ account executive at Berry Industries, (13) _____ computer services company in (14) _____ New York. Her mother, (15) _____ professor of sociology, has worked in (16) _____ Philippines recording (17) _____ history of rural families. Mr. Johnson, (18) _____ newspaper reporter, attended (19) _____ University of Pennsylvania and graduated from Columbia University. His father is (20) _____ psychologist.

## THE COMPOSING PROCESS

### 1. Developing a Paragraph

*Recognizing General Ideas and Specific Details.* After each sentence in the following paragraphs, there is a blank space. As your instructor reads each sentence aloud, mark *G* in the blank space if the sentence is a *general* idea or opinion. Mark *S* in the blank space if the sentence is a *specific* detail or example.

**a.** In India traditional society is divided into groups called castes. _____ The different castes are related to certain occupations. _____ The Brahmins are priests and scholars. _____ The Kshatriyas are soldiers. _____ The Vaisya are businessmen or merchants. _____ The Sundras are factory workers and craftsmen. _____ Traditionally, a person belongs to one of these castes by birth. _____ For example, a child born of a father who makes jewelry is a Sudra. _____ In the past, a person from one caste didn't marry someone from another. _____ A Brahmin never married a Vaisya, and a Sudra couldn't marry a Kshatriya. _____ However, under modern Indian law, all the groups are equal. _____ So the caste system has become weaker, and people sometimes marry outside their traditional group. _____

**b.** In many parts of the world, there are rules about marrying a person from the same place, or outside that place. _____ In Kalaphur, India, a man must take a wife from outside his village. _____ All married women in Kalaphur come from many different villages in the area. _____ Some people think that life is difficult in Kalaphur because the married women don't know each other. _____ In Mexican villages, however, women usually marry within the village. _____ In the village of Tepotzlan, over 90 percent of marriages take place within the village. _____ Over 40 percent of the women marry men from the same neighborhood. _____ Observers say that there is more unity in Mexican villages because most of the people know each other. _____

c. Changes in the American life-style have affected the American family. _____ The number of households headed by women keeps increasing. _____ In 1970 about 5.6 million American homes were headed by women. _____ In 1979 that number had increased to 8.5 million. _____ There are several reasons for this. _____ First, many young working women are living alone in their own apartments. _____ Also, divorce has increased the number of households where the female is the sole parent. _____

2. **Developing a General Idea with Specific Details.** Read the following paragraph on the topic of wedding gifts. Then answer the questions.

   a. (1) In the United States, couples usually receive gifts from their relatives and friends when they get married. (2) Wedding guests usually give gifts to express their good wishes to the couple, but gifts are not necessary for the marriage itself. (3) In other societies, however, gifts are very important, and the marriage may not take place without them. (4) One type of necessary gift is called bride service. (5) A young husband must work for a period of time for his wife's family. (6) He may work as long as fifteen years or until their third child is born. (7) Bride service may seem strange to us, but it is important in societies where people don't have money or material goods to exchange at marriage.

   *Questions.* Place a check (√) before the correct answer to the following questions.

   **(1)** Sentence (1) states the topic of the paragraph: marriage gifts. What is the relationship of Sentence (2) to Sentence (1)?

   _____ It contradicts the idea of Sentence (1).

   _____ It gives a reason for the idea in Sentence (1).

   _____ It gives an example of the idea in Sentence (1).

**(2)** What is the relationship of Sentence (3) to Sentence (2)?

_____ It contradicts the idea of Sentence (2).

_____ It gives a reason for the idea in Sentence (2).

_____ It gives an example of the idea of Sentence (2).

**(3)** Which word in Sentence (3) signals its relationship to Sentence (2)?

_____ gifts

_____ however

_____ marriage

**(4)** What is the purpose of Sentence (4)?

_____ It gives an example of an important marriage gift.

_____ It gives a reason for an important marriage gift.

_____ It shows the time sequence of giving important marriage gifts.

**(5)** What do Sentences (5) and (6) do in relation to Sentence (4)?

_____ They give the author's general opinion about the topic of Sentence (4).

_____ They give reasons for the topic in Sentence (4).

_____ They give specific details for the topic in Sentence (4).

**(6)** What does Sentence (7) do?

_____ It gives more specific details for the main idea.

_____ It gives a general reason for the main idea.

_____ It gives another example of the main idea.

With your class and instructor, review the pattern of this paragraph's development on the board.

3. **Composing a Paragraph with General and Specific Statements.** The following list includes some items that are considered important for a wedding ceremony. Brainstorm additional items.

| | |
|---|---|
| location of the celebration | bridesmaids' dresses |
| time of day and the season | music and dancing |
| wedding dress | flowers |
| groom's suit | _____ |
| | _____ |

An important part of a wedding is the ceremonial cutting of the wedding cake by the bride and groom. Do you have this custom in your culture?

Write a paragraph describing a wedding you observed. Choose three of your listed items on which to focus. Introduce each item with a general idea statement or opinion. Develop each item with specific and concrete details. Completing the following outline will help you to write your extended paragraph.

**Overall Main Idea** _____
_____

**I. General Statement, First Item** _____
_____

    Details 1: _____
            2: _____
            3: _____

**II. General Statement, Second Item** _____
_____

    Details 1: _____

Chapter Eight   Working Relationships: Old and New    297

    2: _____

    3: _____

 **III. General Statement, Third Item** _____

  _____

  Details 1: _____

    2: _____

    3: _____

 **Concluding Statement** _____

 _____

**4. Sentence Combining to Form a Paragraph.** Combine the following sentences into longer, more interesting statements to form a paragraph about wedding gifts in Greece. Leave out all unnecessary words. Use signal words and other connecting expressions to make your paragraph flow smoothly. Rewrite your complete new paragraph on a separate sheet of paper.

 **a.** The *dowry* is a common kind of gift.
 **b.** The gift is for marriage.
 **c.** The marriage is in Greece.
 **d.** Dowries began in ancient times.
 **e.** These times were many centuries ago.
 **f.** The dowry was a gift of money.
 **g.** The dowry was a gift of land.
 **h.** The gift was from the parents.
 **i.** The parents belonged to the bride. (Use possessive.)
 **j.** The gift was to their son-in-law.
 **k.** At that time a wife didn't work.
 **l.** The work was outside the home.
 **m.** She was expected to add to the wealth. (Use signal for reversal of thought.)
 **n.** The wealth belonged to her husband.
 **o.** She was expected to take care of her home. (Use signal of addition.)
 **p.** She was expected to take care of her children.
 **q.** The government of Greece wants to do away with dowries. (Use signal of reversal.)
 **r.** The government is current.

s. The government says that dowries aren't necessary.
t. Some women work outside the home. (Use signal for reason.)
u. Some women earn as much as men do.
v. Families can't afford to give dowries to all their daughters. (Use signal for addition.)
w. These families are poor.
x. To some women dowries are like buying something. (Use signal for last or final item.)
y. That something is a husband.
z. A man may marry a woman.
aa. The reason might be that she has money. (Use signal for reason.)
bb. The reason might not be that he loves her.
cc. Dowries present an interesting question.
dd. Dowries are a difficult question.
ee. This is in parts of Europe.
ff. This is in parts of Asia.

5. **Paragraph Topics**

   a. Large weddings cost a lot of money. Some couples prefer to have a smaller wedding with just close relatives and a few friends or to elope and use the money that they would save to begin their new life together. In your opinion, which is the better way? Be sure to support your general idea statements with specific details, examples, and reasons.

   b. In the United States and many other cultures, it is traditional to give gifts to the bridal couple—the bride and groom. These gifts may be useful, beautiful, or interesting. Describe the kind of wedding gifts most common in your culture. Include a main idea sentence at the beginning of the paragraph that identifies your culture and states the topic of your paragraph.

## ADDITIONAL READING

### Men's Roles, Women's Roles: A Changing View

[1] In the traditional American society of the past, male and female roles were easily defined by the division of labor. Men worked outside the home and earned the income to support their families. Women cooked the meals and took care of the home and the children. These roles were firmly fixed for most people, and there was not much opportunity for men or women to exchange their roles. By

Some women have begun to enter traditionally male occupations such as geological surveying, pictured here.

the middle of this century, however, men's and women's roles were becoming less firmly fixed.

[2] In the 1950s, economic and social success was the goal of the typical American, but in the 1960s a new force developed called the counterculture. The people involved in this movement did not value the middle-class American goals. The counterculture presented men and women with new role choices. Men became more interested in child care. They began to share child-rearing tasks with their wives. In fact, some young men and women moved to communal homes or farms where the economic and child-care responsibilities were shared equally by both sexes. In addition, many Americans did not value the traditional male role of soldier. Some young men refused to be drafted as soldiers to fight in the war in Vietnam.

[3] In terms of numbers, the counterculture was a small group of people. But its influence spread to many parts of American society. Working men of all classes began to change their economic and social patterns. Industrial workers and business executives alike cut down on overtime work so that they could spend more leisure time with their families. Some doctors, lawyers, and teachers turned away from high paying situations to practice their professions in poorer neighborhoods. Some young people joined the Peace Corps to share their skills with people in nonindustrialized countries around the world.

[4]   In the 1970s, the feminist movement, or women's liberation, produced additional economic and social changes. Women of all ages and at all levels of society were entering the work force in greater numbers. Most of them still took traditional women's jobs such as public school teaching, nursing, and secretarial work. Some women, however, began to enter traditionally male occupations: police work, banking, dentistry, and construction work. Women were asking for equal pay for equal work and equal opportunities for promotion. Women's groups were organizing more day-care centers for the children of working mothers.

[5]   Women and men began to join groups and attend meetings where these new roles were discussed. Women in particular needed to hear about the problems of other women who were working in nontraditional areas. At Rutgers University, for example, a conference of some of America's most creative women writers attracted a large crowd. Most of the speakers were older women who had achieved success in their field many years ago. They spoke about some of their greatest difficulties as women in a "man's world." Novelist and playwright Lillian Hellman and magazine writer Emily Hahn, two popular speakers at this conference, encouraged the women in their audience to attempt new roles and activities in their lives.

[6]   Even among older Americans, the grandmother and grandfather generation, there was a broadening of the roles that men and women could play. Advances in medicine and health care were allowing older people to live longer and experiment with new kinds of social activities. Men who retired from work began to take up hobbies such as cooking, painting, or crafts. Previously, these activities had been thought of as "women's work." At the same time, anthropologist Margaret Mead was making Americans more aware of the important part older women played in other cultures. And American grandmothers themselves were changing the definition of their roles. Many, of course, remained traditional grandmothers. Baking cakes, knitting sweaters, and baby-sitting for their grandchildren were their chief activities. But other grandmothers took up jogging, dancing, and writing. They joined senior citizen centers for social activities either with or without their husbands.

[7]   Today the experts generally agree that important changes are taking place in the roles of all classes and age groups of men and women. Naturally, there are difficulties in adjusting to these changes. It is not easy for men and women to learn to share the labor of the workplace. It is not easy for women to meet the demands and pressures of work outside the home and still take care of a family. Not all men are willing to share home and child-care responsibilities with their working wives. But perhaps more men are beginning to feel like Rafael Suarez, Jr., a New York City college student who looks forward to the new type of society. "Who needs the pressure of being a typical male?" asks Rafael. "It's more fun being a human being first."

Many modern mothers like artist Susan Price, seek quality day care for their children so they can reenter the work force.

**Paragraph Completion.** Fill in the blank spaces with a word that is correct in both form and meaning.

In the 1970s, the feminist movement, or (1) _____ liberation, produced additional economic and (2) _____ changes. Women of all ages (3) _____ at all levels of society were entering (4) _____ work force in greater numbers. Most (5) _____ them still took traditional women's jobs (6) _____ as public school teaching, nursing, (7) _____ secretarial work. Some women, however, began to (8) _____ traditionally male occupations: police work, banking, dentistry, and (9) _____ work. Women were asking for equal (10) _____ for equal work, and equal opportunities (11) _____ promotion. Women's groups were organizing (12) _____ day-care centers for the children of working mothers.

## DISCUSSION QUESTIONS

1. Think about a traditionally male occupation such as fire fighting, construction work, or dentistry. Discuss why a woman could or could not do one of those jobs as well as a man.
   Think about a traditionally female occupation such as elementary school teaching, nursing, or telephone operating. Discuss why a man could or could not do one of those jobs as well as a woman.

2. Since the 1960s, increasing numbers of men have taken an interest in parenting, or the care of their children. Do you think that men can be equally good parents as women can? Is the age or sex of the child an important point to consider in terms of whether the mother or father can do a better job of being a parent? Discuss with reference to specific elements of child care.

3. In your native culture, what are some of the activities that are traditional for males? What activities are traditional for females? Do men and women usually socialize together in your culture? Explain. Are female–male roles changing in your culture? What are some specific changes you can point out?

## READING COMPREHENSION

1. **Understanding the Text.**   Circle the number of the correct answer.
   a. Which sentence best expresses the main idea of Paragraph [1]?
      (1) Men's and women's roles were usually quite separate in the past.
      (2) Women usually worked outside the home for wages.
      (3) Men's and women's roles were easily exchanged in the past.
   b. The sentence that best expresses the main idea of Paragraph [2] is
      (1) the first sentence.
      (2) the third sentence.
      (3) the last sentence.
   c. In Paragraphs [2] and [3], the author suggests that the counterculture
      (1) destroyed the United States.

- (2) changed some American values.
- (3) was not important in the United States.

**d.** The main idea of Paragraph [4] is stated in
- (1) the second sentence.
- (2) the fifth sentence.
- (3) the last sentence.

**e.** In Paragraph [4], indicate the best place for the following sentence: *They also became taxicab drivers, pilots, and college presidents.*
- (1) After the first sentence
- (2) After the fourth sentence
- (3) After the last sentence

**f.** The main idea statement of Paragraph [5] is
- (1) the first sentence.
- (2) the second sentence.
- (3) the last sentence.

**g.** Women *in particular* needed to hear about other women in nontraditional fields probably because
- (1) the whole idea of women working in a "man's world" was new.
- (2) women needed to earn more income than men.
- (3) men gave a lot of support and encouragement to working women.

**h.** In Paragraph [6] the main idea is in
- (1) the first sentence.
- (2) the second sentence.
- (3) the sixth sentence.

**i.** In Paragraphs [5] and [6], two expressions that introduce specific supporting illustrations of general statements are
- (1) previously/at the same time.
- (2) for example/such as.
- (3) of course/in particular.

**j.** In Paragraph [7], the author suggests that
- (1) men and women will never share the same goals.
- (2) most men will be happy to take care of their children.
- (3) some men may be willing to change their traditional male roles.

k. The quotation by Rafael Suarez, Jr., in Paragraph [7] suggests that

   (1) he would not permit his wife to hold a job.

   (2) he would share some of the household responsibilities with his wife.

   (3) he wants a job with a lot of pressure.

2. **Answering Information Questions.** Write the answers to each question in complete sentences on a separate sheet of paper.

   a. In the past, which sex took care of the home and children?

   b. In the past, which sex worked outside the home?

   c. Did the counterculture value or reject the goals of the 1950s?

   d. List two specific ways in which the values of the counterculture were different from traditional male values of the 1950s.

   e. Why did some men turn down overtime work in the 1960s?

   f. Why did some young people join the Peace Corps?

   g. What are some traditional female occupations?

   h. What did women's groups do for working mothers?

   i. Does the quotation by Rafael Suarez, Jr., show agreement or disagreement with women's liberation?

3. **The Reading Process: Paraphrasing.** Writers may express the same ideas in different ways. A paraphrase is another, usually simpler, way of saying something. Follow the directions for each item.

   a. The following sentences are paraphrases of some of the ideas in Paragraphs [2] and [3]. In the blank space next to each sentence, write the paragraph and sentence number of the original sentence. The first one is done for you.

   (1) The members of the counterculture didn't want the same things from life as did most middle-class Americans. _Para. 2_ _Sent. 2_

   (2) Fathers took over more of the job of being a parent. _____

   (3) On communes both men and women share the outside work and the child care. _____ _____

   (4) Some men wouldn't go into military service. _____

(5) Men wanted to work shorter hours so they could see their families more. _____  _____

b. In each group of four sentences, put a check (√) next to the two sentences that mean the same thing.

(1) (a) More American households are headed by woman than ever before. _____

(b) There has been an increase in the number of women who return to work after having children. _____

(c) Many American women leave their jobs when they have children. _____

(d) The number of American homes with no adult male member is increasing. _____

(2) (a) In many colleges in the United States men and women live in the same dormitories. _____

(b) Most formerly all-male colleges now admit female students. _____

(c) Women are starting to enter some colleges that used to be only for men. _____

(d) Women in some colleges are taking part-time jobs that used to be held by men. _____

(3) (a) Divorced mothers are returning to college in increasing numbers. _____

(b) More divorced men are asking to have their children live with them. _____

(c) Most children of divorced parents live with their mothers. _____

(d) The number of divorced men raising their children is growing. _____

(4) (a) In the United States, secretaries are usually women. _____

(b) In European and South American offices, secretaries are frequently male. _____

(c) Male secretaries are common in the offices of Europe and South America. _____

(d) European offices are usually better run than American offices. _____

(5) (a) Research shows that the more education a woman gets, the fewer children she usually has. _____

(b) Research reveals that many women now combine going to college with having children. _____

(c) Research shows that educated women have high educational goals for their children. _____

(d) Research indicates an increase in the number of mothers going back for higher education. _____

## VOCABULARY

1. **Expanding Vocabulary.** Circle the number of the correct answer.
    a. Working mothers don't have much *leisure*. *Leisure* means
        (1) happiness.   (2) free time.   (3) money.
    b. When a family's *economic* situation is not good, the children may have to work after school. *Economic* situation refers to the family's
        (1) religion.   (2) size.   (3) amount of money.
    c. Is your *goal* to graduate from college? A *goal* is
        (1) an expert.   (2) an education.   (3) an aim.
    d. In a *typical* office, the secretary is female. *Typical* means
        (1) rare.   (2) usual.   (3) interesting.
    e. Women's work usually *involves* child care. *Involves* means
        (1) improves.   (2) produces.   (3) includes.
    f. It has been the man's *responsibility* to support his family. A *responsibility* is
        (1) a duty.   (2) a boring job.   (3) an invention.
    g. The counterculture had an *influence* on American society. An *influence* is
        (1) an effect.   (2) a communication.   (3) damage.

**h.** *Industrial* workers in the United States are mostly male. *Industrial* refers to people who work in

   **(1)** offices.    **(2)** schools.    **(3)** manufacturing plants.

**i.** Typical female *occupations* are public school teaching and nursing. *Occupations* are

   **(1)** levels of schooling.
   **(2)** types of paid work.
   **(3)** ways of spending leisure time.

**j.** Women workers ought to have the same possibilities for *promotion* as men have. When a person gets a *promotion*, he or she

   **(1)** moves to a better job.
   **(2)** goes to school at night.
   **(3)** changes his or her place of work.

**k.** People in certain occupations are under a lot of *pressure*. *Pressure* means

   **(1)** stress.    **(2)** temperature.    **(3)** comfort.

2. **Using Vocabulary.** The following list contains new vocabulary words or forms of words from the reading. Use each word correctly in one of the blank spaces in the paragraph.

| | | | |
|---|---|---|---|
| involves | responsibilities | leisure | typical |
| influenced | industry | economic | goals |
| occupations | promotion | pressure | |

In a (1) _____ American business office, men's jobs and women's jobs are different from each other. Typing, filing, and other secretarial work usually (2) _____ women. A female typist may get a (3) _____ to a secretary's position, but she will find it harder to move into management. In most firms, men still have the major (4) _____ and enjoy a higher (5) _____ level. But in these higher-level (6) _____ , there is more (7) _____ and less (8) _____ time. The women's movement has (9) _____ women to set higher occupational (10) _____ for themselves. But women who move up in (11) _____ or business often find they have two full-time jobs: the one they are paid for and their housework and child care at home.

3. **Word Families: Noun Formation.** Nouns in English often end in *age, ure, ment, ion,* or *hood*. Here are some examples of nouns with these endings.

| | | | | |
|---|---|---|---|---|
| advantage | leisure | involvement | tradition | parenthood |
| courage | culture | movement | situation | brotherhood |

Follow the directions for each item. Write your answers in the space provided.

a. What noun ending in *age* is the opposite of *advantage*? _____

b. What noun can be made by adding *en* to *courage* and adding one of the noun endings from the word family list? _____

c. What noun ending in *ure* can be formed from the verb *to please*? _____

What noun rhymes with this word and means "to take the size of something"? _____

d. What noun ending in *ure* do we give to that part of our environment that includes plants, animals, and weather? _____

e. The verbs *involve* and *move* add *ment* to become nouns. Make nouns of the following verbs in the same way.

discourage _____ advance _____

replace _____ disappoint _____

f. What noun that ends in *ion* means an explanation for a word? _____

g. What nouns ending in *ion* describe the four basic processes of arithmetic?

_____ _____

_____ _____

h. Write the noun forms ending in *hood* for each of the following conditions.

(1) When women think of themselves as sisters in a universal family _____

(2) What Alaska and Hawaii gained when they became states of the United States _____

(3) The stage of a child's life up to the age of twelve _____

## PARAGRAPH TOPICS

1. The following lists include some of the household activities typically done by women and men in the United States. Write a paragraph about your own family, or another family you know well, and tell about some of the different household jobs done by each sex. Use some of the items in the lists. You may add others of your own. Remember that a good paragraph has some general ideas or opinions and some specific details or examples that explain or support the general ideas.

    | Women | Men |
    |---|---|
    | wash dishes | move heavy furniture |
    | iron | wash windows |
    | vacuum | repair broken items |
    | do laundry | take care of the car |
    | take children to the doctor | put out the trash |
    | cook dinner | hang pictures |
    | shop for food | do carpentry |
    | shop for clothes for the family | |

2. In all cultures, girls and boys are taught how to behave according to their traditional roles. Part of this teaching is in the form of toys, games, and activities that are typical of *either* boys or girls.

    Think about the typical toys, games, or activities that are related to *either* boys or girls in your culture. Describe these toys, games, or activities and what they are intended to teach children about their future place in their society. Begin with a clear main idea sentence that identifies your culture, states whether you are going to discuss girls or boys, and makes some general statement about the topic.

# CHAPTER NINE

# NEW DIRECTIONS IN FAMILY LIFE

## PREREADING

**Role Play.** Imagine that the wife in the photograph (on the next page) has just taken an office job. Think about how this new situation will affect the lives of her husband, her daughter, and herself. With your partners, chose the role of the wife, the husband, the child, and perhaps another child or a grandmother as well. Create a dialogue about this new situation in which all the people involved discuss its effects. You may want to begin with the wife's announcement of her new job, its hours, and other points related to it.

> *Free Write.* Read the following letter to "Dear Abby" and freewrite your response to Jill H.
>
> **Dear Abby,**
>
> I am a seventeen-year-old girl with a twin brother. Whenever my mother needs help with the housework, she always asks me. She never asks my brother because she says that housework is women's work and it will be good training for me when I become a wife. I think that's an old-fashioned, unfair attitude. Whose side are you on?
>
> Sincerely yours,<br>Jill H.

**Vocabulary in Context.** The vocabulary in this exercise will appear in the reading passage. Circle or underline the word(s) in the second sentence that mean the same as the italicized word(s) in the first sentence. The first one is done for you.

This Indian family is a sign of changing family life all over the world. As women become educated and work outside the home, they are having fewer children and simplifying their household duties. But traditional values remain important, too.

1. If you have the *opportunity* to learn a computer language, take advantage of it. This kind of (chance) could be important for your future.

2. Colleges often pay part of a professor's expenses to attend a *conference* out of town. Such educational meetings broaden a person's knowledge of the field and make him or her a better instructor.

3. I don't have the IBM computer *available* right now, but I do have another type free for use.

4. Our archeology site needs a good *supervisor* to make sure valuable items don't disappear. Can you suggest a good director for next summer's work in Turkey?

5. Many people can't *cope with* the problems of small children, while others can deal with youngsters, but have difficulty with teenagers.

6. We all have to *function* in society in a number of roles. We may operate at different times as family members, workers, or students.

7. *Vocational* goals may be difficult to reach if one has many family responsibilities. Yet increasing numbers of people are combining career plans with home, school, and even community service.

8. *Moderately* successful dancers have a difficult time. They don't earn much and have short careers. On the other hand, writers who are only fairly successful can at least look forward to writing for the rest of their lives.

9. The schedules of working actors and actresses are usually *in conflict* with each other. When daily routines are in opposition, it is difficult to keep a marriage together.

10. We all want to *fulfill* our childhood dreams. But how many of us actually satisfy our desires to become baseball players or singing stars?

11. Some teenagers know exactly what career they want to *pursue*. Others, however, change their career goal every year and don't settle on one vocation until they are out of college or even later.

## READING

### One Household: Two Careers

[1] In an increasing number of American families, both the husband and the wife have careers in which they will spend their working lives. These careers often require them to work more than the nine-to-five, five-day-a-week schedule of most people. For example, men and women in sales, or those who own small businesses, may have to work weekends or evenings. Men and women in the medical or police field may work unusual hours or be on call at any time. Teachers, hairdressers, or computer technicians may have conferences or educational programs to attend that take them out of town for several days at a time. Male and female workers who are active in their labor unions may have many meetings to attend that take up a lot of time. When both the husband and the wife in a family are involved in these types of careers, theirs is known as a dual-career family.

[2] The number of American dual-career families is steadily rising. There will be more of these families in the future for several reasons. First, the women's liberation movement has given women the desire and opportunity to work outside the home and enter new occupations. More husbands are sharing the household and child-care responsibilities with their wives, and more day-care services are becoming available. Therefore, wives have more time for the requirements of higher-level jobs. Second, with inflation, both the husband and wife in many families must work in order to provide the basic necessities. Furthermore, if American families want to enjoy a high standard of living, they often need two

Physicians Anna and William Fisher are both pursuing careers as scientist–astronauts.

incomes. If families want to buy more goods, own a home, and send their children to college, the wife's income is often essential.

[3] In some dual-career families the husband and wife are both in the same field. This may make it easier for them to understand each other's needs and requirements. Dual-career couples in the same field can communicate well because they are interested in the same things. Married astronauts Dr. Anna and Dr. William Fisher are an example of one such dual-career couple. They both developed an interest in space and medicine when they were children. Dr. Anna Fisher says, "When I was twelve or thirteen, I knew that by the time I grew up there were going to be space stations and they'd need doctors." Both Anna and William became physicians. Then they applied together for work in the Space Agency. Today they train together as specialists in space travel. After they train for four or five years, they expect a team assignment on a space shuttle or rocket ship.

[4] Drs. Anna and William Fisher have no children. What happens in dual-career families where there are children? A recent article in *Harvard Magazine* discussed this problem. One doctor stated that children raised in dual-career families may feel angry or fearful or may demand their parents' attention. If dual-career parents cooperate with each other, however, and arrange leisure time activities with their children, then the children may not suffer these emotional problems.

[5] Professors Ravinder and Serena Nanda are a dual-career family with two children—Raj, fourteen, and Jai, twelve. In their careers as university professors, both parents must attend many meetings, do a lot of writing, and occasionally speak at conferences out of town. But they try to spend as much time as possible with their children. They try to arrange their schedules so that one parent is home while the other is away. They bring some of their work home so that they can supervise the homework of their two boys. Their sons take on some of the household responsibilities such as doing their laundry and cooking simple meals. The boys are equally proud of their mother's and father's work. When they grow up, perhaps they will be able to cope with dual-career marriages themselves.

Dual-career families like the Nandas appreciate the leisure time they can spend together.

[6]   However, not all dual-career families, whether with or without children, function as well as those described here. Sometimes situations arise that make it impossible for a dual-career couple to stay together unless one gives up his or her own vocational goals. In a recent news magazine article, for example, a moderately successful writer talked about the difficulties of his dual-career household. When he and his wife first got married, he had wanted to be a writer and she had wanted to work with horses. Because neither was making money in these careers, they both took evening jobs in restaurants to earn a living. They both believed that these jobs would be only temporary. As soon as the husband started selling his writing, they planned to buy a place in the country where the wife could raise and sell horses.

[7]   The husband's writing career improved steadily, but he never made quite enough money to give up his extra night work in the restaurant business. His wife became a jockey and a horse trainer in a neighboring state. Their schedules were always in conflict. When he was coming home from the restaurant in the early hours of the morning, she was just leaving for the track. When she came back from the track, he was getting ready to leave for his restaurant work. They became strangers living under the same roof. Eventually, after several years of struggling with this dual-career marriage, they divorced. The wife went back to the Midwest where she could work with horses, and the husband remained in the big city where he could pursue his writing career. If either of them marries again, it will probably be to a mate whose career plans fit in with their own.

**Guided Summary.**   A summary tells about the most important ideas of a passage. A summary may also include the most important details or examples used by the writer. Follow the directions for each item to write your summary of this passage. Write the sentences in correct paragraph form.

1. Complete the following sentence with the main topic of the reading. This will be the first sentence of your summary.
   This passage discusses . . .

2. Compose your second sentence by choosing the best item to complete the given words.
   Paragraph [2] tells why
   a. it is difficult to choose a career.
   b. dual-career marriages are increasing.
   c. children should share household responsibilities.

3. For your third and fourth sentences, complete the following statements.
   a. Dual-career couples in the same field . . .
   b. Astronauts Anna and William Fisher are an example . . .

4. For your fifth sentence, choose the best statement about Paragraph [4].
   a. *Harvard Magazine* contains important articles.
   b. An article in *Harvard Magazine* discusses the advantages of dual-career families.
   c. A *Harvard Magazine* article discusses the problems of children in dual-career families.

5. For your sixth sentence, complete the following statement.
   But the example of the Nanda family shows that . . .

6. Next, complete the following statements:
   a. Not all dual-career marriages, however, . . .
   b. The example of the writer and his wife, the horse trainer, shows that . . .

## DISCUSSION QUESTIONS

1. Do you think a wife should work if her husband earns enough income to support the family? What benefits in addition to money does a person gain from work outside the home?

2. If there are preschool children in the family, how can working parents arrange for their care? What are the best choices for day care for the children of working mothers? What are some of the problems that may arise in a family where both parents work outside the home?

3. If a husband and wife both have careers and one of them has to travel frequently on the job, how should the household responsibilities and child care be arranged? Does the wife have a responsibility to stay home even if it means giving up promotions on the job? Can a husband take care of of his children and house as well as a wife can?

4. Think about a specific dual-income family that you know well. What are some of the benefits and some of the problems in that family?

## READING COMPREHENSION

1. **Understanding the Text.** Circle the number of the correct answer.

   a. In a dual-career family,

      (1) the husband and wife share one full-time job.

      (2) the husband and wife both have long-term careers.

      (3) only the husband has a long-term career.

   b. Paragraph [1] gives medical and police work as an example of

      (1) careers that are mostly for men.

      (2) careers that offer normal eight-hour work days.

      (3) careers that require long or unusual hours.

   c. In the last sentence of Paragraph [1], the word *theirs* means the same as

      (1) this family.   (2) these careers.   (3) these meetings.

   d. According to the passage, the number of dual-career families

      (1) is rising.   (2) is decreasing.   (3) will remain about the same.

   e. In Paragraph [2], the words *First* and *Second* signal the reader to expect

      (1) a negative statement.

      (2) a list of additional items.

      (3) a statement of contrast.

   f. In the fifth sentence in Paragraph [2], the word *Therefore* signals the reader to expect

      (1) a negative.   (2) an example.   (3) a result.

   g. Buying more goods, owning a home, and sending your children to college are examples of

      (1) a low standard of living.

      (2) a high standard of living.

(3) the standard of living in most of the world.

**h.** According to Paragraph [3], husbands and wives who work in the same field

    (1) compete against each other.

    (2) earn extraordinary incomes.

    (3) can communicate easily with each other.

**i.** Dr. Anna Fisher's quotation in Paragraph [3] shows that

    (1) she became a doctor after she got married.

    (2) she always wanted to work in the space and medical field.

    (3) she is a better astronaut than her husband.

**j.** The last sentence in Paragraph [3] tells us that

    (1) long training is necessary before astronauts go into space.

    (2) long training is necessary after astronauts go into space.

    (3) the training to be an astronaut is not difficult.

**k.** In Paragraph [4], the third sentence, the phrase *this problem* refers to

    (1) the difficulties of writing for *Harvard Magazine*.

    (2) the difficulties of holding two jobs.

    (3) the difficulties of children in dual-career families.

**l.** According to Paragraph [4], parents in dual-career families should

    (1) spend free time with their children.

    (2) take frequent vacations away from home.

    (3) suffer emotional problems.

**m.** Paragraph [5] is an example of which sentence in Paragraph [4]?

    (1) The fourth    (2) The last    (3) The first

**n.** The Nanda boys have probably been taught to cook simple meals because

    (1) their parents don't like to eat out.

    (2) their parents are not always home for dinner.

    (3) the parents want the boys to become restaurant workers.

**o.** The Nanda boys will probably be able to cope with their own dual-career marriages because

    (1) they can do their own laundry.

    (2) they take vacations with their parents.

    (3) they have lived in a dual-career household.

p. In your own words, state the main idea of Paragraph [6].

_____

_____

q. The example of the writer who had to work in a restaurant suggests that

   (1) making a living as a writer is easy.
   (2) writers don't need to have income-earning mates.
   (3) beginning writers usually need other jobs to add to their incomes.

r. Which sentence in Paragraph [7] states the *general* reason for the breakup of the marriage?

   (1) The first sentence   (2) The third sentence   (3) The last sentence

2. **Answering Information Questions.** Write the answers to the following questions in complete sentences.

   a. What kind of schedule do most people work?
   b. What kind of people may have to work weekends or evenings?
   c. If a person is active in a labor union, will he or she have many or few meetings to attend?
   d. Is the number of dual-career families increasing or decreasing?
   e. How many incomes are often needed for a high standard of living?
   f. Are day-care centers becoming more or less available?
   g. Why can dual-career couples in the same field communicate well?
   h. When did Anna and William Fisher develop an interest in space and medicine?
   i. Did the Fishers apply separately or together for work in the Space Agency?
   j. What do the Fishers expect after four or five years' training?
   k. How many children do Professors Ravinder and Serena Nanda have?
   l. Do the Nandas write much in their careers?
   m. What are two household responsibilities that the Nanda boys take on themselves?
   n. How do the Nanda boys feel about their mother's and father's work?
   o. Why did the couple described in Paragraphs [6] and [7] take evening jobs?
   p. What was the wife's real career goal?
   q. What was the main cause of the breakup of this couple's marriage?

3. **The Reading Process: Following Key Words.** In reading a paragraph, you must follow the key, or main, topic words that the writer uses all through the paragraph. These words may not always be exactly the same. The writer may

use synonyms, paraphrases, specific parts of a topic, or pronouns in place of the topic word(s). Study Paragraph [5] of the reading passage. This paragraph is about the Nanda parents and children. The key topic words in the first sentence are the following: *Professors Ravinder and Serena Nanda, dual-career family, two children*. The topic is referred to in later sentences by the following words:

| | |
|---|---|
| Sentence 2 | their careers, both parents |
| Sentence 3 | they, their children |
| Sentence 4 | they, one parent . . . the other |
| Sentence 5 | they, their two boys |
| Sentence 6 | their sons |
| Sentence 7 | the boys, their mother's and father's work |
| Sentence 8 | they, they, dual-career marriages, themselves |

**a.** Now read the following paragraph carefully. The key topic phrase in the first sentence is underlined. Circle or underline the other words in the paragraph that refer back to this key phrase. The first one is done for you.

Because of the high divorce rate in America, one California high school has begun a <u>course in marriage training</u>. (In this class,) students are matched up as husbands and wives for the semester. The course offers these couples various marriage problems to solve throughout the semester. In it the student–couples may have to cope with such difficulties as the husband's or wife's loss of a job, the arrangement of child-care schedules in a dual-career family, or even the death of a child. The creator of this new approach to premarriage counseling hopes that it will make young people more thoughtful about marriage. Students who take this marriage-training course should be able to make wiser decisions about their future marriages. Perhaps this instruction will lower the American divorce rate.

**b.** The key topic words that identify the main idea of Paragraphs [6] and [7] are *impossible for a dual-career couple to stay together*. To follow the thread of this example, you must be able to focus on those phrases that relate to the main idea. Check (✓) the items below that relate to the central topic.

    **(1)** Recent newsmagazine article _____

    **(2)** Difficulties of this dual-career household _____

(3) She wanted to work with horses _____
(4) Jobs would be only temporary _____
(5) Planned to buy a place in the country _____
(6) Husband's career improved steadily _____
(7) Schedules were always in conflict _____
(8) Strangers living under the same roof _____
(9) Struggling with this dual-career marriage _____
(10) Wife worked with horses _____
(11) Either of them may marry again _____

## VOCABULARY

1. **New Words.** Pronounce these words following your instructor.

   | Nouns | Verbs | Adjectives | Adverbs |
   |---|---|---|---|
   | opportunity | cope (with) | available | moderately |
   | conference | function | vocational | |
   | supervisor | fulfill | | |
   | conflict | pursue | | |

   a. *Expanding Vocabulary.* Check (√) the phrases in each item that mean the same as the italicized phrase in the sentence.

   (1) There are many *vocational opportunities* in the large cities of the American Southwest.

   places for vacations _____  chances for jobs _____

   many job openings _____  businesses in operation _____

   good career positions _____  vacant apartments _____

   leisure activities _____

   (2) Teenagers are usually *in conflict with* their parents over money, helping around the house, and staying out late.

   agree with _____  oppose _____  struggle against _____

   give up to _____  are fluent in _____

   have basic differences with _____  are in harmony with _____

   (3) I want to *pursue* a teaching career.

handle _____ follow _____ worry about _____
take up _____ prevent _____ continue with _____
take to court _____ proceed with _____

(4) An executive finds it difficult to *function* without a good secretary.

perform _____ make a mistake _____ operate _____
slow down _____ discover _____
take part in business _____ work _____
move quickly _____

(5) Some young mothers find it difficult to *cope with* small children.

capture _____ contain _____ deal with _____
entertain _____ handle _____ content _____

b. *Using Vocabulary.* Follow the directions for each item.

(1) Choose the correct word for each blank space.

pursue(d)       moderately      function        opportunity(ies)
in conflict     available       fulfill         cope(ing)
conference(s)   vocational      supervisor

The Space Agency had many (1) _____ to discuss the qualifications that astronauts would have to (2) _____ before they could be accepted for the space program. Over eight thousand people applied for astronaut training in a single year. Two of the best people (3) _____ were Anna and William Fisher. Both were physicians who knew how to (4) _____ with a variety of medical problems. They would both (5) _____ _____ at a high level psychologically, intellectually, and emotionally. Both of them had (6) _____ their interest in space medicine for several years. At first only Anna was chosen for the program. She became an informal (7) _____ _____ for her husband, helping him with extra training and directing him in various ways to improve his qualifications. Finally, he was accepted for the space program too. Now they are both (8) _____ well with the difficulties of astronaut training. They hope to (9) _____ their dream of becoming the first medical astronauts in space.

(2) Write a complete sentence for each item. Use the italicized words in your sentences. Use the lines provided.

  (a) At what hours is your English instructor *available* for conferences?
  _____

  (b) Do you *function* best in the early hours or late at night?
  _____

  (c) What career goal would you like to *pursue*?
  _____

  (d) Name someone you know who smokes *moderately.*
  _____

  (e) Name two things you might have the *opportunity* to do this summer.
  _____

  (f) Do you like or dislike the *supervisor* on your job? Why?
  _____

2. **Word Families: Number Prefixes.** The word *dual* may be used as a prefix meaning "two." Two other prefixes meaning "two" are *bi* and *di*.

> **My brother is *bilingual*; he speaks French and English.**
> **Two students read a *dialogue* in front of the class.**

Other prefixes that show numbers are the following:

| mono- 1    | quint- 5 | oct- 8  | cent- 100  |
| tri- 3     | sext- 6  | nov- 9  | mille- 1000 |
| quad(t)- 4 | sept- 7  | dec- 10 |            |

Answer the following questions in the space provided.

  a. *Logue* is a part of a word that means "speech." If a dialogue is the speech of two people, how many speakers are there in a monologue? _____

**b.** *Ped* is a part of a word that means "foot." Is a horse a *biped* or a *quadruped*? _____ Is a human being a *biped* or a *quadruped*? _____ What kind of insect is a *centipede*? _____

**c.** Why would a mother with *quintuplets* find it difficult to have a career? _____

**d.** If you played the drums in a *sextet*, how many other people would be in your band? _____

**e.** September, October, November, and December are the number–names of months taken from the early Roman calendar. These months are correct in that calendar because the Roman year did not start in January, but in _____ .

**f.** A *decade* is _____ years. A *century* is _____ years. A *millennium* is _____ years.

**g.** On July 4, 1976, the United States celebrated its *bicentennial* birthday. How old was the United States on that date? _____

**h.** How many sides does an *octagon* have? _____ How many angles does a *quadrangle* have? _____ How many angles does a *triangle* have? _____

## WRITING EXERCISES

### Complex Sentences with *Before* and *After*

Complex sentences sometimes include activities that happen at different times. One part of the sentence happens *before* or *after* the other. The part of the sentence that begins with the time word *before* or *after* is called the *dependent clause*. The dependent clause must be joined to a main, or independent, clause to complete the sentence.

---

Before my sister got married, she worked as a private nurse.
    (dependent clause)              (independent clause)

She became a hospital nurse after she married.
    (independent clause)          (dependent clause)

---

Note that when the dependent clause begins the sentence, it is followed by a comma.

The main verb in both parts of a complex sentence must be in the same or related tenses.

**Simple Present**          **Simple Present and Future**

> Many mothers *go* back to work after their children *are* in school.
> Most couples *will open* a joint bank account after they *get* married.

**Simple Past**          **Simple Past and Past Continuous**

> Before my niece *moved* to New York, she *was living* in California.
> After she *finished* school, she *moved* to New York with her husband.

1. **Sentence Combining.** Join the two sentences in each set by adding the word *before* or *after*. Make whatever small changes are necessary for sentence correctness. Rewrite each new complete sentence. The first one is done for you.

    a. (1) I went back to work.
       (2) My daughter began kindergarten.
       
       *I went back to work after my daughter began kindergarten.*
    
    b. (1) Dr. Anna Fisher was a physician in California.
       (2) She applied to the Space Agency.
    
    c. (1) Dr. Fisher's application was accepted.
       (2) She took many physical and mental tests.
    
    d. (1) The Fishers expect to work in space.
       (2) They have four or five years of training.
    
    e. (1) The Space Agency assigns people to rocket planes.
       (2) They give them long, difficult training.
    
    f. (1) The Fishers relax by skiing.
       (2) Their work for the week is done.
    
    g. (1) The Nanda boys do their homework.
       (2) They come home from school.

**h.** (1) The boys go out to play on Saturday.
(2) They must do their laundry together.

**i.** (1) Mrs. Nanda cooks many meals in advance for her family.
(2) She goes out of town to a conference.

**j.** (1) The Nandas all go on vacation together.
(2) School is over in June.

**k.** (1) I go to work in the morning.
(2) I take my child to school.

**l.** (1) Many older people find interesting things to do.
(2) They retire from their regular jobs.

**m.** (1) My grandmother used to read me a story every night.
(2) I went to sleep.

**n.** (1) We were living near my aunt's house.
(2) We moved next door to my grandparents.

**o.** (1) My baby brother learned to walk.
(2) My mother had to watch him all the time.

**p.** (1) My daughter finishes her homework.
(2) She will play outside with her friends.

**q.** (1) Some families move many times.
(2) They finally find a suitable place to live.

**r.** (1) My aunt had a baby.
(2) She didn't go back to work for a few years.

2. **Sentence Building.** Use each pair of items in a complex sentence with the time word *before* or *after*. You may use the items in any order and add as many words as you like to make a complete, interesting sentence. You may use the verbs in any tense or in the negative. The first one is done for you.

   **a.** work hard, feel tired

   *After I work hard all day, I feel very tired.*

   **b.** leave my house, lock the door
   **c.** have a test, review my notes
   **d.** eat dinner, see a movie
   **e.** take a course, see an advisor
   **f.** quit my job, save money

- g. get married, think
- h. graduate, apply for work
- i. finish work, go bowling
- j. finish this exercise, do another
- k. open the window, go to bed
- l. get a job, answer an advertisement
- m. graduate, pass my courses
- n. eat, get thirsty
- o. go swimming, play
- p. buy my ticket, pack
- q. give my opinion, read
- r. write a paragraph, proofread

3. **Sentence Composing.** Follow the directions for each item.

   a. Tell what you will do after this class is over.
   b. Tell what people need before they can drive a car.
   c. In two separate sentences, tell two things the astronauts did after they landed on the moon. Now combine the two sentences into one, making all the necessary changes.
   d. In two separate sentences, tell two things you should do before you write a paragraph. Now combine the two sentences, making all the necessary changes.
   e. In two separate sentences, tell what children like to do after they come home from school.
   f. In three separate sentences, tell three things you do after you get home from school or work. Then combine the three sentences into one complete sentence, using a series of items.
   g. In three separate sentences, tell three things you do before you leave the house each morning. Then combine the three sentences into one complete sentence, using a series of items.
   h. In two separate sentences, tell two things you must not do after a test has started. Now combine the two sentences into one, making all the necessary changes.
   i. Tell where you lived before you came to this city.
   j. Tell where you plan to live after you finish school.
   k. In two separate sentences, tell two things you do before you buy a new pair of shoes.

l. In two separate sentences, tell two things you must do before you can get a passport. Now combine the two sentences, making all the necessary changes.

## Adverb Use

1. **In What Manner.** Adverbs describe how, *in what manner*, verb action is done.

> **Most people plan their vacations *carefully*. (People *plan*. How do they plan? *carefully*)**

*Rewriting Sentences.* Rewrite each sentence changing the italicized phrase into an adverb that tells how the verb action is done. Use the space provided. The first one is done for you.

a. Dual-career parents have to plan their schedules *in a careful manner*.
   *Dual-career parents have to plan their schedules carefully.*

b. Men and women both work *in an active manner* in labor unions.

c. Children from dual-career families may suffer *in an emotional way*.

d. They may behave *in a fearful manner*.

e. They may speak *in an angry way* to their parents.

f. But if parents and children work *in a cooperative manner*, a dual-career family may work well.

g. The number of dual-career families in America is increasing *in a steady manner*.

h. Dual-career couples can communicate *in an easy manner*.

i.  Children in dual-career families often speak *in a proud way* of both parents' work.
   _____

j.  The baby rested *in a comfortable manner* in its mother's arms.
   _____

k.  After children learn to walk, parents must watch them *in a close way*.
   _____

l.  Children in extended families always behave *in a respectful manner* toward their elders.
   _____

m.  Many older people are living *in a modest way* on small incomes.
   _____

n.  Some of them live with relatives and others live *in an independent way*.
   _____

o.  Carlo works *in a successful way* at keeping his family together.
   _____

*Sentence Expansion with Adverbs of Manner.* First locate the main action verb in each sentence and underline it. Then add an adverb of manner that will explain the way in which the verb action was done. You may use the adjective in parentheses as the base for your adverb, or you may choose your own appropriate adverb. Think about the best position in the sentence for the adverb. The first one is done for you.

a.  The patient <u>rested</u> in the hospital. (comfortable)
   *The patient rested comfortably in the hospital.*

b.  The driver got into the left lane behind the truck. (slow; quick; careful)
c.  United Nations guides speak at least two languages. (fluent)
d.  I counted the bills in my wallet before paying the cashier. (careful)
e.  Most students finished the multiple-choice part of the exam. (easy)
f.  Because she was angry, she spoke to the postal clerk. (loud)
g.  The baby smiled at her parents for the photograph. (nice)
h.  The math student figured out the problem. (quick; complete)
i.  The class worked on its assignment until 10:00. (busy)
j.  The newly married couple danced under the stars. (romantic)

**2. Extent or Degree.** Adverbs tell the *extent or degree* of an adjective or adverb. Some common adverbs of degree are *very, too, extremely, fairly, rather, quite*.

> **Some people plan their vacations *very* carefully.**
> **I had a *rather* difficult schedule last term.**

Note that in English the adverb *too* usually has a negative meaning: You work *too* hard (you should work less). *Too* is not a synonym for *very*, which may be used in either a negative or positive way.

a. *Sentence Completion.* Read the first sentence in each pair. Then choose one of the given adverbs of degree to fill in the blank space. (More than one adverb may be correct in some cases.)

fairly          very        completely    extremely
extraordinarily quite       rather        too

(1) I've read that chapter three times. I know it _____ well now.

(2) That was a dull, uninteresting movie. I was _____ bored by it.

(3) My daughter is five feet, four inches. That's _____ tall for a ten-year-old girl.

(4) Our Russian friend has been here just three months. She's still _____ shy about speaking English.

(5) That tree has more apples than any other in the yard. It produces _____ well every year.

(6) Our new piano is over seven feet long. It's _____ large to fit in the elevator of our building.

(7) My neighbor's three children are so well behaved. They play _____ quietly in the evenings.

(8) John often drives at eighty miles per hour. I don't like to drive with him because he goes _____ fast.

(9) Chinese characters are _____ difficult to learn. But the verbs have no tense endings, so they are _____ easy to remember.

(10) Dinosaur bones may break at the first touch. They are _____ fragile.

(11) I am not going to buy those theater tickets. At $17.50, they are _____ expensive for me.

(12) There isn't any water on the moon. It's _____ dry.

(13) It is fifty degrees below zero in some parts of the North. That is _____ cold.

(14) I got 78 on the last exam and 75 on the one before. I think I'm doing _____ well in English.

(15) My mother was from a poor family. She was _____ happy that she was able to go to college.

(16) We have a few more sentences to complete. We're not _____ ready to begin the next exercise.

(17) Spanish and Italian are related languages. An Italian could learn Spanish _____ easily.

(18) I went out this morning without much breakfast. I feel _____ hungry now.

(19) The doctor told my aunt that she must rest more. She works _____ hard around the house.

(20) My grandmother lives about four miles away. I'll take the bus because it's _____ far to walk.

b. *Pair Dictation.*   Choose five sentences from the Sentence Completion exercise to dictate to a partner. Then take dictation from your partner. Correct your dictations together.

c. *Answering Questions with Adverbs of Degree.*   Write the answers to the following questions in complete sentences that use an adverb of degree. The first one is done for you.

(1) How quickly can you walk to school?
*I can walk to school very quickly in nice weather.*
(2) Is that furniture heavy?
(3) Did you finish the test quickly?
(4) Why didn't you buy those theater tickets?
(5) Were you satisfied with your grades last semester?
(6) Does your biology instructor explain things clearly?
(7) Is John's new girlfriend intelligent?
(8) Is she attractive too?
(9) Did you understand the lecture well?
(10) Why aren't you going outside today?
(11) Was the French exam difficult?
(12) Did that blue dress fit you?
(13) How tall is your brother?

3. **Comparative Adverbs.** Comparative adverbs compare the different degrees in which verb action is done. To use adverbs for comparison, you must normally add the word *more* before the adverb.

> **People communicate *more easily* when they have things in common.**

Note some common exceptions in the comparative adverb form:
*hard* ⟶ *harder*; *well* ⟶ *better*; *badly* ⟶ *worse*; *fast* ⟶ *faster*

*Sentence Composing.* Write a complete sentence to answer each of the following items. Use the sentence pattern in the example.

> **Do teenagers or older people drive more safely?**
> *Older people drive more safely than teenagers.*

a. Do older children or younger children cooperate better?
b. Do men or women work more actively in labor unions?
c. Do boys or girls play more roughly in the gym?
d. Do fathers or mothers work harder at home?

e. Can turtles or rabbits run faster?
f. Do deer or elephants run more gracefully?
g. Do airplanes or spaceships travel faster?
h. Do hunters or farmers live more dangerously?
i. Do men or women act more emotionally?
j. Can birds or mosquitoes fly higher?
k. Do cats or mice behave more intelligently?
l. Does an electric light or a match burn more brightly?

## Punctuation: Quotations

Quotations are the *exact* words spoken by someone. These quoted words and their punctuation are written within quotation marks (" "). The part of the sentence that tells who is speaking is called the narration. The quoted part of a sentence and the narration are separated from each other by a comma.

> **One working mother said, "I ask my children to help around the house."**
>
> **"I ask my children to help around the house," said one working mother.**

Some common verbs used in the narration are *said, stated, remarked, commented, added,* and *answered*.

### Punctuating Quotations

1. A magazine reporter interviewed Dave and Martha Harper, a dual-career couple. Dave has his own insurance business, and Martha runs her own travel agency. The reporter (R) asked Dave (D) several questions. Punctuate Dave's quoted answers correctly.

   a. R: "Why did your wife start her own business?"
      D: **(1)** My wife was a gal with a lot of talent he said
      **(2)** She wanted to do a real service for people he added

   b. R: "How did you feel about your wife working?"
      D: **(1)** Dave said at first I didn't like it
      **(2)** But now I've changed he stated

**c.** R: "Do you help your wife with the housework?"
D: **(1)** I hate most of it commented Dave
**(2)** I do damn little of it he added
**(3)** Then he remarked but I do feel a little guilty about that
**(4)** Marty's always helped me do what I wanted he said
**(5)** He told the reporter I took a long while to do the same for her

2. Ellen Lenz, a writer living in West Berlin, interviewed Tina Breitinger, the divorced mother who started the Granny Emergency Service. Ellen (E) asked Tina (T) several questions. Punctuate Tina's quoted answers correctly.

   **a.** E: "How did you start your service?"
   T: **(1)** I announced it on local radio stations she answered
   **(2)** I gave my phone number and business hours on interview programs she added

   **b.** E: "Did you get many responses at first?"
   T: **(1)** At first the service got off to a slow start said Tina
   **(2)** Then she remarked I wasn't sure it would be a success

   **c.** E: "Has the service been working well?"
   T: **(1)** Tina responded it's been quite successful in a small way
   **(2)** We have seventeen women and two men registered so far she stated
   **(3)** They range in age from fifty-five to seventy-five she added

   **d.** E: "Where do these 'Grannies' take care of the children?"
   T: **(1)** Tina answered they go to a family's home and care for the children there
   **(2)** We pay them for their carfare or gasoline she said
   **(3)** They do it more for love than money she commented

## THE COMPOSING PROCESS

1. **Developing a Paragraph.** In composing a paragraph, you must pay attention to both the content of the paragraph and the correct formation of the sentences that develop it. In the following exercise, the content of the paragraphs is given

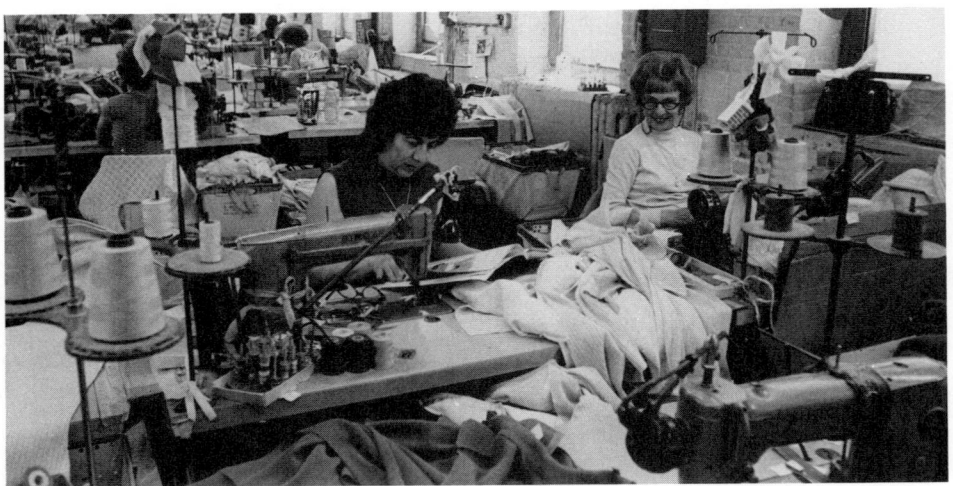

Many immigrant women today, as in the past, bring needed income to their families by working in factories. Dual-income families of all kinds are on the increase today.

to you. The subjects relate to the subject of this chapter: dual-income families. Follow the directions for constructing the basic paragraph. Then expand the basic paragraph as directed.

**a.** The following paragraph tells something about the economic situation of dual-career couples. The first three sentences are given to you. Construct the next five sentences from each set of items provided. Do not change the form or order of the given items. Rewrite your complete new paragraph including the given conclusion.

Many two-income families are looking for new ways to manage their money. It is true that dual-career couples have a double income. But the bigger income can bring bigger expenses too.

(1) two-career couples    often    housekeeper    home
(2) if    children    spend    day-care
(3) spend    more    luxuries    clothes    vacations
(4) dual-career    entertain    eat out    more than
(5) married    higher taxes    single

After Sentence (5) add the following general statements: *Most dual-income families have no choice, however. They have to earn more because it costs more to live now.* Add four or five details to support this general idea following the same pattern as the original paragraph. Conclude your complete expanded paragraph with a sentence about the increase of dual-income families. Use a separate sheet of paper.

    **b.** The beginning of a paragraph about single-parent families is given to you. Unscramble the five sentences that follow. These will tell you some details about being a single parent. Rewrite the entire paragraph including the final sentence on a separate sheet of paper.

        In today's small families, due to death or divorce, many men and women are raising their children without a mate. Many of these single parents do not have their own families close by to help them out. There are many problems for single parents in this situation.

    (1)  working parents    their children    .    at home alone    must leave    after school

    (2)  nervous    .    may    the parents    very    feel

    (3)  cannot    the children    .    give    a lot of attention    the parents    perhaps

    (4)  guilty    about this    feel    .    parents    may

    (5)  may not    time    have    parents    their    own    social life    .    for

Yet many single parents do a wonderful job of raising their children.

    Use the last sentence of the paragraph as the main idea for the next part of your paragraph. Tell about a single parent you know who does a good job of raising his or her children. Use the expression *For example*, to introduce the case you are going to describe. Give specific details of how that single person is doing a good job.

2. **Developing a Paragraph from an Outline.**   The content of a paragraph is given to you below in outline form. The main idea of the paragraph is written in full. First, use the given content notes to develop a complete paragraph about the life of Carlo Caperna. Then, compose a similar paragraph in which you develop the same main idea about yourself or someone you know well. Make a content note outline before writing your original paragraph.

    **Main Idea**

    Carlo Caperna manages to combine modern family living and traditional family ties in his life.

### Modern Family Living

only two children
dual-income family
wife works bank teller
live in small apartment
live in downtown area big city
housekeeper cleans, some cooking
eat light meals or eat out twice a week

### Traditional Family Ties

Carlo's parents live in nearby small town
frequent visits to grandparents
children stay with grandparents on holidays
grandmother sends baked goods to Carlo's family
Carlo's sister-in-law lives same building

### Main Idea

I (or identify someone you know well whom you wish to write about) combine modern family living and traditional family ties.

### Modern Family Living

size of family
employment of wife
use of household appliances for housework
independence of the family unit
personal freedom of family members to follow their interests
separation from relatives
amount of time family has lived in neighborhood
other features of modern family life

### Traditional Family Ties

family cooks traditional food
celebration of traditional holidays
family speaks original national language
traditional customs followed, religious traditions continued
in frequent contact with relatives
visits to native country

family members read newspaper or see movies or television of native culture

other features of traditional family life

*Note:* After you have finished discussing details of modern family living, you will need a sentence signaling reversal of thought—using *but, however,* or *although*—to introduce the details of traditional family ties.

3. **Paragraph Topics**

   **a.** Write a paragraph that tells about a family in which both parents work or go to school. Tell about the kinds of jobs the parents do and the hours they work. Tell something about how they share the household jobs. Tell about the role of the children in the family: who takes care of them and what responsibilities they may have. Begin your paragraph with a main idea sentence that includes a feeling or opinion about this family.

   **b.** It is important for all types of families to spend some leisure time together. Write a paragraph about a pleasant day or vacation that you spent with your family. You may write about a time you remember as a child, or you may write about some current experience. Describe some of the activities you and your family did together and how you felt about spending the day as a family.

## ADDITIONAL READING

### The Family: Past, Present, and Future

[1]   A baby elephant can walk shortly after it is born. Only a few weeks after baby birds are hatched, they can fly away from the nest to find their own food. Most animals mature rather quickly. A human baby, however, is helpless for a long time. Its slow development makes it dependent on adults for many years. Adults must work together to provide the food, warmth, and protection necessary for a child's growth to maturity. They must provide some kind of family for the human child.

[2]   Thousands of years ago, men and women lived by hunting animals and gathering wild plants. People had almost no possessions and no permanent home. They had to move from one area to another to find food. They lived in small units of a mother, a father, and children. This kind of family is called the nuclear family. The nuclear family was well adapted to hunting and gathering societies because it was small enough to move easily from place to place. In early hunting and gathering societies, each nuclear family was independent, but sometimes several related families camped together for companionship. Then they could communicate their ideas and experiences to each other.

In all societies, grandparents are important to family life. They are a link between the past and modern life.

[3] As time passed, people discovered how to plant food and to tame wild pigs, goats, and other animals. When families settled down on farms, they had more children, and they were able to keep the older members of the family with them. This new type of family was called the extended family. It was a useful arrangement in farming societies. It provided many workers for the family farm. When members of the older generation got too old for farm work, they could take care of the young children while the parents worked. When the older members died, the farmland continued in the hands of the younger generation.

[4] Both the nuclear and the extended family exist today. Extended families follow the economic and social traditions of the past. Most of them live on farms or in villages, mainly in Asia, Africa, and South America. Some extended families have moved to the cities and started businesses in which all members have a share. The extended family offers companionship because daily activities are carried out by a number of relatives working together. When a family member becomes too old or too sick to work, he or she can still participate in family decisions. Older people don't lose their sense of dignity or purpose. Children who grow up in extended families usually are respectful and caring toward older people. The majority of the world's people live in this way and have these ideas.

[5] The modern nuclear family is typical of Western industrial societies. This type of family has a different set of values and needs from those of the extended family. The nuclear family is well adapted to the needs of modern industry because it can move from place to place, wherever there is work. The nuclear family is also adapted to apartment living in urban centers, small homes in suburban areas, or individual farmhouses. Such a family may live far from relatives. The children may not have a close relationship with grandparents, uncles, and

aunts. Children in a nuclear family are often closer to friends than they are to older or younger members of the family. In the nuclear family, children are educated to become independent and follow their own careers. A person is expected to be economically and socially independent in old age.

[6] There are some disadvantages to the nuclear family structure that concern people today. The nuclear family can be broken easily by divorce or by the death of a parent. Even with two parents, children in nuclear families sometimes don't get the attention they need, especially if both parents are working long hours. Moreover, there is the problem of caring for the elderly without strong family support. Loneliness can be a problem for young and old alike. Nevertheless, the nuclear family will survive. In fact, social scientists predict that there will be more independent nuclear families in the future as the world becomes more industrialized. There will be fewer places left for the extended family farms and businesses that were so common in the past. But perhaps some of the ideals of the extended family will still survive and give additional strength to modern family life.

## DISCUSSION QUESTIONS

1. What are some of the advantages of large families? Some of the disadvantages? What are some of the advantages of small families? Some of the disadvantages? Do you live in a small nuclear family or a large extended family? Explain the positive aspects of your family situation.

2. Do you think life is better for a family on a farm or in a village or in a large city? Explain your answer with specific details. Where did you grow up—in the country or in the city? What are some advantages of each place?

## READING COMPREHENSION

1. **Understanding the Text.** Circle the number of the correct answer.
    a. In Paragraph [1], the development of animals
        (1) is described as similar to that of human children.
        (2) is contrasted to the development of human children.
        (3) is said to be slower than that of human children.
    b. Hunters and gatherers
        (1) sometimes lived with related families on farms.
        (2) lived permanently in small villages.
        (3) depended on wild plants and animals for food.

c. According to Paragraph [3], the extended family was a benefit to people who

   (1) were lazy.
   (2) farmed the land.
   (3) wanted a private life.

d. The extended family is

   (1) both an economic and a social unit.
   (2) only an economic unit.
   (3) primarily a social unit for the care of the aged.

e. In Sentence (5) of Paragraph [4], the word *because* signals the reader to expect

   (1) a contrast.
   (2) an example.
   (3) a reason.

f. The extended family continues as a permanent economic unit because

   (1) farms and businesses are handed down from generation to generation.
   (2) all the members have companionship.
   (3) the older generation has a sense of dignity.

g. Movement, distance from relatives, and independence are typical characteristics of

   (1) the majority of the world's families.
   (2) the modern nuclear family.
   (3) extended families in cities.

h. In Paragraph [5], Sentence (8), the first word *Their* refers to

   (1) friends.
   (2) grandparents.
   (3) children.

i. In Paragraph [5], the last sentence, the words *A person is expected to be* mean the same as

   (1) a person must be.
   (2) a person is supposed to be.
   (3) a person will be.

j. Social scientists predict that

(1) there will be fewer divorces in the future.
(2) the nuclear family won't survive.
(3) the extended family structure will change.

2. **Summary Completion.** Choose the correct word from the columns following the paragraph to fill in each blank space in the paragraph.

Two types of family structures (1) _____ in the past. The nuclear family was adapted to a life of (2) _____ and gathering. The members of the (3) _____ family lived together in a permanent place. Both types of families (4) _____ today. The extended family is an (5) _____ unit as well as a social unit. There is companionship for the workers and dignity for (6) _____ members. The nuclear family has a different set of (7) _____ . Children in a nuclear family are educated to become (8) _____ in their own careers. In the future there might be (9) _____ in the structure of the family, but family life will survive.

(1) gathered, approached, developed, rested
(2) planting, growing, arranging, hunting
(3) nuclear, extended,
(4) exist, control, depend, decide
(5) economic, active, American, interesting
(6) literate, ideal, older, personal
(7) people, ideals, units, ages
(8) weak, lonely, independent, elderly
(9) parents, predictions, scientists, changes

3. **Answering Information Questions.** Write the answers to the following questions in complete sentences on a separate sheet of paper.
   a. Name three things that adults must provide for a child.
   b. In the hunting and gathering societies, did people live in nuclear families or in extended families?
   c. In which areas of the world do most of the extended families live today?
   d. How do children who grow up in extended families behave toward older people?

e. In what type of homes do nuclear families live today?
f. Do modern nuclear families usually live close to or far from their relatives?
g. In the nuclear family, is an old person expected to be dependent or independent?
h. Will there be fewer or more nuclear families in the future?

## VOCABULARY

1. **Expanding Vocabulary.** Circle the number of the item that explains the meaning of the italicized word.

    a. My friend is staying with us at present, but the arrangement isn't *permanent*.
    *Permanent* means

    (1) short-lived.   (2) well furnished.   (3) long-lasting.

    b. Polar bears are *adapted* to living in a cold climate.
    *Adapted* means

    (1) unsuited.   (2) adjusted.   (3) allowed.

    c. The sun *provides* warmth and light on the earth.
    To *provide* something means to

    (1) supply it.   (2) feel it.   (3) warm it.

    d. My daughter enjoys the *companionship* of her cousins.
    *Companionship* means

    (1) easy life.   (2) daily schedule.   (3) close company.

    e. Although they were poor, my grandparents lived with a sense of *dignity*.
    A sense of *dignity* is a feeling of

    (1) worthiness.   (2) brotherhood.   (3) hardship.

    f. People have a better chance of *survival* in a car accident if they use seat belts.
    *Survival* means

    (1) getting hurt.   (2) being careful.   (3) remaining alive.

    g. Fruits taste best when they *mature* on the tree.
    When something *matures*, it

    (1) falls easily.   (2) develops fully.   (3) grows poorly.

    h. Many grandparents communicate well with members of the younger *generation*.

A *generation* is

(1) an age group.   (2) a national group.   (3) a social group.

i. The city of Pittsburgh is the heart of an *industrial* area of Pennsylvania. In an *industrial* area there would be a lot of

(1) farms.   (2) factories.   (3) clean air.

j. Would you rather live in an *urban* center or in the countryside? *Urban* refers to

(1) farmlands.   (2) villages.   (3) cities.

2. **Using Vocabulary.**   Follow the directions for each item.

   a. Write a complete sentence for each item. Use the italicized words in your sentences.

   (1) Why would *survival* on the moon be difficult?
   (2) Name two things public elementary schools *provide* for the children.
   (3) Do you get along well with people of your parents' *generation*?
   (4) Is *urban* living more expensive or less expensive than living on a farm?
   (5) Where in your neighborhood can older people go to find good *companionship*?

   b. The word *mature* is a verb. It is also an adjective. The noun form is *maturity*. Fill in the blank space with the correct verb, adjective, or noun form, depending on the sentence.

   (1) A _____ student sits quietly in class and listens to the instructor.

   (2) When a person _____ , he or she is called a young adult.

   (3) Doctors say that females _____ at an earlier age than males.

   (4) My children are only nine and eleven years old; they have not yet reached _____ .

3. **Word Families: Prefix Meanings.**   A prefix is a syllable at the beginning of a word that changes or adds to the meaning of a word. If you know the meaning of a prefix, it will help you understand word meanings and build your vocabulary.

Follow the directions for each item.

a. *di* = apart, separate: *divide, divorce, distance*
   Choose the correct word with the prefix *di* to fill in the blank spaces.

   (1) When a wife and husband separate permanently, we say they get a _____.

   (2) You should _____ a birthday cake equally so that each child gets a part of it.

b. *sub* = under, secondary: *subway, substitute, submarine, subject, suburban*
   Choose the correct words with the prefix *sub* to fill in the blank spaces.

   (1) A ship that can travel underwater is called a _____.

   (2) The place that is secondary to a main urban area is referred to as a _____ area.

   (3) A _____ is an underground transportation system.

   (4) If your teacher is absent, you may get a second, or _____, teacher in his or her place.

c. *co, col, com* = together, with: *communicate, common, cooperate, company, collection*
   Choose the correct words with *co, col,* or *com* to fill in the blank spaces.

   (1) When people work well together, we say they _____ with each other.

   (2) If you gather together a number of stamps from different countries, you will have a fine stamp _____.

   (3) When people talk together and understand each other, we say they _____ well.

d. *ex* = out of, from: *exit, existence, extended, express*
   Choose the correct words with the prefix *ex* to fill in the blank spaces.

   (1) When a family stretches out to include two or three generations, we call it an _____ family.

   (2) If there is a fire in your school, you should go out of the building by the nearest _____.

e. *pre* = before, in advance: *prefix, prediction, prefer, prepositions, premature, prepare*

Choose the correct words with the prefix *pre* to fill in the blank spaces.

(1) Before you eat, you must _____ the food and set the table.

(2) A _____ is a syllable that comes before the other parts of a word.

(3) People who tell something in advance are making a _____ _____ about the future.

(4) The words *in, on, to,* and *from* are placed before nouns; they are called _____ .

## PARAGRAPH TOPICS

1. Write a paragraph that describes a special relationship you have with a member of the older generation in your family, such as an aunt, an uncle, or a grandparent. Describe the person, tell where he or she lives, and how the relationship developed. Tell what the advantages are and how both of you benefit. If the relationship is past, use the appropriate tense and time expressions. Begin your paragraph with a main idea sentence that includes a feeling or opinion about this relationship.

2. Some parents think an older person is better able to care for small children than a younger person. If you were a parent who needed help with your children, whom would you choose? Give specific reasons for your choice.

NAME _____

INSTRUCTOR _____

# UNIT III REVIEW

1. **Sentence Completion.** Fill in the blank spaces with the appropriate word(s) as directed by the Key following the paragraph.

   Until 1976 Ted Koppel (1) _____ in a high-pressure job as a television news reporter (2) _____ ABC. In the first thirteen years of his marriage, (3) _____ wife, Grace Ann, stayed home with (4) _____ four children. But then Grace Ann wanted her own (5) _____ . So she (6) _____ to law school. (7) _____ she was accepted, Ted agreed to give up his job for a year and take the (8) _____ for the housework and children. Ted didn't change roles (9) _____ . One of the (10) _____ things he had to learn was that his time was no longer his own. He had to make a daily schedule (11) _____ gave (12) _____ time to write, take care of the house, and (13) _____ the children. (14) _____ a child got sick, Ted couldn't cope with all his work. In many ways, his new job kept him (15) _____ than his high-pressure job in television.

   **Key**
   - **(1)** Past continuous tense of the verb *work*
   - **(2)** Preposition of place
   - **(3)** Singular male possessive pronoun
   - **(4)** Plural possessive pronoun
   - **(5)** Synonym for "a responsible job that a person will keep for most of his or her life"
   - **(6)** Simple past tense of the verb *apply*
   - **(7)** Time word showing that one event happened later than another
   - **(8)** Synonym for *duties*
   - **(9)** Adverb form of *easy*
   - **(10)** Superlative form of the adjective *important*

(11) Relative pronoun for nonhuman items
(12) Singular male object pronoun
(13) Synonym for "watch over"
(14) Word that introduces the conditional part of a sentence
(15) Comparative form of the adjective *busy*

2. **Word Forms.** Fill in the chart with the correct forms of the given word. (Some parts of speech may have more than one word.)

|    | Verb      | Noun           | Adjective | Adverb |
|----|-----------|----------------|-----------|--------|
| 1  | X         |                | typical   |        |
| 2  | involve   |                |           | X      |
| 3  | X         | responsibility |           |        |
| 4  | X         | loneliness     |           | X      |
| 5  | enrich    |                |           | X      |
| 6  |           | conferences    | X         | X      |
| 7  | apply     |                |           | X      |
| 8  | X         |                | jealous   |        |
| 9  | X         |                | proud     |        |
| 10 | cooperate |                |           |        |

*Word Form Completion.* Fill in the blank space in each sentence with the correct form of the word from the same numbered item on the Word Form chart. Use verbs and nouns in their singular or plural forms as necessary. For dictation with blanks, close your book.

(1) American women _____ earn less money than men.

(2) A teacher's _____ with her students is important.

(3) Working parents must teach their children to act _____ .

(4) Even children in large families may suffer _____ .

(5) A job helping others offers true _____ .

(6) _____ often take place in New York City.

(7) Did you fill out an _____ for your promotion?

(8) Children are sometimes _____ of their parents' work.

(9) A husband should be _____ of his wife's work.

(10) Members of a dual-career family must work _____ .

3. **Group Paragraph Reconstruction.** Read the following paragraph about Carlo Caperna and his family. Then on the board construct a Subject–Main Verb chart of the sentences. Include one or two key words from the paragraph for each sentence.

   Read your paragraph aloud or silently several times. Then close your books. Now, with your group, try to reconstruct the paragraph, using only the chart on the board.

   (1) Carlo Caperna and his family combine modern city life with traditional family ties. (2) The Capernas live in Turin, a major industrial city in Italy. (3) They own a small but comfortable apartment with three bedrooms and a small balcony. (4) Carlo's parents live in a nearby small town. (5) The Caperno grandparents sometimes come into Turin for Sunday visits, but more frequently, Carlo and his family go out to the country to see the older people. (6) Grandmother Caperno loves to bake breads and cakes for the children, and Grandfather Caperno takes the children for walks through the small town. (7) Carlo grew up in this town, so he knows it well. (8) He is glad that his children have the opportunity to experience traditional Italian life with their grandparents. (9) But he and his wife could never return to the quiet life of the small town. (10) They enjoy the excitement of Turin's cultural activities and their interesting jobs. (11) They are content with their combination of a modern and traditional life-style.

4. **Developing a Paragraph.** Read the following poem aloud. Then discuss the questions that follow the poem.

   The Bear's Song
   (Haida: Queen Charlotte's Island, British Columbia)

   I have taken the woman of beauty
   For my wife;
   I have taken her from her friends.
   I hope her kinsmen will not come
   And take her away from me.
   I will be kind to her.
   Berries, berries I will give her from the hill
   And roots from the ground.
   I will do everything to please her.
   For her I made this song and for her I sing it.

   A man from the Bear clan of the Haida tribe of Native Americans is singing this song for a special occasion. What is the occasion? What are the man's

Today, many women as well as men participate in active sports for health and fun. What sports do women and men play together in your culture? Which sports do men and women usually play separately?

feelings about the woman? What gifts will he give her? What do you think these gifts mean?

Write a paragraph using the questions and class discussion as a basis for your content. Begin with a main idea statement that identifies the poem and tells who is speaking. Include your feelings about the poem and whether you find it interesting. Think about whether the singer's emotions are similar to those you would feel on the same occasion. Explain this idea.

5. **Paragraph Topics**

   a. Think about the story of Harriet Tubman in Chapter 7. Do you know of a person, man or woman, who lived (or is living) his or her life helping other people? Write about this person, telling who he or she is and what kind of generous and helpful things he or she did (or does) for others.

   b. Read the following paragraph about a high school boy who wanted to join the girls' volleyball team. Discuss the situation with your class. Then write a paragraph about it in which you express your opinion as the main idea statement.

John Gidman is sixteen years old. Earlier this year he joined the volleyball team at his high school. But he had to quit after only a few games. Why? It is a girls' team, which means it is for girls only. If a girl wants to play on a boys' team, she can. The choice is hers. But boys can't make the same choice. The coaches are afraid that the boys will be too competitive, and they will push the girls aside. John Gidman thinks that the rules that put him off the team are unfair. There is no boys' volleyball team for him to join. Should John get his chance on the girls' team? What's your opinion?

# APPENDIX A

# BASIC TERMINOLOGY FOR ENGLISH-LANGUAGE STUDY

1. **Parts of Speech**

   *Noun:* A word that names a person, place, thing, quality, idea, or action.

   > **Peter Rodriguez, girl, country, chair, attention, democracy**

   *Pronoun:* A word used in place of or as a substitute for a noun. (See Writing Exercises in Chapter 2.)

   > **The instructor gave the exam to the students at 9:00 A.M.**
   > ***He* asked *them* to stop writing at 9:35.**

   *Verb:* A word that expresses a state of being, feeling, or appearance.

   > **You *seem* ill today.**
   > **I *am* nervous about my exam.**

   A word that expresses physical or mental action.

   > **I *thought* about you yesterday.**
   > **My friends *play* soccer very well.**

*Adjective:* A word that describes a noun. Articles (a, an, the) and numbers are adjectives.

> **Many students find English *a difficult* subject.**

*Adverb:* A word that tells how often or in what way verb action is done. (See Writing Exercises in Chapter 1 for more examples.)

> **Young people *often* have part-time jobs.**
> **New Yorkers speak *rapidly*.**

A word that tells us the degree to which an adjective is true. (See Writing Exercises in Chapter 9 for more discussion of adverbs.)

> **My cat is *very* healthy.**

*Preposition:* A word that generally has some meaning of place, direction, time, or connection with a noun. (See Writing Exercises in Chapter 1 for a list of common prepositions and their use.)

> **Please put the book *for* John *on* the table *in* the hall.**

*Conjunction:* A word that joins related words, phrases, or clauses of similar form.
*and, but, or* may connect independent clauses or other kinds of parallel expressions

> **Many women work outside the home, *but* they still have household responsibilities.**

*if, because, when, while, before, after, although* begin dependent clauses. These clauses must be connected to independent clauses.

> *Because* you speak French, you may learn Spanish easily.

2. **Phrases**
   A group of two or more words forming a unit of thought.
   *Prepositional Phrase:* A phrase that begins with a preposition.

   > **The United Nations is located** *in New York City.*

   *Infinitive Phrase:* A phrase that begins with *to* and is followed by the basic form of a verb.

   > **Archeologists like** *to explore* **ancient cities.**

3. **Clauses**
   A group of words with a subject and a complete main verb.
   *Independent Clause:* A group of words that can stand by itself as a complete sentence.

   > **Last week he saw a white tiger at the zoo.**

   *Dependent Clause:* A clause that cannot stand by itself as a complete sentence because it begins with such words as *if, because, when, while, before, after, who, which,* or *that*.

   > **It is difficult to live on the moon** *because there is no water.*
   > **Professor Jones knows** *which students will pass the course.*

4. **Punctuation**
   *Period:* Closes off a finished thought that can stand by itself as a complete sentence.

> **I enjoy this class.**

*Comma:* Separates parallel items in a series.

> **Many words from German, Latin, and French are found in English. Computer science is a new, interesting, and important field of study.**

Follows a dependent clause that begins a sentence.

> **When you have finished your exam, leave your paper on the desk.**

Marks off signal words and expressions.

> **Some languages do not use a Latin alphabet. Russian, for example, uses the Cyrillic alphabet.**

Precedes *but, and,* and *or* in a compound sentence.

> **Weight lifting used to be a sport only for men, but today many women are lifting weights.**

*Quotation Marks:* Surrounds direct speech, that is, the exact words spoken by someone.

> **At 12:00 the professor said, "The exam will begin."**

5. Articles

*Indefinite Article: a, an*

Placed before a singular countable noun when the noun is mentioned for the first time and represents no specific person or thing. (See Unit II Review for Article chart.)

> There is *a* cat in my backyard.

When the noun is an example of a class of things.

> *A* bicycle has two wheels.

Placed with a noun complement.

> She is *an* interesting person.

*Definite Article: the*
Placed before a singular or a plural noun when someone or something is mentioned a second time.

> I saw a man in the park. *The* man was walking his dog.

When someone or something is made definite by the addition of a clause or a phrase.

> *The* women that I met were friendly.
> *The* boy in the red sweater is my son.

When there is only one of something.

> *The* sky is blue. *The* weather is fine.

Placed before names of seas, oceans, rivers, groups of islands, mountain ranges, and geographical areas.

> **She lives in *the* West near *the* Rocky Mountains.**

Placed before countries representing a union.

> ***the* United States, *the* Soviet Union, *the* Dominican Republic**

Placed before the superlative degree of adjectives.

> **Paul is *the* best student in the class.**

Placed before singular nouns that represent a class of objects.

> ***The* rose is a beautiful flower.**

6. **Verb Summary**
   *Basic Form:* Simple verb, no endings for person or tense.

> *hold    study    speak    write*

*Infinitive:* to + basic form of verb.

> **The movie is going *to begin* at noon.**

*Simple Present:* Basic form of verb, except for Third Person singular, which adds *s*. For habitual or general action.

> **Every summer Jean *visits* his family in Haiti.**
> **Both girls and boys *need* physical exercise.**

*Present Continuous: am, is,* or *are* + *ing* form of main verb. For actions that are taking place right now.

> **Two people *are waiting* to use the telephone.**

For actions that suggest continuous activity.

> **When *I'm studying*, I like peace and quiet.**

*Simple Past:* Basic form of verb + *ed*, or irregular form. For actions that were completed in the past.

> **Yesterday I *finished* my work by dinner time.**
> **Traffic *was* slow because a car *broke* down in the middle of the highway.**

*Past Continuous: was* or *were* + *ing* form of main verb. For continuous action in the past.

> **The class *was practicing* verb forms all last week.**

For interrupted past actions, usually with another clause in the simple past.

> **Our team *was playing* well until our best batter injured his arm.**

7. **Modals + Basic Form of Verbs.** A modal is a helping part of a verb. Modals tell about certain conditions related to the main verb and are used to express ability, possibility, probability, or advisability. The main verb following a modal is always in the basic form. (See Writing Exercises in Chapter 6 for a detailed discussion of modals.)

Study the following explanations and examples of some common modals.

To show present ability or possibility

> **We *can* go to the library after class.**

To show past ability or possibility less certain than *can*

> **We *could* go to the library after class if we eat lunch now.**

To show present or future possibility and permission

> **Students *may* take Monday off as a holiday.**

To show possibility less certain than *may*

> **Stanford University *might* expand its Asian history classes.**

To show necessity or strong probability

> **He *must* attend the lecture today to take notes.**

To show obligation, advisability, or expectation.

> **Both teachers and students *should* come to class prepared.**

To show future certainty or probability.

> **I *will* pass the test.**
> **If you went to class, you *would* know about the quiz.**

8. **Useful Signal Expressions**

| Thought Relationship | Signals Marking Independent Clauses | Signals Marking Dependent Clauses |
|---|---|---|
| Time | now<br>later<br>then<br>next<br>afterward | before<br>after<br>when<br>while |
| Sequence | first<br>second . . .<br>finally | |
| Addition of items | in addition<br>moreover<br>also<br>too<br>and (connector) | |
| Addition of description (adjective clause) | | who<br>which/that |
| Contrast | however<br>nevertheless<br>in contrast<br>on the other hand<br>but (connector) | although/even though |
| Reason | | because<br>since |
| Result | therefore<br>as a result<br>thus<br>consequently<br>so (connector) | |
| Condition | | if |
| Example | for example,<br>for instance<br>such as (to introduce noun examples) | |

## Commonly Used Irregular Verbs

| Basic Form | Simple Past | Past Participle | Basic Form | Simple Past | Past Participle |
|---|---|---|---|---|---|
| arise | arose | arisen | forget | forgot | forgotten |
| awake | awoke | awoken | freeze | froze | frozen |
| be | was | been | get | got | gotten |
| beat | beat | beaten | give | gave | given |
| become | became | become | go | went | gone |
| begin | began | begun | grow | grew | grown |
| bend | bent | bent | have | had | had |
| bet | bet | bet | hear | heard | heard |
| bite | bit | bitten | hide | hid | hidden |
| bleed | bled | bled | hit | hit | hit |
| blow | blew | blown | hold | held | held |
| break | broke | broken | hurt | hurt | hurt |
| bring | brought | brought | keep | kept | kept |
| build | built | built | kneel | knelt, kneeled | knelt |
| burst | burst | burst | | | |
| buy | bought | bought | know | knew | known |
| cast | cast | cast | lay | laid | laid |
| catch | caught | caught | lead | led | led |
| choose | chose | chosen | leap | leaped, leapt | leapt |
| come | came | come | | | |
| cost | cost | cost | leave | left | left |
| deal | dealt | dealt | lend | lent | lent |
| dig | dug | dug | let | let | let |
| do | did | done | lie | | |
| draw | drew | drawn | (to recline) | lay | lain |
| dream | dreamed, dreamt | dreamt | (to tell a falsehood) | lied | lied |
| drink | drank | drunk | light | lit, lighted | lit |
| drive | drove | driven | lose | lost | lost |
| eat | ate | eaten | make | made | made |
| fall | fell | fallen | mean | meant | meant |
| feed | fed | fed | meet | met | met |
| feel | felt | felt | pay | paid | paid |
| fight | fought | fought | put | put | put |
| find | found | found | quit | quit | quit |
| flee | fled | fled | read | read | read |
| fly | flew | flown | | (*pronounced* "red") | |
| forbid | forbade | forbidden | | | |

| Basic Form | Simple Past | Past Participle | Basic Form | Simple Past | Past Participle |
|---|---|---|---|---|---|
| ride | rode | ridden | stand | stood | stood |
| ring | rang | rung | steal | stole | stolen |
| rise | rose | risen | stick | stuck | stuck |
| run | ran | run | sting | stung | stung |
| say | said | said | stink | stank | stunk |
| see | saw | seen | strike | struck | struck |
| seek | sought | sought | swear | swore | sworn |
| sell | sold | sold | sweep | swept | swept |
| send | sent | sent | swim | swam | swum |
| set | set | set | swing | swung | swung |
| shake | shook | shaken | take | took | taken |
| shoot | shot | shot | teach | taught | taught |
| shrink | shrank, shrunk | shrunk | tear | tore | torn |
|  |  |  | tell | told | told |
| shut | shut | shut | think | thought | thought |
| sing | sang | sung | throw | threw | thrown |
| sink | sank, sunk | sunk | understand | understood | understood |
| sit | sat | sat | wake | woke, waked | woken |
| sleep | slept | slept | wear | wore | worn |
| slide | slid | slid | weave | wove | woven |
| speak | spoke | spoken | weep | wept | wept |
| speed | sped | sped | win | won | won |
| spend | spent | spent | wind | wound | wound |
| spin | spun | spun | withdraw | withdrew | withdrawn |
| spit | spit, spat | spat | write | wrote | written |
| split | split | split |  |  |  |

# APPENDIX B

# PARAGRAPH CORRECTION SYMBOLS

| | |
|---|---|
| ap. | apostrophe error *(Tonys parents are going to the Far East.)* |
| cap. | capitalization *(A visit to the brooklyn botanical gardens is a delightful experience.)* |
| caret ∧ | something left out *(My neighbor was walking∧dog last night at 10:00.)* |
| frag. | fragment; incomplete sentence; dependent clause used as a sentence *(For example.; Many college students holding part-time jobs.; Although I like my neighborhood.)* |
| omit ℓ | *(I received ~~the~~ good instruction in English at the University of California.)* |
| ¶ | paragraph; begin new paragraph for a new topic. |
| pl. | plural error; disagreement in number between plural nouns and related words *(There are many good reasons for continuing your education.; Many students at our college want to become accountant.)* |
| punct. | punctuation error: comma or semicolon incorrectly used *(Because, I have to work part-time, I can't study too much.; Although it's raining; the game will go on.)* |
| RO | run-on sentences: two independent clauses incorrectly joined by a comma *(I only watch the news on TV, everything else is junk.)* |
| sp. | spelling *(Do your two children have seperete rooms?)* |
| s–v | subject–verb disagreement *(The world of older people have changed a lot.)* |
| VF | verb form or tense wrong *(I was lived in Hawaii for two years.)* |
| WF | wrong form or word: noun–adjective–adverb confusion *(Not having a car is very inconvenience for me.)* |
| WW | wrong word *(There are many attentive [for attractive] restaurants in most large cities.)* |

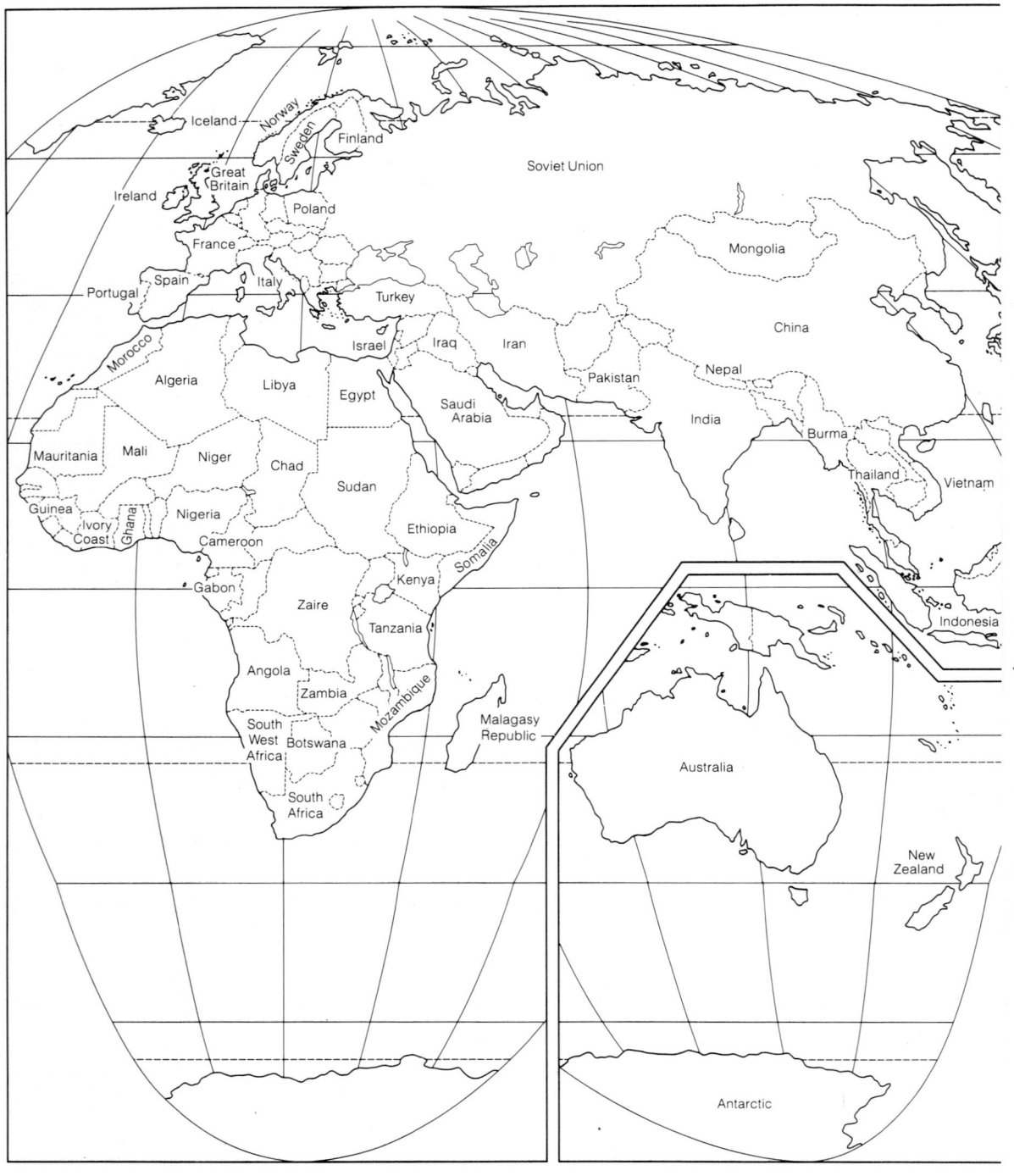

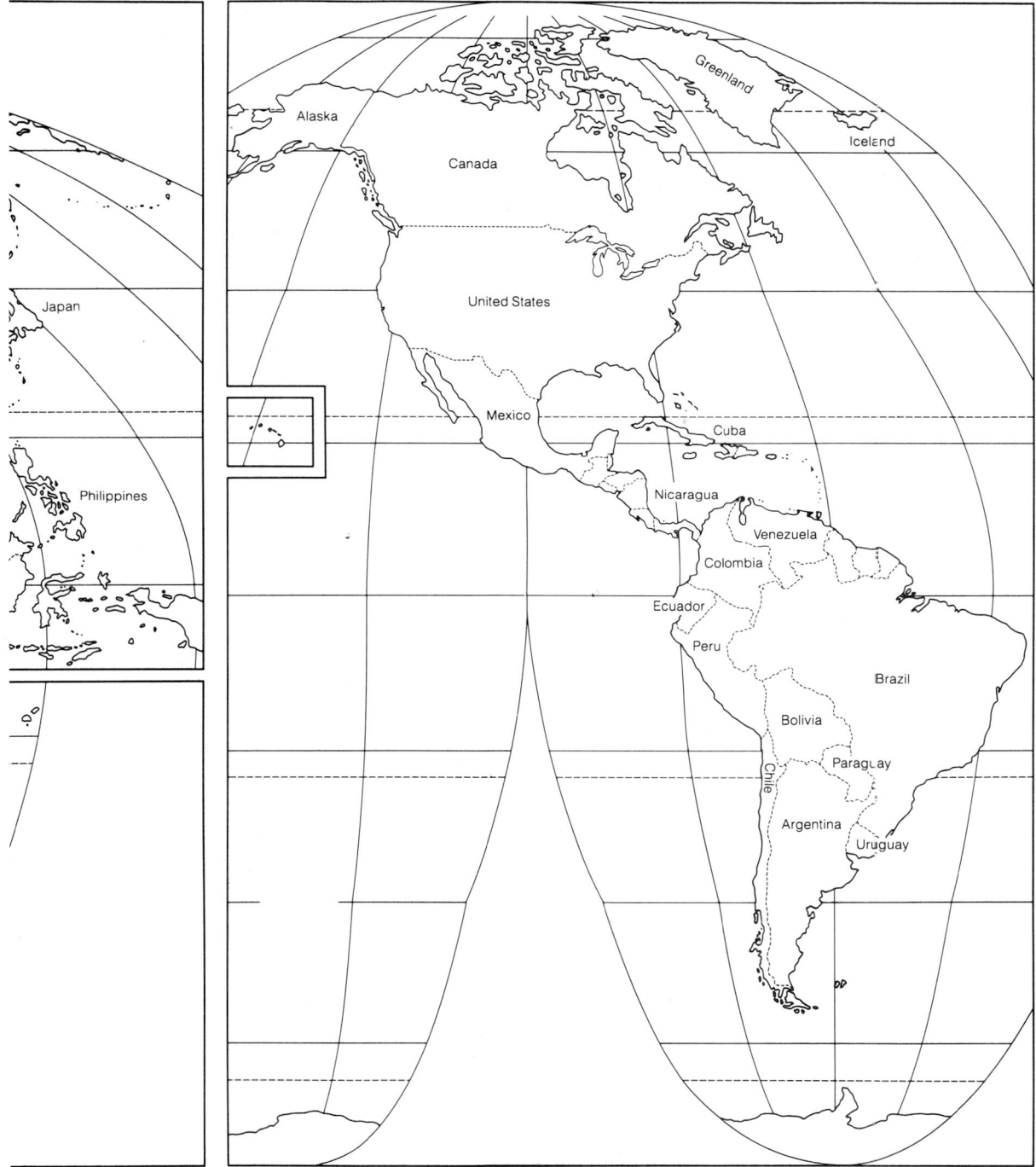

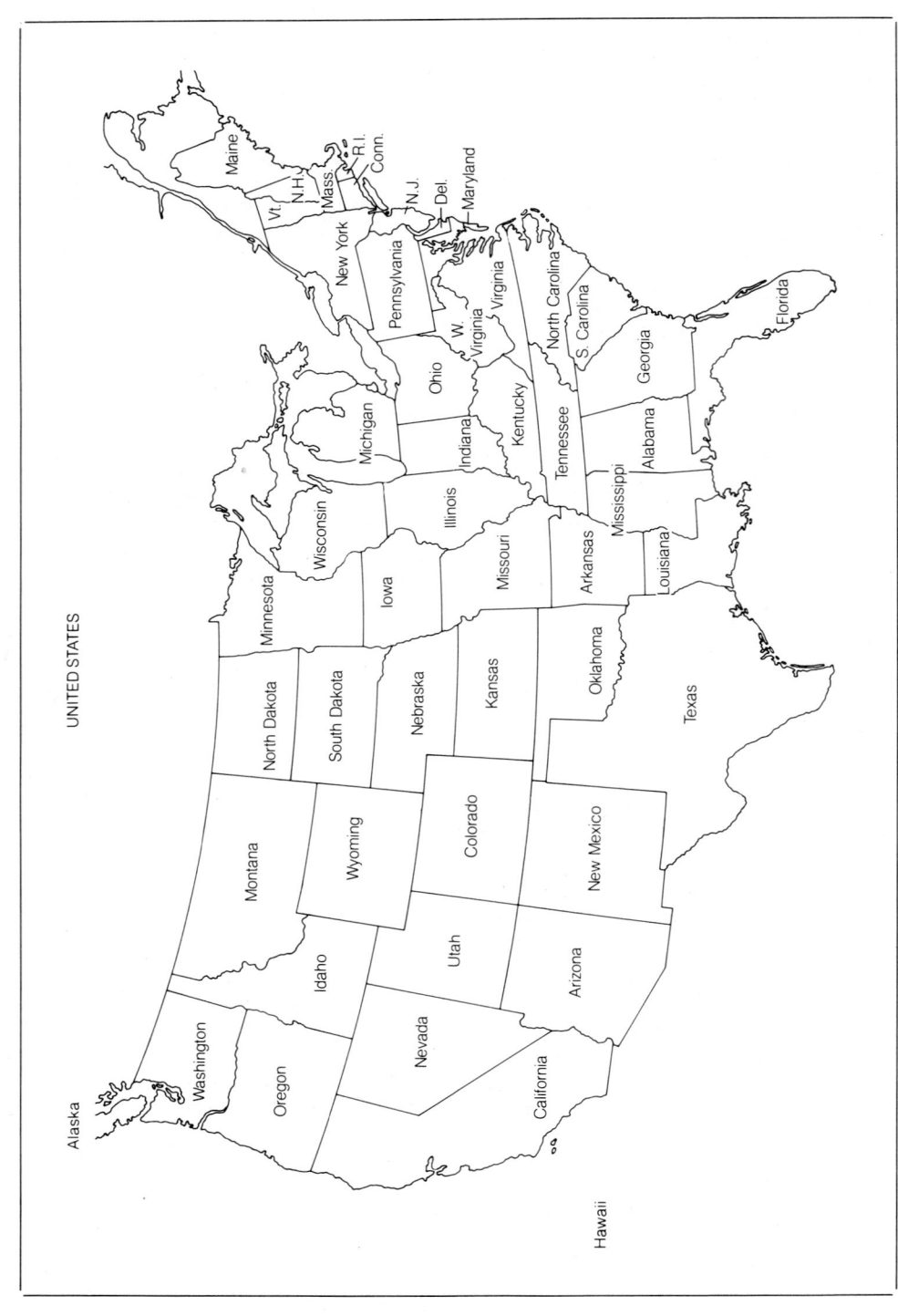

428.052
G819p
3rd ed.

Gregg,J.Y. & J.Russell

Past,Present,and Future

428.052
G819p
3rd ed.